The Changing Electoral Map of England and Wales

Endorsements/praise page

'Under Britain's first-past-the-post electoral system, the outcome of elections depends not only on how many votes a party wins but also on how its support is distributed geographically. In this fascinating book, Furlong and Jennings uncover how the geography of party support in England and Wales has changed dramatically over the last forty years as a result of the country's transition to a post-industrial society whose consequences have varied from place to place. It is essential reading for anyone who wants to understand the long-term forces that enabled the Conservatives to win many Red Wall seats in the North of England in 2019, when, at the same time, London has become a Labour dominated city.'

Sir John Curtice, Professor of Politics at the University of Strathclyde and Senior Research Fellow at the National Centre for Social Research

'Furlong and Jennings have provided a masterful and timely insight into Britain's electoral geography and its changes over time. Deep in explanation, nuanced in insight, its packed full of essential information, correcting overly simplistic stereotypes with authoritative analysis. Anyone who wants to understand Britain's electoral geography needs to read it.'

Jane Green, Professor of Political Science and British Politics, Nuffield College, University of Oxford

'Awash with illuminating electoral statistics and maps, this is a truly excellent analysis of the changing shape of British politics.'

Lord Hayward OBE, psephologist and political analyst

'Furlong and Jennings have provided a tour de force of analysis that augments and expands on the trends around changing political identity and geography of England and Wales. This book is essential reading for those who want to understand British politics.'

James Kanagasooriam, Chief Research Officer, Focaldata and inventor of the 'Red Wall' concept

'The 2019 election turned the political map on its head. This book is a must read for anyone who wants to know how party allegiances are shifting again and how that could shape and define future elections and the country'.

Lisa Nandy MP

'By moving beyond simple Red Wall / Blue Wall dichotomies with a more subtle breaking down of 'left behind' communities into three different types, this book provides an invaluable explanation as to what has happened in British politics – and provides thoughtful pointers towards what is yet to come'.

Dr Mark Pack, President, Liberal Democrats

'Dramatic shifts in party support at recent British elections have substantially altered the country's political map in sometimes surprising ways. In this important new book, Jamie Furlong and Will Jennings provide a compelling analysis of how the changing social and economic geography of England and Wales over the last four decades has influenced that shifting geography of party support. Anyone hoping to understand Britain's political geography has much to learn from this book'.

Charles Pattie, Professor of Geography,
University of Sheffield

The Changing Electoral Map of England and Wales

Jamie Furlong and Will Jennings

OXFORD

UNIVERSITY PRESS

OXFORD
UNIVERSITY PRESS

Great Clarendon Street, Oxford, OX2 6DP,
United Kingdom

Oxford University Press is a department of the University of Oxford.
It furthers the University's objective of excellence in research, scholarship,
and education by publishing worldwide. Oxford is a registered trade mark of
Oxford University Press in the UK and in certain other countries

Published in the United States of America by Oxford University Press
198 Madison Avenue, New York, NY 10016, United States of America

British Library Cataloguing in Publication Data
Data available

Library of Congress Control Number: 2024937972

ISBN 9780192847959
ISBN 9780198927082 (pbk.)

DOI: 10.1093/9780191943331.001.0001

Printed and bound by
CPI Group (UK) Ltd, Croydon, CR0 4YY

Cover image: Alasdair Rae

MIX
Paper | Supporting
responsible forestry
FSC® C013604

Acknowledgements

This book has been many years in the making and reflects a joining together of many streams of research and practice of the authors. It began in February 2015 with a late-night email from Jamie to Will and Andy Hinde at the University of Southampton asking if they would consider supervising a Ph.D. project forecasting future elections from changes in constituency demographics. After securing funding from the Economic and Social Research Council (ESRC), Jamie's thesis exploring the changing electoral geography of England and Wales began in October 2015 and was completed in December 2019, just prior to the redrawing of Britain's electoral map at the 'get Brexit done' election. Outside our regular meetings during this period, Will had been working closely with another Southampton colleague, Gerry Stoker, on the growing electoral and values divide between 'cosmopolitan' and 'left behind' England. That work similarly started to identify how the changing social and economic profile of places was giving rise to divergent electoral fortunes of the Conservative and Labour Parties in different parts of the country. In the aftermath of the referendum on the UK's membership of the EU, an article by Will and Gerry on 'Two Englands' was picked up in early 2017 by Labour MP for Wigan, Lisa Nandy, who made a series of influential interventions on the geographical divides exposed by Brexit and the threat they posed to the Labour Party's electoral future—leading to the founding of a think tank, the Centre for Towns, led by Lisa, Will, and Ian Warren. While Labour's vulnerability in 'left behind' towns did not cost it electorally in 2017, as the unexpected surge in support for Jeremy Corbyn's Labour during the campaign shocked many, it did leave the Conservatives poised to strike against its opponent in the future. Indeed, at the 2019 general election the Conservative Party under Boris Johnson made dramatic inroads into Labour's heartlands in the North and Midlands of England, winning many constituencies that it had never held before. As the dust settled from that election, we decided that it was time to join our research together to document how Britain's electoral geography had been transformed by recent events and historical processes.

We have accrued many professional and personal debts during this project. This book would never have been possible without the financial support of the ESRC studentship for Jamie's Ph.D. He would also like to thank many of the staff associated with the ESRC South Coast Doctoral Training Partnership (DTP)—in particular: Glenn Harris, Gemma Harris, Professor Pauline Leonard, and Professor Amos Channon. Each gave an immeasurable amount of support and advice and always kept the well-being of Ph.D. students as a top priority. The Ph.D. itself would never have been completed without the immense support of the supervisors, Dr Andrew Hinde and the co-author of this book Will Jennings. They offered boundless support and made invaluable contributions to the thesis and the direction of this research. Thanks also go to Professor Charles Pattie and Professor Gerry Stoker for their very useful comments as examiners at Jamie's Ph.D. viva, which have shaped the direction of this book.

Jamie would also like to extend his gratitude to Dan Devine, Chloe Harvey, Matthew Ryan, James Dawber, Mandy Moore, Sandra Jurasszovich, Roger Tyler, Mia Tackney, Nele van der Wielen, Kristine Nilsen, Rob North, Dana Thomson, Cori Ruktanonchai, Neema Begum, and Stuart Wilks-Heeg, all of whom were called upon for their statistical or political expertise at various points in this project. Beyond this we are deeply grateful to our fellow psephologists and political scientists—perhaps most of all to Ron Johnston, who sadly is no longer with us, but whose work as *the* pioneer of British electoral geography has been an inspiration to both Jamie and Will and has informed so much of this book. In addition, we would like to thank Jane Green, Paula Surridge, John Curtice, Dave Cutts, Ed Fieldhouse, Paul Widdop, Maria Sobolewska, Patrick English, Tim Bale, Jon Mellon, Justin Fisher, Phil Cowley, Stephen Fisher, Chris Prosser, Robert Ford, Jack Bailey, Lizzie Simon, Lawrence McKay, Christopher Wlezien, James Kanagasooriam, Patrick Sturgis, and Anand Menon for the many thought-provoking exchanges and conversations we have had over the years regarding Britain's changing political divides and electoral geography. This book has built on each of those conversations in some way. We owe special thanks to Alasdair Rae, for producing the fantastic cover to the book (using real electoral data!), and to all the interviewees who spoke to us for the fieldwork conducted in Merseyside and Lincolnshire.

From his time working at the Labour Party, Jamie offers special thanks to Tim Waters, Tom Adams, and former employee, Lena Mangold—all of whom appointed Jamie as a Targeting Analyst (2017–19) and Targeting and Analysis Manager (2019–21). Many of the statistical skills and political knowledge that made this book possible are the result of your guidance and your insights. Will is extremely grateful to colleagues at Sky News—Michael Thrasher, Isla Glaister, John Woollard, Ed Conway, Sam Coates, Nick Phipps, and Jonathan Levy—where he worked as part of the election analysis team in 2017 and

2019, for their insights and support. From his time co-directing the Centre of Towns, Will is thankful to Lisa Nandy, Ian Warren, and Mark Gregory for their time collaborating on how to tackle the country's spatial divides, and for the many enjoyable and stimulating conversations we had running the think tank. He also owes a huge amount of thanks to the teams from his other ESRC projects, that overlapped with writing of this book, for their support and patience—Dan Devine, Viktor Valgardsson, Jennifer Gaskell, Lawrence McKay, Hannah Bunting, John Kenny, Andra Roescu, Stuart Smedley, and Nick Or.

We would like to express our gratitude to our Editor at Oxford University Press, Dominic Byatt, for his support for the book and patiently waiting on its delivery (Will's first introduction to the mysteries of academic book publishing was at a workshop given by Dominic in Oxford about twenty years ago!). Many thanks also to Vicki Sunter for her support as we prepared the final manuscript and materials. We benefited hugely from the insights and knowledge of an anonymous reviewer and hope that the final manuscript does justice to the wise and constructive feedback we received in drafting it.

During the period of writing-up the initial Ph.D. and working at the Labour Party, Jamie owes an awful lot to the kind friends and family that put him up in London. Thank you to Arran Olivares Whitaker, Alex Ascherson, and Tony Furlong, all of whom welcomed Jamie late at night after a day at work and an evening spent working on the Ph.D.

Jamie would also like to offer a heartfelt thank you to his mum (Diane) and his dad (Tony, who sadly passed away during this project) for a lifetime of encouragement and giving opportunities that neither of them have had in their own lives. He would also like to say thank you to his brother, Tony, and sister, Katie, for their love and support during their father's illness and death.

Finally, the biggest thanks of all from Jamie goes to his wife, Haley, who moved to the UK because he was offered a Ph.D. at Southampton. Thank you for the help to get out of bed some mornings, the coffee, the patience during all the late-night writing, and the comfort during a really challenging period of life.

Will would like to thank his wife, Natalie, and his son Arthur, who have—as ever—been extremely patient about his nocturnal writing habits and provided great company over an intense few years.

This book was completed in late 2023, at a time when the electoral tide seemed to be on the verge of another momentous recalibration, with Labour nearly twenty points ahead in the polls and an election due in 2024 (or January 2025 at the latest). Whether the relationships we observe here persist, and structure Britain's electoral map once again, or there is some return to historical geographies of voting, only time will tell. Regardless of the outcome, however, we believe that the long-term structural factors shaping the demographic composition of various places, and the positions taken by political parties, mean that we are unlikely to see a complete reversal of trends in the spatial distribution of support observed over the past forty years. Rather, as we show in this book, it is quite likely that major electoral results may conceal ongoing changes in the underlying relationship between the demographic profile of places and their support for political parties.

Contents

List of Figures   xii
List of Tables   xvii

1. Redrawing the electoral map   1

2. How changing demography drives electoral change   37

3. Electoral change in England and Wales   62

4. How places vote   85

5. Relative decline (and growth) and the changing
   electoral geography of England and Wales   119

6. In search of Red and Blue heartlands   151

7. Why place matters: Insights from Merseyside and Lincolnshire   184

8. Conclusion   215

References   231
Index   247

List of Figures

1.1. Demographically left behind constituencies, 1945–2019   2

1.2. Economically left behind constituencies, 1945–2019   3

1.3. Precariously left behind constituencies, 1945–2019   4

1.4. Cosmopolitan inner-city suburbs, 1945–2019   5

1.5. University towns and cities, 1945–2019   7

1.6. Change in SNP vote in Scotland (2010–2015) by Labour vote (2010)   9

1.7. Change in Labour vote vs Leave vote in England and Wales, 1979–2019   12

1.8. Change in Conservative vote vs Leave vote in England and Wales, 1979–2019   13

1.9. Change in Labour vote (2010–2019) vs combined Liberal Democrat/Green Party vote (2010) in England and Wales   14

1.10. Change in Conservative vote (2015–2019) vs UK Independence Party vote (2015)   15

1.11. Party vote share for working-class voters, 1979–2019   20

1.12. Working-class vote as a share of party's vote, 1979–2019   21

1.13. Women's vote as a share of party's vote, 1979–2019   21

1.14. Labour Party vote share by age, 1979 vs 2019   22

1.15. Conservative Party vote share by age, 1979 vs 2019   22

1.16. Working age voters (18–64 years old) as a share of party's vote, 1979–2019   23

1.17. Older voters (65+ years old) as a share of party's vote, 1979–2019   23

1.18. Party vote share for university graduates, 1979–2019   24

1.19. University graduates' vote as a share of party's vote, 1979–2019   25

2.1. Party positions on the left–right economic dimension, 1979–2019   59

2.2. Party positions on the liberal–authoritarian dimension, 1979–2019   59

3.1. Party vote share by region, 1945–2019   65

3.2. Labour Party vote share by region relative to national vote share, 1945–2019   66

3.3. Conservative Party vote share by region relative to national vote share, 1945–2019   67

3.4. Region as a predictor of party constituency vote share, 1945–2019   68

3.5. Labour and Conservative vote share in selected core city constituencies, 1950–2019   70

3.6. Labour and Conservative vote share in selected industrial town constituencies, 1950–2019   71

3.7. Labour and Conservative vote share in selected rural constituencies, 1950–2019   72

3.8. Labour and Conservative vote share in selected Welsh rural constituencies, 1950–2019   73

3.9. Labour-Conservative vote margin by population density, 1945–2019   74

3.10. Size of constituency majority by marginality, Great Britain, 1945–2019   77

3.11. Increments of majority increase by marginality, 1945–2019   79

4.1. Correlation between traditional working-class occupations and Labour and Conservative vote share, 1979–2019   93

4.2. Mean party vote share (1979 and 2019) by social class   95

4.3. Mean party vote share (1979 and 2019) by manufacturing employment   97

4.4. Correlation between age and Labour and Conservative vote share, 1979–2019   97

4.5. Mean party vote share (1979 and 2019) by age   98

4.6. Correlation between urban-ness, ethnic diversity, gross migration, and Labour and Conservative vote share, 1979–2019   99

4.7. Mean party vote share (1979 and 2019) by ethnic diversity   100

4.8. Correlation between cosmopolitan occupations, degree-level qualifications, and Labour and Conservative vote share, 1979–2019   101

4.9. Mean party vote share (1979 and 2019) by cosmopolitan-ness   102

4.10. Mean party vote share (1979 and 2019) by degree-holders   103

4.11. Correlation between economic deprivation and Labour and Conservative vote share, 1979–2019   104

4.12. Correlation between precarious occupations, secure employment and Labour and Conservative vote share, 1979–2019   105

4.13. Mean party vote share (1987 and 2019) by occupational precariousness   106

4.14. Standardized coefficients predicting Labour vote share, 1979–2019   109

4.15. Standardized coefficients predicting Conservative vote share, 1979–2019   110

A4.1. Correlation between distance from nearest cosmopolitan place and distance from the nearest university and Labour and Conservative vote share, 1979–2019   116

A4.2. Mean party vote share (1979 and 2019) by unemployment   117

A4.3. Correlation between home ownership, professional occupations, and
       Labour and Conservative vote share, 1979–2019   117

A4.4. Mean party vote share (1979 and 2019) by home ownership   118

5.1.   Labour to Conservative swing (1979–2019) by change in semi-skilled
       and unskilled occupations (1981–2011)   126

5.2.   Labour to Conservative swing (1979–2019) by change in 16–29 age
       group (1981–2011)   127

5.3.   Labour to Conservative swing (1979–2019) by change in over-65 age
       group (1981–2011)   128

5.4.   Labour to Conservative swing (1979–2019) by change in ethnic diversity
       (1981–2011)   129

5.5.   Labour to Conservative swing (1979–2019) by change in university
       graduates (1981–2011)   130

5.6.   Labour to Conservative swing (1979–2019) by change in social housing
       (1981–2011)   132

5.7.   Labour to Conservative swing (1979–2019) by change in unemployment
       rate (1981–2011)   133

5.8.   Labour to Conservative swing (1979–2019) by change in poor health
       (1981–2011)   134

5.9.   Labour to Conservative swing (1979–2019) by change in home
       ownership (1981–2011)   135

5.10. Change in Labour and Conservative vote share (2005–19) by change in
       employment in precarious occupations (2005–11)   137

5.11. Change in Labour vote share (2005–19) by change in employment in
       house price to logged income ratio (2005–14)   138

5.12. Change in Labour and Conservative vote share (1979–2019) by ranking
       of socio-economic decline (1981–2011)   141

5.13. Predictors of change in Labour vote share (1979–2019)   144

5.14. Predictors of change in Conservative vote share (1979–2019)   145

6.1.   Labour constituency vote shares at the 1979 general election (1983
       boundaries)   153

6.2.   Labour constituency vote shares at the 2019 general election   154

6.3.   Conservative constituency vote shares at the 1979 general election (1983
       boundaries)   157

6.4.   Conservative constituency vote shares at the 2019 general election   158

6.5.   Labour over- and under-performance mapped by standardized residuals
       at the 1979 general election (1983 boundaries)   160

6.6. Labour over- and under-performance mapped by standardized residuals at the 2019 general election   161

6.7. Conservative over- and under-performance mapped by standardized residuals at the 1979 general election (1983 boundaries)   163

6.8. Conservative over- and under-performance mapped by standardized residuals at the 2019 general election   164

6.9. Standardized residuals and Labour/Conservative vote shares in Merseyside, 1979–2019   165

6.10. Standardized residuals and Labour/Conservative vote shares in Lincolnshire, 1979–2019   166

6.11. LISA cluster map showing statistically significant clustering of Labour vote shares at the 1979 general election (1983 boundaries)   168

6.12. LISA cluster map showing statistically significant clustering of Labour vote shares at the 2019 general election   169

6.13. LISA cluster map showing statistically significant clustering of standardized residuals (under- and over-performance) from the 1979 model predicting Labour vote shares (1983 boundaries)   170

6.14. LISA cluster map showing statistically significant clustering of standardized residuals (under- and over-performance) from the 2019 model predicting Labour vote shares   171

6.15. LISA cluster map showing statistically significant clustering of Conservative vote shares at the 1979 general election (1983 boundaries)   172

6.16. LISA cluster map showing statistically significant clustering of Conservative vote shares at the 2019 general election   173

6.17. LISA cluster map showing statistically significant clustering of standardized residuals (under- and over-performance) from the 1979 model predicting Conservative vote shares (1983 boundaries)   174

6.18. LISA cluster map showing statistically significant clustering of standardized residuals (under- and over-performance) from the 2019 model predicting Conservative vote shares   175

7.1. A row of independent shops in Crosby   189

7.2. A not atypical suburban street of large, detached homes and big gardens   189

7.3. One of many gated houses in the area   190

7.4. The grand entrance to Sacred Heart Catholic College—a Catholic comprehensive school in Crosby   190

7.5. A banner declaring 'we're not English we are Scouse' at Anfield, Liverpool Football Club   196

7.6. Liverpool fans unveil a banner supporting Jeremy Corbyn during the
Premier League match at Anfield, Liverpool Football Club, Sunday 7
May 2017   196

7.7. A leaflet used by Phil Dilks in the run up to the 2013 Local Elections in
Deeping St James   203

7.8. North Street, Bourne, does not give the impression of an economically
thriving area   204

7.9. The unusual geography of the Fens of south Lincolnshire, close to
Spalding   205

List of Tables

A1.1. Social class measures in the British Election Study, 1979–2019   35

2.1. Varieties of left-behindedness   50

2.2. Constituencies with highest share of manufacturing, routine/semi-routine occupations, over-65s, and housing tenure, 1981–2011   52

2.3. Constituencies with highest share of cosmopolitan industries, managerial-professional occupations, university graduates, under-30s, and ethnic minorities, 1981–2011   55

3.1. Majority size and electoral efficiency, Great Britain, 1945–2019   78

A3.1. Labour vote share (%) by region, 1945–2019   81

A3.2. Conservative vote share (%) by region, 1945–2019   82

A3.3. Liberal/Alliance/Liberal Democrat vote share (%) by region, 1945–2019   83

A3.4. Nationalist party vote share (%) in Scotland and Wales, 1945–2019   84

4.1. Classification and measurement of demographically left behind areas   86

4.2. Classification and measurement of economically left behind areas   87

4.3. Classification and measurement of precariously left behind areas   88

4.4. Pre-existing census and electoral data sets used for this research   91

4.5. Party vote share in England and Wales, 1979 vs 2019 general elections   92

4.6. Summary of bivariate correlations between constituency characteristics of left-behindedness and Labour and Conservative vote shares   107

A4.1. 'Cosmopolitan industries': 2001 and 2011 harmonization   114

5.1. Socio-economic profile of Gravesham vs England and Wales   120

5.2. Change in the socio-economic profile of Gravesham vs England and Wales   121

5.3. Measurement of whether an area is becoming left behind for each classification   124

5.4. Change in renting and change in vote share, by region   136

5.5. Mean vote share changes (1979–2019) across constituencies by categories of socio-economic change   141

5.6. Mean vote share changes (1979–2019) across deindustrialized constituencies compared to all constituencies   143

A5.1. Predictors of change in Labour and Conservative vote share, 1979–2019   150

6.1. Labour and Conservative vote shares in 1979 (at 1983 boundaries): a comparison between constituencies in and around Barnsley with Leeds   155

6.2. Labour and Conservative vote shares in 2019: a comparison between constituencies in and around Barnsley with Leeds   156

6.3. Proportion of schools affiliated to the Catholic Church by constituency in Merseyside — 178

6.4. Proportion of schools affiliated to the Catholic Church by constituency in Lincolnshire (excluding Lincoln and North East Lincolnshire) — 178

6.5. The twenty constituencies in England and Wales with the highest proportion of schools that are affiliated to the Catholic Church — 179

6.6. Mean standardized residual values across Merseyside and Lincolnshire for old and new models predicting Labour vote share — 180

6.7. Mean standardized residual values across Merseyside and Lincolnshire for old and new models predicted Conservative vote share — 180

A6.1. Regression summaries of the new OLS models predicting Labour vote shares at the 2019 and 2017 general elections — 181

A6.2. Regression summaries of the new OLS models predicting Conservative vote shares at the 2019 and 2017 general elections — 183

7.1. Summary of the interviewees and their connection to politics in Merseyside/Lincolnshire — 186

1

Redrawing the electoral map

At 11.32pm on 12 December 2019, the declaration of the third result of election night, for the constituency of Blyth Valley, confirmed that the electoral map of Britain was in the midst of a tectonic shift. The seat—a former coal-mining and shipbuilding town on the coast in south-east Northumberland that had been held by Labour since 1950—had just been won by the Conservatives with a swing of over 10 points, overturning a Labour majority of over 8,000 votes. Three hours later and 40 miles south, Bishop Auckland, another town with a long coal-mining history (which like Blyth Valley voted convincingly in favour of leaving the EU), elected a Conservative MP for the first time since the constituency's creation in 1885, ending the Labour Party's hold that dated back to 1935. It was not just the voting habits but also the populations of these former industrial towns that had changed. Over the past half century, both places had aged considerably, and in the case of Bishop Auckland the number of people under 45 had actually shrunk between 1961 and 2011 (Office for National Statistics 2021). These two towns had experienced a significant decline of employment in their traditional industries, with a much-reduced manufacturing sector and coal-mining gone.[1] The last coal mine in Blyth, the Bates Colliery, closed in 1986, while the last in the Bishop Auckland area, Haggs Lane Drift, shut down in 1987. The constituencies were archetypal of what have often been referred to as 'left behind' places—former industrial towns with populations that on average were older, predominantly white, working class with lower levels of qualification.[2] Throughout this book, we refer to these places as *demographically left behind* (contrasting them with places that are *economically left behind* in terms of their socio-economic deprivation or *precariously left behind* due to presence of a population in insecure employment). Over successive decades, the foundations that had made these places Labour strongholds—including a strong local trade union presence linked to industry—had crumbled. In

---

[1] Between 1979 and 2019, the proportion of people employed in manufacturing in Bishop Auckland fell by 61% (to 15%) and by 60% in Blyth Valley (to 11%).

[2] This characterization of left behind *places* follows Ford and Goodwin's (2014) original development of the concept of 'left behind' to capture the demographic and attitudinal characteristics associated with support for UKIP at the individual level.

The Changing Electoral Map of England and Wales. Jamie Furlong and Will Jennings, Oxford University Press.
© Jamie Furlong and Will Jennings (2024). DOI: 10.1093/9780191943331.003.0001

many such places Labour's vote had begun to decline as early as the 1960s, and although support for the party in those communities rallied as a reaction against the Thatcher and Major governments, it resumed that downward trajectory from the high point of 1997 (see Figure 1.1).[3]

Even as the Conservative Party made large inroads into Labour's traditional heartlands across the North of England, the Midlands, and Wales, not everywhere has followed the same trend. While Labour have been, relative to the Conservatives, losing support across several elections in post-industrial towns, their vote share has held up in seats with the most significant economic challenges, largely in bigger cities. In constituencies like Liverpool Walton, Birmingham Hodge Hill, and Birmingham Ladywood—city constituencies with high levels of household deprivation (ranked 1st, 2nd, and 7th respectively on the Index of Multiple Deprivation for England), poor health, unemployment, and social renters, Labour's support held up relative to the national swing against it (see Figure 1.2). The party has retained its grip in larger cities where levels of poverty are highest—areas we refer to as economically left behind in contrast to the demographically left behind towns

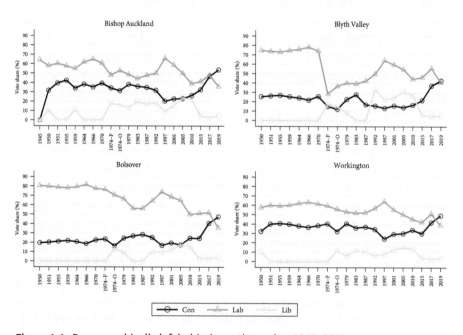

Figure 1.1 Demographically left behind constituencies, 1945–2019

[3] In Blyth Valley, Labour's vote slumped to 29% (from 74%) at the general election of February 1974 due to the sitting Labour MP (Eddie Milne) who had been deselected by the party standing against it as an independent candidate, winning the seat. Milne stood again as an independent in the elections of October 1974 and 1979. Though Labour won the seat back at the first attempt, this substantially depressed support for the party in the constituency at these elections.

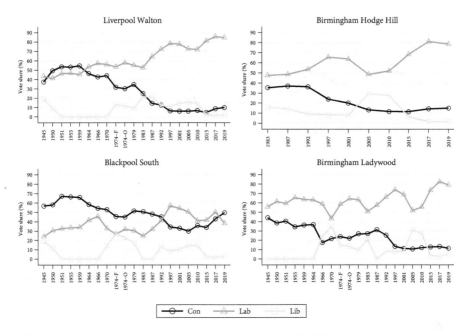

Figure 1.2 Economically left behind constituencies, 1945–2019

that have drifted towards the Conservatives. This is in part a consequence of the poverty of these city constituencies, but also because of their other characteristics, such as ethnic diversity and a younger age profile. Yet it remains the case that, while the Conservative Party picked up some seats with above average rates of deprivation in 2019, the overall pattern remained that *the most disadvantaged areas* that may be considered more economically left behind tended to stick with Labour.

Similarly, the Conservatives were less successful in overhauling Labour majorities in areas characterized by the presence of what has been called 'the new working class' (Ainsley 2018). These are areas with many people living on low to middle incomes in insecure jobs (Standing 2011), typically in service sectors such as social care, retail, and catering. This reflects the growing prevalence of highly precarious, casualized forms of employment in Britain's economy. One such example is Leicester, home to a rampant gig economy in textiles, with its garment factories becoming a focus of allegations regarding widespread exploitation of workers during the Covid-19 crisis (Johnson 2020). While Labour suffered large swings against it in both Leicester West and Leicester East in 2019, the party's vote remained relatively high—a pattern that held true across many other areas with high levels of precarious forms of employment (see Figure 1.3).

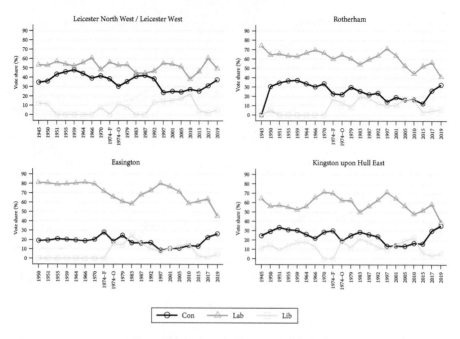

Figure 1.3 Precariously left behind constituencies, 1945–2019

While many bricks in Labour's 'Red Wall'—historically strong seats across Northern England and the Midlands—had crumbled in 2019 (Kanagasooriam and Simon 2021), its vote proved rather more durable in the most deprived areas, and in places where the local economy consisted of a greater number of insecure, low-paid jobs. As we will argue in the remainder of this book, the narrative of working-class, left behind areas deserting Labour for the Conservatives requires some nuance and qualification. While Labour has seen its vote collapse in certain sorts of left behind constituency, its support has been more resilient in other areas that could just as easily be termed left behind, marked by high levels of deprivation or precarious employment—despite the loss of the party's relative electoral dominance since the landslide of 1997. A key distinction—illuminated in Chapter 5—is that the Conservatives have gained from Labour in areas that are becoming, relative to other areas, increasingly left behind, but not in those areas that are the most economically left behind. The former—declining areas but not the most severely deprived—are typically seats in post-industrial towns; the latter—often economically improving but still with the highest levels of deprivation—are typically seats in large cities. These divergent fortunes for either party in relatively improving and declining areas is key to understanding the changing geography of recent general election results.

There is another side to the story of the changing electoral geography of England and Wales in the shifting allegiances of some relatively affluent, 'cosmopolitan' suburbs of major cities—home to large numbers of professionals, university graduates, and well-paid public sector employees (see Figure 1.4). The leafy suburbs of Manchester Withington and Sheffield Hallam, each located in the southern corridor of a major Northern city, were once Conservative Party strongholds where the professional classes lived in large Victorian family houses. At the 1951 general election, the Conservatives won 65% of the vote in Withington and 71% in Hallam. By 2019 these numbers had fallen to 11% and 26% respectively. Over time both constituencies have become even more desirable for young professionals and families, as they are home to independent delicatessens, book shops, cafes, and bars selling craft beer. But the Labour Party's electoral fortunes did not simply mirror the Conservative collapse thanks to the robust local competition offered by the Liberal Democrats, who for a long time attracted the sort of voter that Labour now increasingly appeal to—that is, younger, white, middle-class professionals/university graduates living in large urban centres. In fact, up until 2015, Labour's vote had appeared to be steadily declining in Sheffield Hallam, and the constituency had become a safe Liberal Democrat seat. But at the 2015 election, Labour gained nearly 20 points and came close to ousting Deputy Prime Minister Nick Clegg, creating the foundations for it to win

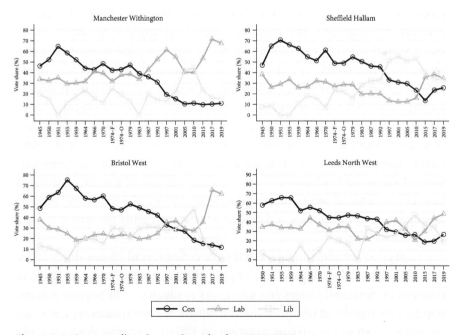

Figure 1.4 Cosmopolitan inner-city suburbs, 1945–2019

the constituency in 2017 and later retain it against the odds in 2019 (faring better than the national swing and avoiding a backlash over the scandal-hit tenure of the former Labour MP). In contrast, Labour's vote in Manchester Withington had been on an upward trajectory since 1983, before the party lost the seat to the Liberal Democrats at the 2005 and 2010 general elections as the popularity of the New Labour government waned. The national collapse of the Liberal Democrats in 2015 helped Labour into a commanding position in Withington, and by 2017 the party was on 72% of the vote in the constituency—over 50 points ahead of its nearest rival.

Bristol West shares many of the same characteristics as Withington and Hallam, covering a large part of the city's leafy inner suburbs with larger houses and civic parks in affluent districts like Redland and Clifton—home to professionals and university graduates, with the University of Bristol the largest employer in the constituency—but also encompassing more deprived areas such as Lawrence Hill and Easton. The constituency was held continuously by the Conservative Party for 112 years between 1885 and 1997. At the 1955 general election, the party's vote had reached over 70% and it remained steadfastly above 40% until Labour's landslide in 1997. By 2019 it had collapsed to barely 10%, while the combined Labour and Green Party vote reached 87% (with the Liberal Democrats having stepped aside due to the Unite to Remain electoral pact).

Across the well-to-do suburbs of Manchester, Sheffield, and Bristol, a common factor behind these trends was an electorate that, over time, had become younger, more diverse, and more educated—making it more amenable to the direction taken by the Labour Party and less receptive to what the Conservatives had to offer. The rate of electoral change in just a decade should not be understated: Withington went from being a marginal seat in 2010 to having a 50-point Labour lead in 2019, Hallam went from a Liberal Democrat lead of over 30 points in 2010 to a narrow Labour win in 2017, Bristol West went from a 20-point Liberal Democrat win in 2010 to a 50-point Labour advantage in 2019. In each seat, the collapse of the Liberal Democrats from 2015 onwards played a crucial role in the size of the swing towards Labour—combined with the long-term decline of Conservative support among young professionals and graduates who are highly prevalent in these areas.

A final group of constituencies that have defied recent electoral trends are university towns (see Figure 1.5)—again characterized by the presence of younger, professional classes and university graduates, with sizeable student populations registered to vote in the constituency. These places typically had backed Remain in the 2016 referendum on Britain's membership of the EU. In 2017, Labour enjoyed a shock win in Canterbury, ending over a century of

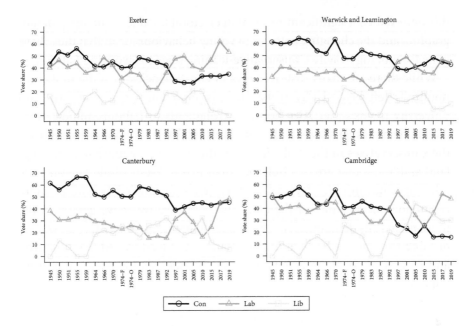

Figure 1.5 University towns and cities, 1945–2019

continuous Conservative control of the seat, and in 2019 increased its narrow majority, resisting the national swing. The constituency has over 30,000 students attending two university campuses in the town (the University of Kent campus and Canterbury Christ Church University), while one in four workers are employed in the education sector (McLennan 2019), making it fruitful terrain for a party that increasingly relies on younger voters and graduates (Sturgis and Jennings 2020).

Warwick and Leamington, a constituency with a high proportion of professional classes (68%) and university graduates (37%), and home to some students from the nearby University of Warwick (with the university confusingly located not in Warwick but on the outskirts of Coventry), has similarly gone from being a safe Conservative seat—once held by party leader and PM Anthony Eden—to being a Labour-held marginal. Labour enjoyed rather more substantial majorities (a little over 15%) in Cambridge and Exeter, places again with a younger population than the national average (with 64% and 55% aged under 45 respectively) and in the former case many university graduates (47% compared to the national average of 27%). Both constituencies had seen a gradual decline in the Conservative vote share, from consistently above 50% during the 1950s, to less than 20% in Cambridge and a little over 30% in Exeter. While not as calamitous as the collapse in support observed in the affluent suburbs of Manchester, Sheffield, and Bristol, this represented a significant reversal in electoral fortunes. Changing demographics and the changing patterns of voting behaviour mean that these have gone from being heavily Conservative-leaning seats to favouring Labour.

While there are many distinct types of constituencies—(a) the most economically left behind city seats; (b) cosmopolitan urban seats; (c) and university towns—that have become strongholds of Labour support, simple mathematics tells us why this has not translated to recent victories over the Conservatives in the polls. In short, there are many more seats in England and Wales that are like Bolsover than Bristol West. While Labour have piled up votes in cities (typically either economically left behind or more cosmopolitan, or a mix of the two), the Conservatives have gained in the more numerous demographically left behind areas, as well as across swathes of small-town and suburban England that have at least leaned Conservative, and in some cases more dramatically swung towards the party away from Labour.[4]

A tale of two electoral realignments?

During just four years between 2015 and 2019, the electoral geography of Great Britain underwent not one but two critical junctures.[5] At the 2015 general election, Labour was reduced to just one seat in Scotland (from forty-one seats in the previous election), seeing a swing of nearly 25 points to the Scottish National Party (SNP)—who won a majority of seats north of the border for the very first time. The SNP made its largest gains in Labour's former strongholds (see Figure 1.6), areas in which voters were more likely to vote in favour of Scottish independence in the 2014 referendum. In Glasgow North East, a constituency that had voted Yes to independence, with an 8% unemployment rate, one in ten people reported as being long-term sick, over a third employed in routine occupations (and fewer than 17% with a university degree), ranking as one of the most deprived constituencies in Scotland, the percentage split of the Labour–SNP vote went from 68–14 in 2010 to 34–58 in 2015, a swing of 38 points. Similar reversals occurred in Glasgow South West (63–16 to 33–57), Glasgow East (62–25 to 32–57), and other constituencies

---

[4] In the 2019 general election, disproportionately large swings from Labour to the Conservatives were found in constituencies where the vote to leave the European Union in 2016 was estimated to be 60% or more (Ford et al. 2021, pp. 463–5).

[5] The Scottish Parliament election in 2011 had foreshadowed the realignment at the 2015 general election. While Labour's vote only fell slightly, the SNP resoundingly took first place, gaining around 12 points aided by the collapse of the Liberal Democrats—who saw their vote more than halve from the previous election.

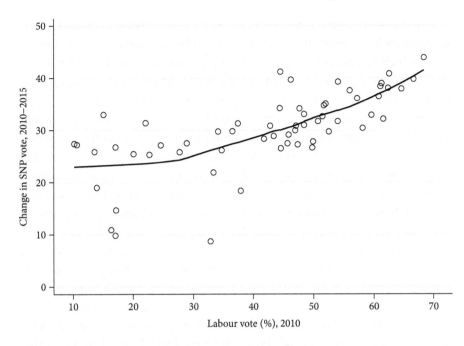

Figure 1.6 Change in SNP vote in Scotland (2010–2015) by Labour vote (2010)

in the city. Between 1987 and 2010 Labour had held every seat in Glasgow,[6] but in 2015 it was wiped out completely—even in areas where most people had voted against Scottish independence.

The constituencies where the SNP usurped Labour in the electoral pecking order were places where, unsurprisingly, Scottish national identity tended to be strongest, but also which suffered from high rates of unemployment, deprivation, and poor health. In the solitary seat that Labour held onto, the more affluent Edinburgh South (with 47% graduates), which had voted 61% to 39% to remain part of the UK in 2014, Labour's vote actually increased—despite a large rise in SNP support (from 8% to 34%). The fact that Labour's last bastion standing in Scotland was a seat it had first won in 1987, while losing its working-class heartlands on the Clyde, reflected the changing demographic composition of its vote—as well as the rise of the SNP as an electoral force. The immediate effect of this realignment of voting behaviour in Scotland, combined with a disappointing electoral performance more generally in 2015, was to significantly reduce Labour's chances of winning a majority in Westminster in the near future.

---

[6] One constituency (Glasgow Springburn) was held by the Speaker of the House of Commons, former Labour MP Michael Martin, between 2001 and 2010 (and so was not contested by the main parties as a result).

The aftermath of the referendum on Britain's membership of the EU was to dramatically impact the electoral geography of England and Wales, as well as further undermining chances of a Labour revival north of the border. At the 2017 general election, the immediate effects of that geographical shift were hidden by the unexpected gains made by the Labour Party under Jeremy Corbyn, increasing its vote share by 9.6 points to 40% (its highest national vote share since 2001) and achieving a swing from the Conservatives of just over 2 points. While the Conservatives saw their vote increase in Leave-supporting constituencies, Labour's advances were spread much more evenly across the Brexit divide (Jennings and Stoker 2017). This meant that Theresa May's Conservatives did not translate the changing geography of their support into many new seats. A few surprise results hinted at the electoral shift that was around the corner—with Labour picking up the once solid Conservative seats of Canterbury and Kensington, but losing Mansfield (a constituency it had held since 1923). Indeed, despite the small national swing to Labour, the Conservatives gained substantial ground in many demographically left behind areas, something that went largely unnoticed as predicted seat gains barely materialized. From Stoke-on-Trent Central to the Rother Valley, the Conservatives were finally in touching distance of constituencies that they had never taken from the Labour Party. In Scotland, Labour did manage to regain six seats, but found itself in third place, as the Conservatives took on the mantle of the party of Brexit against the Remain-supporting SNP, increasing their vote share by over 13 points.[7]

It was at the general election of 2019 that the Brexit realignment came to electoral fruition in England and Wales. Ahead of the election, polling analyst James Kanagasooriam had warned of the vulnerability of Labour's 'Red Wall'—constituencies that historically voted more heavily for Labour than would have been predicted by demographics alone.[8] Typically former industrial towns in the Midlands, North of England, and Wales, these areas had tended to vote to leave the EU in June 2016 creating an opportunity for the Conservatives to drive a wedge between Labour and their supporters in

---

[7] Unionist-Brexiters and Separatist-Remainers made up 48% of the electorate. Labour was left without a clear political tribe in the new alignment produced by the combination of Scottish nationalism and Brexit—doing best among No-Remainers (34% of voters) (see Prosser and Fieldhouse 2017).

[8] The concept of the 'Red Wall' was originally reported in the *Financial Times* on 6 November 2019 (Payne 2019), having been outlined in August 2019 by James Kanagasooriam (Kanagasooriam 2019). A similar approach was articulated nine months earlier by Furlong (2018). The methodology associated with it is explained in Kanagasooriam and Simon (2021). We generally avoid using the 'Red Wall' concept to analyse the changing electoral geography. While the concept is useful to describe a huge area of Northern England where Labour have been fairly dominant, the popular application of this idea (especially in the media) usually lacks nuance and ignores the political, cultural, and sociodemographic heterogeneity of this area. Parts of Greater Manchester, for instance, might share more in common with suburban London than the rest of Lancashire. Similarly, even in more rural areas there is significant diversity: compare the gentrifying former mill towns of the Calder Valley (e.g. Hebden Bridge, Todmorden) with the former coal-mining villages of the Rother Valley (e.g. Maltby).

the party's traditional heartlands. While Labour lost support across the country in December 2019, it did far worse in areas that had voted heavily for Brexit—losing twenty-eight of its sixty-nine constituencies where the Leave vote was 60% or higher (with the fall of its vote of nearly 14 points almost double that in other seats it held). The Conservatives, on the other hand, saw their vote share increase by around 6 points in those areas, with their support largely unchanged in areas below that threshold.

The election confirmed unmistakably that the traditional map of British politics was no more, with the Conservatives winning seats that had been held by Labour for generations. Labour suffered symbolic losses in constituencies it had held since the establishment of the party as an electoral force in the interwar years—seats such as Bassetlaw (1929), Sedgefield (1935), Workington (1918), Wrexham (1935), and, as discussed earlier, Bishop Auckland (1918).[9] The party saw its vote collapse in many of its traditional heartlands—what we refer to as demographically left behind towns. These are towns with rich mining and manufacturing heritages that were once home to a thriving union movement but had in recent decades experienced sustained social and economic decline. In contrast, Labour's new strongholds were major cities and a handful of university towns that had voted to Remain in the EU in 2016. The Conservative electoral coalition now stretched across its traditional base in the 'Home Counties' to many of these former industrial towns—with its vote highest in areas that favoured Leaving the EU.[10]

While Brexit undoubtedly played a critical role in breaking the historical ties between voters and the Labour Party in many former industrial towns, these shifts are the product of much deeper transformations in the electoral geography of British politics. Those changes have been driven by a combination of demographic trends and the changing link between demographic predictors and vote choice. Simply put, places have changed and so too have the voting habits of people in those places. The 2015, 2017, and 2019 general elections were 'critical elections' (Green 2021) in highlighting the geographical realignment of British politics. However, they must be understood as part of a gradual process of change that has occurred over several decades. Many demographically left behind constituencies were drifting away from the Labour Party and towards the Conservatives well before a referendum on Britain's membership of the EU was called—even if the Brexit vote itself encapsulated the demographic cleavages and ideological axis

[9] Bassetlaw was won by National Labour in 1931 but held by Labour at every other election since 1929, Workington was briefly held by the Conservatives after a by-election in 1976 but had voted Labour at every general election since 1918. Bishop Auckland was won by the National Liberals in 1931 but voted Labour otherwise.

[10] The bivariate correlation between the Conservative vote share in 2019 and the Leave vote in 2016 was 0.54 ($p = 0.000$). The correlation for Labour's vote was a weaker -0.29 ($p = 0.000$).

around which our electoral geography was already rotating. Brexit was an accelerator of these dynamics, rather than the root cause.

In Figure 1.7, we plot the relationship between *change* in Labour's vote share (relative to the party's overall national performance) in each constituency since 1979 (to 2005, 2010, 2015, 2017, and 2019) and the estimated Leave vote share in 2016.[11] This reveals a gradual process of realignment of Labour's vote over a fifteen-year period. In 2005, the long-term direction of Labour's vote was slightly more favourable in seats that would later vote Leave. By 2010, there was little correlation between the long-term change in Labour's vote and the Brexit-friendliness of constituencies. By 2015, this relationship had reversed, and Labour was starting to see a relative decline of its vote in Leave-voting areas contrasted against relative gains in Remain areas. The slope of this relationship sharpened again in 2017, and by 2019 was pronounced. While Brexit clearly structured the geography of Labour's vote in 2019, the trends towards this point were already under way by 2010.[12]

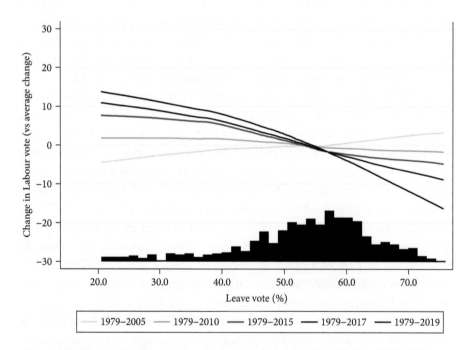

Figure 1.7 Change in Labour vote vs Leave vote in England and Wales, 1979–2019

---

[11] We use 2005–19 as these are the elections where estimates of EU referendum vote are available (Hanretty 2017) and can be mapped against our harmonized data for 1979.

[12] Linear regression of the Leave vote in 2016 on change in the Labour constituency vote between 1979 and 2005 produces a slight positive coefficient (0.10, $p < 0.01$) and explains a small fraction of variance in

A similar but distinct pattern is observed for the Conservatives in Figure 1.8. In 2005, the party was already making relatively greater electoral gains in its vote (compared to 1979) in constituencies that would later vote Leave in 2016. That tendency remained somewhat unchanged between 2005 and 2015. In fact, the 2015 general election saw the party do slightly worse in Leave-leaning areas—due to the challenge from the Eurosceptic UK Independence Party (which won 14% of the vote in England and Wales). It was in 2017 that the geography of long-term change in the Conservative vote became sharply associated with Brexit: the party's largest gains since 1979 were in areas that had voted by more than 55% to leave the EU, while it fared worse in Remain-voting areas. By 2019, the strength of this relationship had increased further, with the long-term trajectory of the Conservative vote highly positively correlated to the percentage share of the Leave vote.[13]

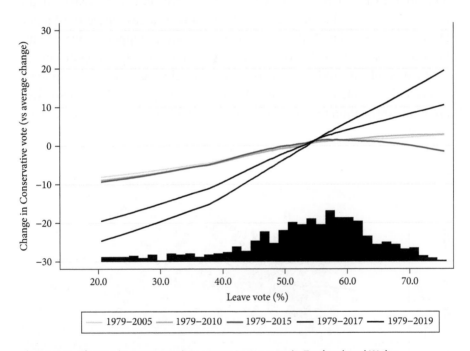

Figure 1.8 Change in Conservative vote vs Leave vote in England and Wales, 1979–2019

the data (Adjusted R-squared = 0.01). For change in the Labour vote between 1979 and 2019, the coefficient is strongly negative (−0.58, $p > 0.001$) and explains a substantial proportion of the variance (Adjusted R-squared = 0.27).

[13] Linear regression of the Leave vote in 2016 on change in the Conservative constituency vote between 1979 and 2005 produces a modest positive coefficient (0.22, $p < 0.001$) and explains some variance in the data (Adjusted R-squared = 0.08). For change in the Conservative vote between 1979 and 2019, the coefficient is strongly positive (0.88, $p > 0.001$) and explains over 50% of the variance (Adjusted R-squared = 0.54).

For both Labour and the Conservatives, this changing alignment of relative electoral gains (since 1979) against the Leave/Remain axis was highly significant; with Labour in particular incurring losses in its Brexit-voting heartlands, but the Conservatives weakened in urban and suburban areas that voted Remain. However, the electoral map of England and Wales was not completely inverted by Brexit: the correlation of the imputed Labour vote share in 1979 and its vote share in 2019 is $r = 0.72$, while this is $r = 0.59$ for the Conservatives. Instead, Brexit *accelerated* changes in sociodemographic patterns of voting: previously the geography of each party's vote had limited association with support for the UK leaving the EU—but by 2019 Brexit significantly structured how support had changed for the parties in different parts of the country.

Two further important changes relate to electoral competition—related both to Brexit and the constituency periods we observed earlier. In the period since 2015, Labour have made inroads in areas where the Liberal Democrats did well in 2010. While Liberal Democrat support is often highly localized, between 1997 and 2010 they were particularly successful in the South West of England, spa towns, and in middle-class cosmopolitan areas of big cities (including in South West London specifically). These were predominantly, though not wholly, areas in which the Remain vote share

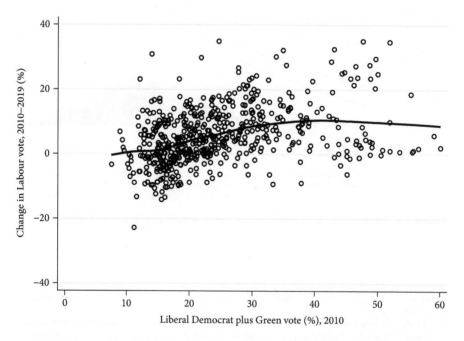

Figure 1.9 Change in Labour vote (2010–2019) vs combined Liberal Democrat/Green Party vote (2010) in England and Wales

was above the national average. Figure 1.9 shows that, generally, in areas with higher combined Liberal Democrat and Green vote shares in 2010, Labour have had a slightly above average increase in vote share between 2010 and 2019. Much of this change is once again driven by urban seats such as Sheffield Hallam, Bristol West, and Leeds North West—all solidly Liberal Democrat in 2010 and solidly Labour in 2019.

The Conservatives, on the other hand, tended to do well in 2017 and 2019 where UKIP had significant levels of support in 2015. Figure 1.10 shows this pattern most clearly: the higher the UKIP vote in 2015, the more positive the change in Conservative vote shares across constituencies between 2010 and 2019. This, to some extent, mirrors the trend in Figure 1.8 related to the Leave vote: UKIP support was unsurprisingly centred around constituencies that subsequently registered convincing majorities in favour of leaving the EU and saw big swings to the Conservatives in the 2017 and 2019 elections. In Boston and Skegness, where 75.6% of the electorate voted to leave the EU, the Conservatives increased their vote share from 43.8% in 2010 to 76.7% in 2019. Similar stories are found in Clacton and Castle Point—constituencies that had either formerly been held by UKIP or where the party had secured a substantial share of the vote at the 2015 general election.

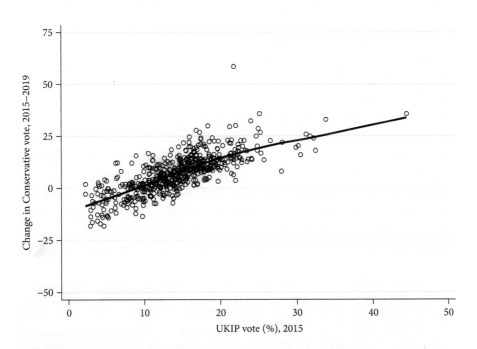

Figure 1.10 Change in Conservative vote (2015–2019) vs UK Independence Party vote (2015)

The historical roots of Britain's electoral geography

The political preferences of individuals are not randomly distributed in space (Rodden 2010). In any political system these distributions reflect the long-term path of social and economic development, and how the dominant political divides—or 'cleavages' (Lipset and Rokkan 1967)[14]—in society are organized geographically. In Britain, as in many countries, industrialization played an important and lasting role in shaping the socio-economic and electoral geography we observe today. Specifically, population changes followed by critical changes in party competition and electoral rules were important precursors to establishment of the *socio-economic* cleavage that would dominate British politics for nearly a century (and which structured its ideological conflict along class lines).[15]

Through the 1800s, the industrial revolution saw the growth of urban populations in Britain, especially in the North of England, Midlands, and Wales. The decline of employment in agriculture and the growing number of job opportunities, and higher wages, available in factories, mines, mills, and docks, led to substantial migration from rural areas to towns and cities.[16] Urban settlements sprang up rapidly close to coal seams and iron ore deposits, as well as in mill towns and trading ports, with access to railways and waterways a crucial factor for industrial (and population) growth. The construction of housing for workers and their families close to new industries added to the build-up of densely populated urban areas. These changes contributed to a growing class consciousness and identity as a result of shared living and working conditions of the large numbers of people in urban areas.

While these demographic trends were important, the conditions for the emergence of Britain's modern party system—whereby Labour replaced the Liberal Party as the main party of opposition to the Conservatives—did not come into force until the first quarter of the twentieth century. This realignment of the party system was enabled by two key changes in party competition and electoral rules. The first of these was the MacDonald-Gladstone pact in 1903 whereby the Liberal Party stood aside for Labour (then known as the Labour Representation Committee) in several constituencies at the 1906 election to avoid splitting the anti-Tory vote (Stephens

---

[14] Bartolini and Mair (1990, p. 215) identify *three elements* of any political cleavage: (i) socio-structural (conflict exists between different groups or interests), (ii) psychological (perceptions exist of distinct group identities, values, and interests), and (iii) organizational (the identities, values, and interests of different parts of society are mobilized by political parties).

[15] This class cleavage has been referred to in different ways by researchers, e.g. 'labour-capital' and 'owner-worker' (Lipset and Rokkan 1967), 'socio-economic' (Curtice and Steed 1982). Ultimately, however, all these accounts are concerned with the same idea.

[16] Law (1967, p. 139) reports high levels of urban population growth in industrial and mining areas as well as seaside resorts between 1801 and 1911.

1982). This enabled Labour to win twenty-nine seats, a substantial improvement on the two seats it had won in 1900. Those constituencies were mainly located in urban industrial areas in the North (e.g. Clitheroe, Manchester North East, Newcastle-upon-Tyne), the Midlands (e.g. Wolverhampton West), and in London (e.g. Deptford, Woolwich). The second major change to occur was enacted through the 1918 Reform Act following the First World War, representing the largest single expansion of the electorate in British history (from 7.7 million to 21.4 million people). This abolished property qualifications for voting for men, significantly expanding the working-class composition of the electorate, though expansion of the suffrage to women over 30 remained conditional on property qualifications.

While the national tides of politics have ebbed and flowed, for a century the electoral map of Britain was defined by the class composition of different regions and constituencies.[17] Traditionally, the working class in industrial urban areas tended to vote for Labour while more middle-class electorates in wealthier towns and rural areas tended to vote for the Conservatives. Like other industrialized countries, electoral advances made by the left were largely concentrated in urban areas, though Labour's heartlands ranged from smaller industrial towns to major cities.[18] As we will discuss in Chapter 2, subsequent economic developments, such as the decline of former industrial towns, ports, seaside resorts, and fishing towns and the growth of new towns and university towns, have seen shifts in the social composition and economic context of many places in England and Wales. Some areas have experienced relative decline in terms of their population and economic activity, while others have prospered. Not only have these developments shaped the course of Britain's economy, they also have influenced the nature and spread of the British electorate, leading certain social and economic groups to be sorted into particular types of area, thereby altering the demographic composition of parliamentary constituencies and making them more or less receptive to the appeals of different political parties. Even holding the ideological preferences of different groups completely constant between elections, changes in the populations of constituencies would see some change hands.

Some geographical changes in the relative electoral strength of the Conservative and Labour parties since 1945 go beyond what would be

---

[17] As Curtice and Steed (1982, p. 261) observed, 'in a society in which voting behaviour is principally determined by class, perhaps the simplest explanation of a long-term change in a constituency's political affiliation is a change in its class composition'.

[18] It is notable that the explosive centrifugal process of urban development in the North of England (and to a lesser extent the Midlands) during the industrial revolution left scattered and less tightly connected urban areas that included smaller towns as well as major cities, in some contrast to countries where industrialization was more heavily concentrated in major cities.

expected based on the demographic composition of constituencies alone. Writing over forty years ago, Curtice and Steed (1982, p. 256) identified an emerging North–South cleavage and an urban–rural cleavage during the 1955–9 parliament which persisted over the ensuing decades; with the North and urban areas moving towards Labour, while the South and rural areas moved towards the Conservatives. Johnston et al. (1988) made a similar observation of 'a nation dividing', whereby Labour tended to 'increase its electoral support in the north of the country and within major cities, while the Conservatives have built up support in the south, the suburbs and in rural areas' (Pattie et al. 1997, p. 147). Patterns of electoral geography that diverge from the demographic composition of areas will be our focus in Chapter 6.

Electoral geography and changing patterns of voting behaviour

There has been much debate over whether electoral geography matters at all, if the patterns of voting that we observe at election time are simply a matter of where different groups have been left on the electoral chess board. Others have sought to highlight the danger of the ecological fallacy, that aggregate-level election results do not necessarily equate to corresponding changes in behaviour at the individual level. In this book, we do not seek to settle the argument definitively, first because we believe that the relationship between the composition of particular places and voting patterns at the aggregate level is intrinsically important (i.e. it can significantly impact the electoral efficiency of a party's support as well as profoundly colouring its geographical identity). Further, the demographics of particular areas reflect fundamental forces of social and economic change, which are inseparable from long-term political choices about how society and the economy should be organized. While we believe that the demographic composition of places is crucial, we also recognize the potential for the voting habits of people in certain places to diverge from what would be expected according to their demographic composition alone. The idea of contextual effects is therefore implicit to our focus in Chapter 7 on those places—Merseyside and Lincolnshire—where Labour and Conservative support cannot be straightforwardly predicted based on demographic and socio-economic composition.

Ultimately, electoral geography is jointly a product of the demographic composition of places and how particular demographic groups behave at the ballot box. Changes in electoral geography can therefore reflect either changes in the population of a constituency, changes in voting behaviour, or a combination of the two. Of course, this is not to deny the importance of context—voters do not live in a vacuum but their voting behaviour, as well as broader values and attitudes, can be influenced by everything from family, friends, and the workplace to regional and local place-based identities and cultures.[19] Nor is it to suggest that demography or voting behaviour tends to be wholly static. Recent decades have seen fundamental shifts in the socio-economic basis of voting behaviour. A long line of research from the 1970s onwards has identified trends of class dealignment (e.g. Crewe et al. 1977; Evans and Tilley 2017) as social class has become an increasingly weak predictor of voting behaviour at the individual level. At the same time, effects of education (Sobolewska and Ford 2020) and age (Sturgis and Jennings 2020) on vote choice have strengthened, while a gender gap has begun to open up in recent elections (Campbell and Shorrocks 2021). These changes have occurred in the context of an electorate that is increasingly volatile (Fieldhouse et al. 2020), and in which attitudes towards Brexit shape political identities (Hobolt et al. 2021) and voting behaviour (Ford et al. 2021). They have also occurred in the context of a population that has changed significantly over time: voters on average have got older, more middle-class, and more educated. It is crucial to understand shifts in voting behaviour in light of these broader demographic trends.

In Figures 1.11–1.19 we illustrate changes in the voting behaviour of some of these groups using survey data from the British Election Study (BES) for each general election between 1979 and 2019, in some instances also plotting alongside this how much of the party's overall support is made up by each group. The former reveals the relative propensities of voting behaviour and the latter indicates the socio-structural basis of support for each party in absolute terms. Notably, this time period has seen Labour's advantage among working-class voters fall precipitously,[20] from highs of over 60% in 1997 and 2001 to less than 40% in 2015 and 2019, while the Conservatives have steadily gained among this group since 1997, and stood at above 40% in 2019 (see Figure 1.11). Some of the electoral consequences of this shift have been offset by the shrinking share of the electorate that the working class makes up. Thus, while the Conservatives have increased their support among working-class

---

[19] There is a long legacy of quantitative research on contextual effects at different spatial scales on voting behaviour. In the UK, this has been led by work by Ron Johnston and Charles Pattie. For example, on regional effects see Pattie et al. (2015), Johnston et al. (2007), and Johnston and Pattie (1998), on neighbourhood effects see Johnston et al. (2004), Johnston et al. (2005), and on social network effects see Pattie and Johnston (2000) and Pattie and Johnston (1999).

[20] Measures of social class in the BES differ slightly between some elections. We recode these into the broad categories of middle class ABC1s (including higher managerial, lower managerial, skilled non-manual, and lower non-manual) and working class C2DEs (including skilled manual, unskilled or semi-skilled manual, and unemployed). See Appendix Table A1.1 for further details.

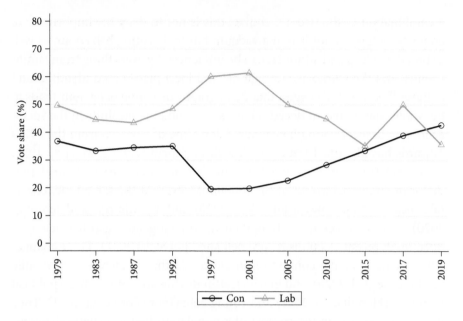

Figure 1.11 Party vote share for working-class voters, 1979–2019

voters, in 2019 this group made up just around a third of the party's vote (see Figure 1.12).

Historically, Labour won marginally more of its support among men than women, but in 2017 and 2019 this pattern was reversed and the relative gender gap is the largest that it has been for forty years (roughly 12 points, with 56% of Labour voters being women and 44% being men). This is shown in Figure 1.13. Age has long been linked to vote choice, with studies finding that individuals are more likely to vote Conservative as they grew older (Tilley and Evans 2014). In 1979, Labour's vote was fairly consistent across all age groups (see Figure 1.14), but the Conservative vote rose gradually as people got older (see Figure 1.15). By 2019, however, the age gradient of support was much steeper for both parties: Labour secured its highest level of support among people in their twenties, with its vote declining steadily in older age bands, while Conservative support rose sharply from the mid-thirties. Labour's vote now is made up predominantly of working-age people (18–64 years old), while the Conservative vote has fallen steadily among this group over time (see Figure 1.16). In contrast, the Conservatives' reliance on over-65s has doubled since 1979, with this group now making up two in five of the party's voters (see Figure 1.17).

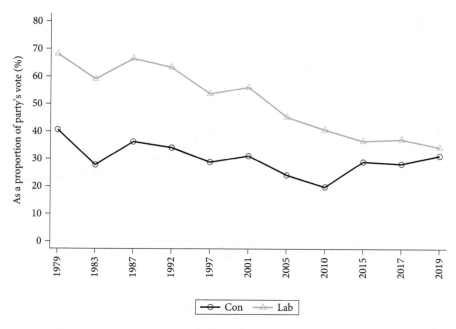

Figure 1.12   Working-class vote as a share of party's vote, 1979–2019

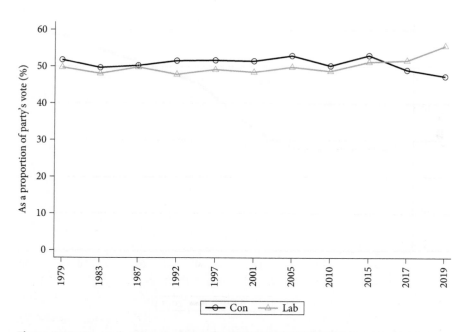

Figure 1.13   Women's vote as a share of party's vote, 1979–2019

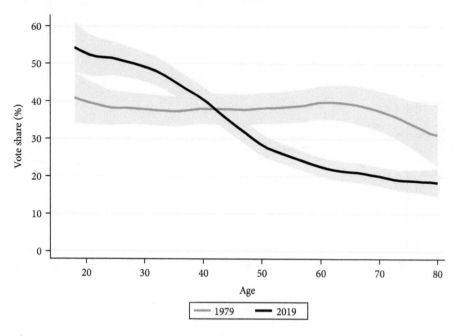

Figure 1.14   Labour Party vote share by age, 1979 vs 2019

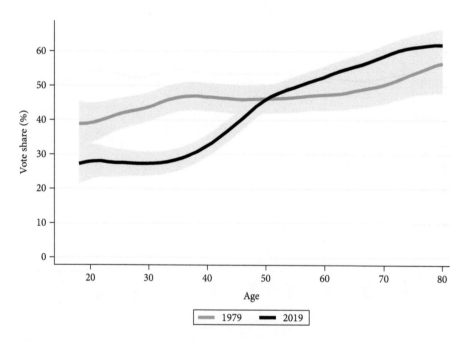

Figure 1.15   Conservative Party vote share by age, 1979 vs 2019

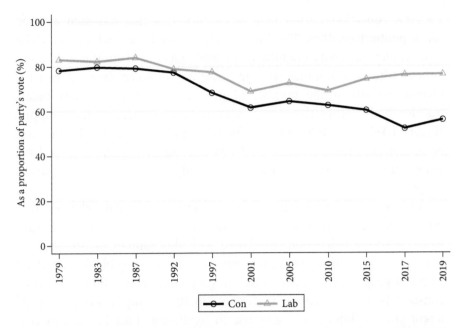

Figure 1.16 Working age voters (18–64 years old) as a share of party's vote, 1979–2019

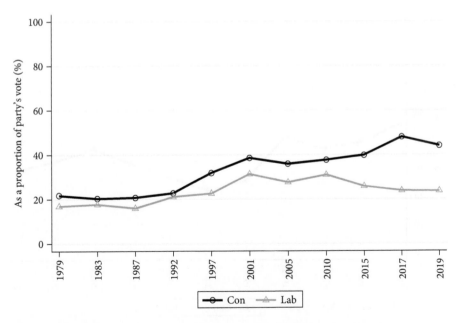

Figure 1.17 Older voters (65+ years old) as a share of party's vote, 1979–2019

Lastly, educational attainment is another area that has seen a reversal of political loyalties. The Conservative Party once held a comfortable lead among university graduates, but lately has found itself overtaken by Labour who now dominate among this group of voters (see Figure 1.18). Overall growth in the number of graduates in British society means that for both parties this group is growing as a share of their support (Figure 1.19). The same story can be told in reverse for people who hold no educational qualifications—the Conservatives having gained ascendance among this group, but it is declining rapidly as a share of both parties' support.

These are not the only groups whose voting habits have changed during the period of our study, though they are among the most important shifts in voting behaviour. Combined with the number of people living within each area, these preferences represent the building blocks of Britain's electoral geography. Even holding the geographical distribution of voters constant between elections, such shifts in the voting preferences of different groups alone would give rise to significant shifts in Britain's electoral geography. But as we discuss in Chapter 2, there have been dramatic changes in the demography of different parts of the country over this same period.

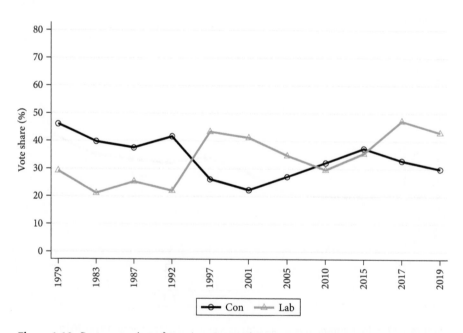

Figure 1.18 Party vote share for university graduates, 1979–2019

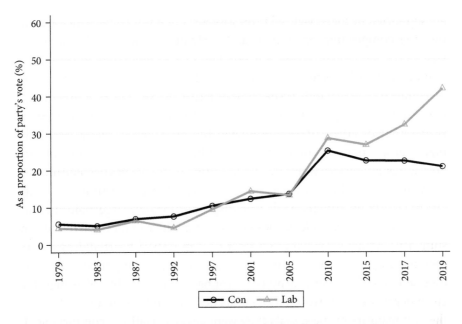

Figure 1.19   University graduates' vote as a share of party's vote, 1979–2019

Changes in the socio-structural foundations of voting behaviour in part reflect a response of voters to ideological convergence (Evans and Tilley 2012) and social representation (Heath 2015) by political parties. On the economic dimension of party competition, the move of the Labour Party to the centre (between 1983 and 2010) and decline in the number of Labour MPs with a working-class background has contributed to class dealignment. At the same time, the appeals of the major parties have shifted on the cultural dimension—Labour has increasingly adopted liberal positions on social issues—appealing in particular to younger voters, university graduates, and ethnic minorities—while the Conservatives' (continued) emphasis on social conservativism, lately turbo-charged by the issue of Brexit, has increasingly attracted the support of white working-class and older voters with fewer qualifications (see Sobolewska and Ford 2020; Ford et al. 2021). Since 2010, the parties have diverged somewhat on economic grounds again—with Labour adopting more traditional stances on spending and public ownership under Ed Miliband and Jeremy Corbyn—while the Conservatives have retained their appeal to the more economically liberal parts of the professional classes, until recently promoting fiscal prudence. It is too soon to speak of a full-blown class *realignment* of British politics, as Labour still secures a not insignificant proportion of working-class support and the Conservatives still are supported by many well-off professionals. But it is no longer the case that the class composition of an area can clearly predict how its electorate will vote.

While Labour's electoral coalition remains intact in some parts of its former industrial heartlands (especially in larger urban centres with younger populations), the party's dominance is now more narrowly centred on Britain's major cities, university towns, and other places characterized by higher proportions of young graduates, ethnic minorities, and low-income post-industrial service workers. The allocation of its vote has become increasingly 'inefficient' in recent elections, in a reversal of the situation in the 1990s. Labour have increasingly won disproportionately large majorities in a number of city seats while becoming less competitive in more marginal constituencies, many of which are former post-industrial heartlands. By 2019, they piled up votes in a minority of seats—large, cosmopolitan, ethnically diverse cities characterized by both younger graduates but also high levels of deprivation. However, those seats do not win Labour an election—in the vast majority of these seats they were already relatively comfortable. In *all* other types of seat—from far-flung suburbs of smaller cities to market towns, seaside towns, and post-industrial villages, Labour moved backwards and the Tories forwards. Most of the country does not look like central Manchester, inner London, Liverpool, or Leeds. The Conservatives, in contrast, have seen their support declining among professional groups—notably among graduates—but have rising appeal to working-class voters, and dominate among the pensioner class. The result has been that the party has seen its vote share decline in parts of major cities and university towns where it once was competitive, and those places where the local economy or culture attracts a higher proportion of younger, educated voters. It made steady gains, though, in former industrial areas and peripheral coastal areas characterized by ageing populations and dwindling local economies, whilst retaining its base in rural heartlands.

Alongside these trends for the two mainstays of the electoral politics of England and Wales, there has been considerable electoral volatility since 1979 for other parties—notably in the rise and fall of the Liberal Democrats and a succession of Eurosceptic parties—the Referendum Party, UKIP, and the Brexit Party—all of which have left an indelible mark on British politics. The Greens have emerged as an electoral force in a few places (notably Brighton and Bristol), while north of the border the ascendance of the Scottish National Party has dramatically realigned Scottish politics as we have discussed already. The rise and fall of the Liberal Democrats and UKIP in particular are associated with accelerations in the changing geography of Labour and Conservative support. In more highly educated areas where the Liberal Democrats had historically been very competitive (e.g. Sheffield Hallam, Leeds North West, Canterbury, Bristol West), Labour have recently gained significant ground at their expense. In contrast, some of the most pronounced recent swings from Labour to the Conservatives have been located in those areas of the North, Midlands, and Wales (e.g. Hartlepool, Great Grimsby, Mansfield) where in 2015 UKIP challenged Labour's dominance and subsequently collapsed. What underlies many of these political shocks is not just the changing nature of party competition but the changing relationships between demography, geography, and votes for Labour and the Conservative Party. The story of this book is that while the geographies of Labour and Conservative support have been impacted by the fluctuating popularity of smaller parties, Brexit, and changing party leaders, they are also the product of longer term demographic and economic changes.

Analytical themes

Places, not people

Our analytical strategy in this book builds on a number of related and interconnected themes. First, there is an important distinction between understanding electoral change through the lenses of places and people. Studies of voting behaviour at the individual level (as we have just set out) are important in highlighting the role of social structure and political attitudes in electoral choice, but a focus on geography enables insights on how changes in the spatial distribution of party support reflect both shifts in demographic composition of places and in the appeal of political parties to particular social groups. Ultimately parties fight elections in a way that seeks to attract the votes of individuals, but elections are made up of a large number of battlefields (i.e. constituencies), across which votes are distributed. Understanding the geography of electoral behaviour enables us to understand the terrains on which parties contest elections. Simply, in a first-past-the-post electoral system, neither Labour nor the Conservatives can win a majority with a vote that is inefficiently distributed across the geography of the country. To gain a crucial advantage, the parties must be aware not only of the sociodemographic composition of their vote, but how this varies from one constituency to the next, and most crucially, how the changing characteristics of places themselves are leading to growing or declining levels of support amongst different types of voter.

We recognize that the distribution of individuals is not coincidental and reflects various push and pull factors that lead to populations in particular places having particular profiles. We develop this argument about the structural social and economic forces of demographic change in Chapter 2. While these processes entail a sorting of populations into certain places, in this book we do not get into questions of how individuals self-select into areas in a way that reinforces spatial divides in voting patterns. Gallego et al. (2016, p. 546) find geographical sorting in the British context driven by self-selection: 'an individual's existing political preference is a strong and significant predictor of the political orientation of the area into which he or she moves'. In a study of immigration attitudes in large European cities, Maxwell (2019, p. 472) notes the presence of both sorting and self-selection effects: 'Large European cities have more positive immigration attitudes than rural areas because those cities have larger percentages of residents who are highly educated and professionals and because people with positive immigration attitudes self-select into large cities'. The sorts of people who move to urban centres tend to be more socially liberal in outlook, even after controlling for demographics. That self-sorting may occur does not undermine our thesis, and indeed it is consistent with the claim that the electoral geography of England and Wales has been redrawn though changes in voting behaviour and demography. That citizens sort themselves in the 'right' sort of place that reflects their political identities and values only highlights the importance of electoral geography. Our analysis is able to point to the specific demographic predictors that are becoming stronger or weaker predictors of party support—hinting at the need for further investigation.

Change vs statics

Secondly, our strategy emphasizes the importance of differentiating between the level and change in electoral support as the unit of analysis. While it may be possible to identify an increase in support from election to election for a given party in places that are more economically deprived, for example, its absolute level of support in these areas may remain quite low. One key insight of this book is therefore that, while Labour's support has, between 2005 and 2019, fallen somewhat in areas that have been economically declining, the party remains dominant in areas with the most significant deprivation. As such, we make a distinction between areas that *are*, relative to other constituencies, economically left behind and those that are, relative to the changes seen elsewhere, *becoming* more economically left behind. By exploring how socio-economic and demographic changes are associated with changing vote shares, we are able to hint at these processes of realignment that are ongoing, but may be far from complete.

Correlational and residual analysis

Thirdly, our application of correlational analysis allows us to understand the link between the demographic composition of places and patterns of voting (both in relation to levels and change in vote share), while the residuals from multivariate regression analyses make it possible to discover those places where that relationship appears to break down. Our approach thus can identify those places where the Conservative or Labour vote is higher than would be predicted by demographics alone—hinting at the importance of local context in shaping electoral behaviour. It also enables us to identify areas where the parties have tended to under- or over-perform at different points in time, further illuminating our understanding of the changing electoral geography of England and Wales.

A rising tide lifts all boats

An important observation is that wider changes in the national electoral tide can for periods allow significant changes in electoral geography to go widely unnoticed, especially in first-past-the-post systems. A party that is popular nationally may experience declining relative support in its electoral strongholds but with little impact on electoral outcomes (in terms of seats won), especially if it starts from a high base. Only once a party's overall support falls below a certain level may spatial variations in its electoral performance then become (painfully) evident. This was the case in the 2019 general election, where the Conservatives won many seats in towns in Northern England where Labour's vote had been declining for many years but in previous elections it had managed to hang onto the seats narrowly. The combination of Brexit (with many of those constituencies having voted heavily to leave the European Union) and the long-term decline of Labour support among working-class voters in those areas ultimately led to a change in party control. In landslide elections like 1997, a party may win seats by small margins that demographically it really shouldn't. The analogy of a tide therefore emphasizes that parties that are popular nationally may win in places where demographics would usually suggest they shouldn't.

Getting to grips with what it means for places to be 'left behind'

A further important contribution of this book is its attempt to refine and clarify the conceptually messy category of 'left behind' places—as a means of understanding the electoral trends observed in them. This term originally became a shorthand for places identified as ripe for the electoral advance of the UK Independence Party, and subsequently became inextricably linked to the Brexit vote in 2016, and the 'levelling up' agenda of the Johnson government in the aftermath of its resounding victory in the 2019 general election. We differentiate between areas that can be characterized as left behind according to economics (specifically areas with higher levels of deprivation), demographics (based on their composition in terms of social class, education, and age—consistent with the group of voters identified in Ford and Goodwin's seminal *Revolt on the Right*), and precarious employment (typically younger workers in low-paid, insecure jobs—what might be called the 'new working class'). When considered in this way, prevailing narratives about Labour's loss or abandonment of left behind communities appear more as stereotypes of a varied and complicated process. While the Conservatives have made significant gains in Labour's traditional strongholds—winning support in largely older, white, working-class constituencies, Labour remain dominant in the poorest areas. Indeed, poverty remains the most important positive predictor of Labour's support, and the party is increasingly dominant in areas home to large numbers of younger people in precarious employment, often drawn from more ethnically diverse groups.

However, whilst Labour's support remains high in areas with high levels of deprivation and precarious employment, many of these places—typically larger urban centres—have experienced economic growth, such that they might be considered 'improving', even if this is unequally distributed. At the same time, Labour has increasingly struggled in those places that have experienced *relative economic decline*—often where traditional industries have dwindled. Although it may be simplistic to suggest Labour has ceased to be the party of the worst off in society, it has lost its grip on areas once dominated by traditional industries which in many cases have experienced sustained periods of decline. As those places have declined, so too have local social institutions and party organization. While major cities (where Labour remains strong) like London are subject to the most serious levels of deprivation, studies of social mobility identify 'cold spots' in particular in former industrial towns and coastal towns (Social Mobility Commission 2017). In contrast to the most deprived inner-city areas, these declining areas are notable for their absence of, and poor connectivity to, key educational, cultural, and civic assets—everything from health services to pubs and libraries (Local Trust 2019).

On this note, this book makes an important contribution to seeing left behindedness as something that describes a process as much as it does characteristics at a particular point in time. Indeed, when one considers the different types of left behind place and the different processes in which places become increasingly left behind, we encounter complex and variegated trends in Britain's electoral geography. This book is a call for more nuance and less simplistic narratives. It is a call for more detailed analysis and rigour. And finally, it is a call for more care in the way in which we use concepts like the 'Red Wall' and 'left behind' to avoid painting overly simplistic conclusions that do not fit with the complex reality of Britain's changing electoral geography.

Places that go against the grain

One of the puzzles of the electoral geography of England and Wales is the places where voters do not faithfully follow the script set by their social and economic profile. Where are the places that defy our expectations? What can these paradoxical cases tell us about British politics? We use spatial analytical methods to identify areas that do not vote in line with what would be typically predicted by their demographic composition alone. Such an idea lay behind the concept of what became popularly known as the 'Red Wall' ahead of the 2019 general election—constituencies where Labour's vote was higher than would be expected given the makeup of their electorate (typically older, dominantly white, working-class populations). In 2019, the bond between voters in these places and the Labour Party was finally broken—an acceleration of a process a long time in the making, but seemingly exacerbated by Brexit and the Corbyn leadership—leading a large swathe of constituencies to turn blue. There are areas, on the other hand, where Conservative support is higher than would be predicted by their social and economic characteristics. These are of interest too, not least since such areas forewarn of the possibility that one day those places might be subject to a shock of their own.

Based on quantitative analysis, two areas—Merseyside and Lincolnshire— are identified as places that do not fit the trends governing other parts of the country. Drawing on interviews with local political actors, we present qualitative case studies considering in some detail the place-based factors that help explain the over-performance of Labour on Merseyside and the dominance of the Conservatives in Lincolnshire. Through this approach, we emphasize the possibility that to fully understand the evolution of electoral geography, particularly those places that go against the grain, one must consider more than just demographics. Indeed, voting does not occur in a vacuum—people are situated in neighbourhoods, towns, cities, and wider regions that all have their own distinct cultural characteristics and political histories that influence voting behaviour.

Plan of the book

We here outline how the remainder of the book is organized, and the rationale behind each of the chapters. In Chapter 2 we outline the mechanisms of social and economic change that are giving rise to changes in the electoral geography of Britain and other advanced industrial economies in recent decades. Our central argument is that important changes in sociodemographic structure have a distinct geographical expression in terms of the composition of places, and these in turn are linked to the relative propensity of those places to vote for the Labour or Conservative Parties. The structural shifts considered by the chapter include deindustrialization and changing patterns of employment, the expansion of higher education, the forces of agglomeration in professional and precarious jobs, the high levels of inward migration, and ageing of the electorate, and how these relate to the changing nature of places.

Chapter 3 provides a broad overview of long-term trends in the electoral geography of Britain; first considering the relative popularity of the parties in particular regions over time, and then differences in the voting habits of major cities, industrial towns, and rural areas, before examining the link between population density and voting patterns. It shows how Labour's vote has historically tended to be less efficient than the Conservative Party's vote (i.e. its translation of raw votes to seat is less proportional than its opponent's), and importantly that the gap in has grown recently in terms of electoral inefficiency.

Chapter 4 explores the changing relationship between the compositional characteristics of parliamentary constituencies, in terms of their socio-economics and sociodemographics, and the Labour and Conservative Party vote share between 1979 and 2019. The extended time period that is considered enables evaluation of long-term trends and short-term fluctuations in the electoral geography of England and Wales. Our analysis highlights key differences between social and economic indicators that are associated with constituencies being *demographically, economically* and *precariously* left behind. The importance of making this distinction is that some highly deprived, 'left behind' areas do not share the same electoral trajectory as others that are usually associated with the term (based on an image of older, white, post-industrial towns). We show that, while there has been a significant swing from Labour to the Conservatives in many former Labour strongholds with dominantly white, working-class populations with lower educational levels (areas we term demographically left behind), Labour has continued to dominate in areas with the highest levels of economic deprivation and higher proportions of the insecurely and precariously employed—often seats in larger urban areas.

Building on the previous analysis of levels, Chapter 5 considers the relationship between *change* in the social and economic characteristics of constituencies and *change* in party support over the period between 1979 and 2019. Change is potentially important because electoral trends may differ in those areas that have experienced relative decline or prosperity in their social and economic fabric. People feeling left behind is typically linked by researchers to feelings of resentment, loss of social status, and nostalgia, and we seek to establish whether socio-economic decline of certain places is associated with a swing from one party or the other. Employing a similar left behind conceptualization to that of Chapter 4, we find that areas that have become more demographically left behind (relatively older, whiter, more working-class, and less educated) have also seen a growth in Conservative support. In deindustrializing areas of the North, the Midlands, and Wales, we show that post-industrial cities that have, more recently experienced a growth in middle-class employment, have become, relatively speaking, more favourable to Labour, while post-industrial towns that have experienced the most prolonged decline have gone the opposite way.

Chapter 6 seeks to advance our understanding of the spatial structure of party support, and in particular to identify those constituencies and regions in which the statistical models from the previous two chapters systematically under- or over-predict support for each party, and how this has changed over time. Specifically, we show how the areas in which Labour and the Conservative Party have 'over-performed' and 'under-performed' have changed between 1979 and 2019. Labour's electoral strongholds have shifted from former coalfield constituencies to Merseyside, with the former areas becoming more electorally marginal as would be predicted given their demographic makeup. In contrast, the Conservatives have tended to out-perform expectations in Lincolnshire and the West Midlands outside of Birmingham, with this trend generally strengthening between 1979 and 2019.

The final empirical chapter, Chapter 7, is based on two qualitative case studies—the areas of Merseyside and Lincolnshire—where election results do not neatly fit with predictions based on their demographic composition. We draw on interviews with local political actors and experts, identifying the place-based factors that might account for these electoral outliers. This mixed methods approach is important in recognizing that the unexplained residuals of models might not be explained using quantitative methods alone. Through these cases we show how local and regional identities, culture, histories, and party organizing can have significant impacts on electoral competition—at least from the perspective of local activists and observers.

Our final chapter, Chapter 8, reflects on the insights that have emerged from our theoretical and empirical analysis, as well as considering the potential future implications of these findings for British politics. Ultimately, we believe the book offers a definitive exploration of how the electoral geography of England and Wales has been transformed since 1979, and the precise influence of the changing nature of places on fundamental shifts in the basis of party support.

Conclusion

This book argues that there has been a gradual realignment—with notable accelerations and decelerations—of the geographical basis of electoral competition in England and Wales. This is a product of the changing social and economic composition of places and the appeals to voters made by parties. We argue that these trends in electoral geography are interlinked with the dominant policy paradigm of British politics of the last forty years. Similar dynamics are observed in other advanced industrial democracies. Accordingly, Ford and Jennings (2020: 309) argue:

> the literature on both political sociology and party competition has neglected the ways in which all of these developments in social structure are intrinsically entangled with the contemporary capitalist model in advanced industrial countries: knowledge economies requiring highly skilled labor (and corresponding decline of employment in traditional industries), open economies that rely on migrant labor, and a focus on urban agglomeration as a driver of growth. These dynamics—shaped through the dominant policy model of advanced industrial economies—have driven the growth of the graduate class, the decline and marginalization of the working class, high migration and rapidly rising ethnic diversity, and the growing geographical segregation of populations between core and peripheral

areas . . . These are not coincidental features of advanced industrial societies but defining features of their political economy, which are central to shaping electoral competition.

Our book thus seeks to draw a long historical arc from the historical foundations of Britain's electoral geography, forged in the era of the industrial revolution and formation of a party system dominated by the Conservative and Labour Parties. The post-industrial period has seen a reshaping of that electoral geography. The contemporary economic model—and its shaping of social and economic change—has produced, and continues to produce, a gradual realignment of the geographical basis of electoral competition in England and Wales. As such, the result of the 2019 general election—and the Conservative gains in long-held Labour seats—represented one moment in an ongoing structural shift in the electoral politics of England and Wales. Indeed, both the 2019 and 1997 general elections are significant in that they are moments where there were accelerations in this ongoing, long-term process of geographical realignment. Over time, the ebbs and flows of the electoral tide have exposed more or less of the changes occurring underneath the surface—with Labour's 1997 landslide disguising some of the underlying changes in its vote, whereas its heavy defeat in 2019 exposed how vulnerable it had become in certain places. A recovery of support from a volatile electorate at the next general election may once again conceal the ongoing transformation of how the party's vote is distributed. Those shifts are not irreversible, but they reflect strong tendencies in the demography of places (trends in Britain's social and economic geography) and in the voting behaviour of particular demographic groups of voters.

Appendix

Table A1.1 Social class measures in the British Election Study, 1979–2019

Years covered	Social class measures used
1979	National Readership Survey social grade (A, B, C1A, C1B, C2, D categories), with respondents assigned a social class using their father's social grade if no information is available.
1983	Goldthorpe-Llewellyn class (ABC1: high grade professional and managerial, low grade professional and managerial, routine non-manual, and petty bourgeoisie; C2DE: manual foreman and technicians, skilled manual, semi and unskilled manual), using respondents' father's social class if no information is available.

Continued

Table A1.1 *Continued*

Years covered	Social class measures used
1987–1997	Registrar General's social class scheme (ABC1: professional, managerial/technical, skilled non-manual; C2DE: skilled manual, partly skilled, unskilled), using respondents' father's social class if no information is available.
2001	National Readership Survey social grade (A, B, C1, D2, D, E categories).
2005	Registrar General's social class scheme (ABC1: professional, managerial/technical, skilled non-manual; C2DE: skilled manual, partly skilled, unskilled), using respondents' father's social class if no information is available.
2010	Occupational class (ABC1: professional or higher technical work, manager or senior administrator, clerical, sales or services, small business owner; C2DE: foreman or supervisor of other workers, skilled manual work, semi-skilled or unskilled manual work), using parent/partner's social grade if no information was available or had never had a job.
2015–2019	National Statistics Socio-economic classification (ABC1: large employers and higher managerial and administrative occupations, higher professional occupations, lower managerial, administrative and professional occupations, intermediate occupations, small employers and own account workers; C2DE: lower supervisory and technical occupations, semi-routine occupations, routine occupations), using parent's social grade if no information was available or never had a job.

2

How changing demography drives electoral change

The core argument of this book is that, over the past forty years, changes in the sociodemographic and economic geography of England and Wales, combined with changes in the respective appeals of the Labour and Conservative Parties to voters—have significantly altered the basis of electoral geography. These trends match wider developments in electoral politics in Western Europe and the United States, where support for parties and candidates on the right and radical right has become increasingly concentrated in peripheral, rural, and former industrial areas, while left-liberal and green parties have tended to make advances in major cities and prospering towns (Rodden 2010, 2019; van Gent et al. 2014; Scala et al. 2015; Marcinkiewicz 2018; Reid and Liu 2019; Fitzgerald 2020; Damore et al. 2020; Faggian et al. 2021; Rickardsson 2021; Dominicis et al. 2022; Armstrong et al. 2022; Harteveld et al. 2022; Taylor et al. 2023). Such electoral shifts are variously characterized as reflecting the increased salience of a 'parochial–cosmopolitan', 'nationalist–cosmopolitan', 'open–closed', 'liberal–authoritarian', or 'urban–rural' dimension of political competition.

Behind these developments in electoral geography is a fundamental transformation of the economic model of advanced industrial societies that has resulted in significant changes in their demographic makeup. As Rodden (2010, 2019) argues, the geographical distribution of ideological preferences in industrial societies does not occur by chance, but rather reflects long-term processes of economic activity and residential choices—with those processes combining sorting, self-selection, and contextual effects.[1] Changes in *how* voters are distributed across a country can impact party competition by creating, or reinforcing, geographical cleavages (Ford and Jennings 2020). The

---

[1] 'Sorting' refers to the movement of people into areas that share their demographic characteristics or attitudes. It can occur naturally through processes of economic and demographic change that result in homophily of the people resident in an area. 'Self-selection' refers to the *intentional* movement of people into areas due to their desire to join communities that share their characteristics, values, identities. The degree of partisan sorting has been subject to extensive debate in the context of the US (e.g. Bishop and Cushing 2008; Brown and Enos 2021). 'Contextual effects' relate to changes in attitudes or behaviours that arise due to living and/or working in a particular area.

The Changing Electoral Map of England and Wales. Jamie Furlong and Will Jennings, Oxford University Press.
© Jamie Furlong and Will Jennings (2024). DOI: 10.1093/9780191943331.003.0002

segregation of populations can have powerful effects on social cognition, and thereby group identities and intergroup relations, with profound consequences for political conflict (Enos 2017). Crucially, political parties are not unwitting bystanders in these processes. Sometimes they shape social and economic change through their policy decisions in government, subsequently seeking to capitalize on them electorally or attempting to resist the electoral tide in their traditional strongholds. At other moments, even out of power, parties signal their commitment to particular groups in society through taking symbolic stances on issues (Sobolewska and Ford 2020).

The electoral consequences of these demographic shifts are especially significant in majoritarian, first-past-the-post systems such as the UK's parliamentary system or the electoral college for US presidential elections—since *where* votes are located can have significant, disproportionate effects. Historically, Rodden (2010, 2019) argues, the urban concentration of left parties in North America and Western Europe has restricted their electoral representation. For modern left-liberal parties, this dilemma has become more acute, with the clustering of demographic groups that tend to vote for them—notably university graduates, professionals, ethnic minorities, and younger people—in major urban areas, which often leaves their support inefficiently distributed. For right-leaning parties, a longer term challenge persists. Population projections suggest that ethnic minority groups will grow most rapidly outside of the largest cities in Britain over the next forty years (Rees et al. 2017). As ethnic diversity will increasingly come to characterize not only inner-city areas but also more politically marginal suburbs and smaller towns, there is a distinct threat to seats held by parties on the political right. University graduates also make up a growing share of the population in many wealthy post-industrial economies, and the growing connection between education and social liberalism presents a further challenge to the right in more affluent areas where many graduates eventually live—areas which, historically, have favoured the Conservatives.

In Britain, five key shifts have transformed the social and economic structure of the country over the past half century, altering their geographical distribution, with profound consequences for patterns of party support. These five trends are: (i) the decline of industry, manufacturing, and traditional working-class occupations (and conversely growth in service sector employment), (ii) an expansion of higher education, focused in major cities and university towns, (iii) the shift to a global knowledge economy with a clustering of jobs and innovation in major cities and high-tech towns—coexisting with a low pay service economy subject to high levels of precariousness and poor working conditions, (iv) high levels of inward migration (from both

EU and non-EU countries), again often concentrated in major urban centres, and (v) an ageing population, located especially in smaller towns and more peripheral areas (as younger working age populations have moved away to study and work). In combination, these trends have transformed the social and economic geography of England and Wales, changing the composition of the electorate in different parts of the country.

These transformations of social structure are intrinsically entangled with the contemporary capitalist model found in many advanced industrial countries: knowledge economies requiring highly skilled labour (and corresponding decline of employment in traditional industries), deregulated and open economies that rely on migrant and precarious labour, and a focus on urban agglomeration as a driver of economic growth (e.g. see Iversen and Soskice 2019). These dynamics—shaped through the dominant policy model of advanced industrial economies—have driven the growth of the graduate class, the decline and marginalization of the working class, high migration and rapidly rising ethnic diversity, and the growing geographical segregation and sorting of populations between core and peripheral areas. The clustering of younger populations in urban centres reflects sorting and self-selection into educational and employment opportunities, reinforced by social and cultural amenities available in those places. On top of outward migration of younger generations, the relative ageing of peripheral areas reflects technological advances in healthcare and long-term improvements in living and working conditions, in part due to the historical decline of industrial employment. As we will see, these changes in social and economic structure have distinct geographical expressions, which in turn shape the contours of electoral geography in England and Wales. Elements of these trends are to be found in other countries, but they also have a distinctive national flavour in the British context. As we show, there are different kinds of 'left behind' places and these are headed in very different political directions.

The changing social and economic structure of England and Wales

The first major change in Britain's social structure is perhaps its most well-known, at least as regards its impact on the dealignment, and later the realignment, of the class basis of British politics. *Deindustrialization*—defined as a declining share of industrial employment—was experienced across Western European economies from the 1950s onwards (Beatty and Fothergill 2020). In Britain, 35% of the workforce (8.6 million people) worked in manufacturing in 1959 (Bank of England 2016). By 2019, this had fallen to 7.7% (2.7 million people).[2] That downward trend accelerated sharply in the 1980s—with over 3 million jobs lost in manufacturing and heavy industry during the first Thatcher government alone (Tomlinson 2021). Consequently, many parts of the country have experienced long-term decline of traditional industry—with mines, factories, and plants permanently closed and jobs lost—which has had lasting effects for local communities and generations of workers. These jobs have been replaced by service sector employment, increasing the size of the professional middle class as well as shifting some low-paid manual jobs to precarious service roles (e.g. social care, hospitality, and sales).

While deindustrialization has affected predominantly urban areas of Britain, its geography cannot be understood by some simplistic North–South, city–town, or London–rest of the UK dichotomy. Just as towns and cities of the North, Midlands, and Wales lost their mills and mines, coastal areas have experienced similar decline of their traditional industries—most notably in domestic tourism, fishing, ship building, and port activities. But as Tomlinson (2020, p. 202) argues, the effects of deindustrialization are *highly spatially differentiated*: 'de-industrialization began in the cities, cities distributed throughout the regions of Britain, not least in London'. Common to the economic revitalization of these major cities was a shift towards (as we detail below) a service-based, financialized economic model.[3] Urban areas, which began with higher rates of industrial employment, tended to suffer the greatest job losses. This was not a simple 'North–South' story, as large parts of the Midlands and places in the South East like Stevenage, Luton, Harlow, Welwyn, Hatfield, and Slough, saw substantial reductions in employment in manufacturing between 1979 and 2019. While this structural economic change impacted the demographic composition of many electorates (reducing the proportion of working-class voters in most constituencies), it left social and economic scars too—especially in those areas that struggled to make the transition to Britain's post-industrial economy.

The process of deindustrialization was thus pivotal in the shaping of both places we refer to as demographically left behind and those we refer to as economically left behind. Former industrial towns, particularly those in the North, lagged behind other areas in terms of productivity, rates of

---

[2] Office for National Statistics. Workforce jobs via NOMIS database.

[3] Note that, while much has been made of impacts of globalization on British politics, those effects were felt later than deindustrialization—as a lot of the industrial decline was down to technological improvements to productivity and changing patterns of consumption, though closure of uncompetitive industries was a factor in some instances.

unemployment, incomes, and deprivation (Martin et al. 2021). Even as geographical inequalities have stabilized, former industrial towns and coastal areas remain substantially poorer than many other areas, with the exception only of some inner-city areas, many of which deindustrialized earlier (Agrawal and Phillips 2020). Notably, the loss of traditional industries has been linked to a range of negative social outcomes—higher rates of offending (Farrall et al. 2020), deprivation (Local Trust 2019), poor health (Riva et al. 2011), and social mobility 'cold spots' (Social Mobility Commission 2017). Despite *relative* industrial decline, many peripheral areas continue to be home to older populations with lower levels of educational attainment and higher rates of employment in routine occupations than the national average (with fewer professional jobs). In certain places, the post-industrial phase has seen employment shift towards the public sector, with the NHS and higher education emerging as the biggest employers. Some coastal towns have succumbed to a downward spiral, as Sarah O'Connor (2017) insightfully chronicled in her award-winning *FT* feature on Blackpool, with the town importing ill-health, unemployment, and precarious labour and exporting skilled labour and good health. The shadow of deindustrialization thus looms large in the social and economic geography of England and Wales. While the UK's national economy has made certain advances in innovation and dynamism since the 1970s, the loss of industry has seen many of the country's more peripheral areas enter a cycle of relative decline (Pike et al. 2016) and made them more vulnerable to shocks.

The second mega-trend, the *expansion of mass higher education*, represents one of the major social transformations in post-war Western Europe, with countries investing heavily in increasing the availability of university education (Ford and Jennings 2020). In 1950, less than four out of a hundred young people in Britain went to university. By 1970, the number was close to one in ten, and by 1990—just before expansion of higher education sector under the Major government, granting university status to many former polytechnics—it had reached nearly one in five.[4] By 2021, the higher education entry rate among 18 year olds reached 38.2%, nearly two in five young people (House of Commons Library 2023). This dramatic transformation has not only underpinned the rise of the UK as a knowledge-based economy, as employment shifted away from traditional industries, but significantly contributed to the changing demography of different places. The Sutton Trust (2018) found that 75% of young people move away from home to attend university (although

---

[4] The overall rate of participation in higher education was 3.4% in 1950, 19.3% in 1990, and 33% in 2000 (see House of Commons Library 2012).

nearly half of those live within 60 miles of home). Over a relatively short period of time, millions of young people have left their families and local communities to study in nearby or rather more distant university towns and cities.

Patterns of educational migration are heavily linked to social class and ethnicity. Place also plays an important role, as young people in Southern England are more likely to leave home and commute long distances to university compared to their counterparts in Northern England (Sutton Trust 2018). This graduate diaspora is one of several factors that have contributed to the divergent demographic paths of university towns and cities, and peripheral towns and areas. Despite the ageing population nationally, populations in university towns and major cities have become younger. Around a quarter of the graduates of research-intensive Russell Group universities end up employed in London within six months of graduation. Simultaneously, nearly three-quarters of students who left London to go to university elsewhere return to the capital to work after graduation (Centre for Cities 2016). Many of those who pass through the 'London escalator', living and working in the inner city of the capital post-university, end up deposited in the suburbs, with spill-over of the graduate diaspora from the city steadily altering the composition of outlying commuter towns in the South of England (Warren 2017). Because university graduates have developed distinctive social identities, values, and interests (Surridge 2016; Sobolewska and Ford 2020; Simon 2022; Scott 2022), the concentration of graduates in particular parts of the country is linked, as we will see, to uneven effects on the electoral geography of England and Wales.

A third mega-trend relates to processes of *urban agglomeration and globalization* (Rickard 2020)—promoted and facilitated by successive British governments—which have seen economic activity increasingly clustered in mega-city regions (e.g. Greater London) and smaller high-tech towns (e.g. Cambridge) which act as magnets for population and skills (Sassen 2019; Moretti 2012). At the same time, peripheral towns, cities, and regions have experienced relative depletion of their human and economic capital (Martínez-Fernández et al. 2012). These economic processes have contributed to the sorting of populations with distinct characteristics into particular places—and intersect with the processes of deindustrialization and educational expansion described above. Mega-cities, most notably London, but also city regions such as Birmingham, Manchester, and Leeds, attract younger, more skilled populations and migrants due to opportunities for education, employment, and cultural consumption. In contrast, many more peripheral towns and rural areas are experiencing rapid population ageing, combined with outflows of economic activity and people (especially young people with higher educational qualifications). These outflows are most acute in areas that have already experienced the decline of traditional industries, such as coastal and former industrial towns.

Processes of agglomeration and globalization—where some areas benefit but others lose out due to their employment and productive profiles (Autor et al. 2020)—are therefore reinforcing a geographical cleavage through polarization in the mixes of people living in different areas: the young, educated, more ethnically diverse populations of major cities are more likely to hold socially liberal values, whereas the older, less educated, and more ethnically homogeneous populations of outlying smaller towns and regions tend to hold more populist and socially conservative outlooks (Jennings and Stoker 2019; Maxwell 2019).

At the same time, it is argued that the offshoring of manufacturing employment has polarized occupational structures—with the elimination of middle-level skilled jobs and movement of high-tech skilled jobs to urban clusters exacerbating regional disparities in income and employment (Storper 2013). These high-tech hubs still depend on a low-paid emergent service 'class-in-the-making', otherwise known as the 'precariat'—people employed in relatively insecure occupations that tend to cluster in urban areas (Savage et al. 2013). The precariat is an unforeseen consequence of the spread of flexible labour and the growth of inequalities since the 1980s, leaving them with distinctive relations of production characterized by 'casualization, informalisation, agency labour, part-time labour, phoney self-employment and the new mass phenomenon of crowd-labour' (Standing 2015, p. 6). Their employment lacks the salary of the middle class and the stable, fixed-hour contracts and options to unionize associated with the working class. Subsequently, they belong to neither. These increasingly insecure employment conditions are 'impacting upon areas and communities that have not been previously characterised by precarity', with particularly strong effects felt in education, the creative industries, and care work (Lazar and Sanchez 2019, p. 9). For Ainsley (2018), people working on low to middle incomes in service sector employment such as social care, retail, and catering, comprise a 'new working class' that is ethnically diverse, disparate, and lacking in any collective identity. The result is high levels of localized inequality in major cities, between the more affluent, educated populations working in knowledge economies and the low-paid service class supporting them. In these areas, economic insecurity is exacerbated by high housing costs.

Like many other Western European countries, Britain has experienced a significant rise in ethnic diversity driven by *mass migration* over the past half century. Between 1979 and 2019, immigration more than tripled, from 195,000 to 681,000 people per year, while net migration rose from just 6,000 to 271,000 over the same time period. Aside from 1979 itself, net migration was negative throughout the 1960s and 1970s (i.e. more people left the country than entered it). Early waves of Commonwealth immigration in the 1960s and 1970s were followed by a rise in EU migration in the 2000s (in particular following enlargement of the EU in 2004) and refugees fleeing conflicts in Africa, the Middle East, and former Yugoslavia (see Ford et al. 2015). These migrant-origin groups are not homogeneous and have developed distinctive political identities and voting behaviour over time (see Heath et al. 2011, 2013; Sanders et al. 2014a, 2014b; Sobolewska and Ford 2020). Crucially, they cluster geographically (often, at least initially, in poorer urban areas) and tend to occupy lower-status, less secure parts of the labour market, meaning that parts of the country have developed large migrant communities, with histories of varying age. Historical diasporas (and chain migration) continue to shape the ethnic composition of populations today.

For example, there are substantial South Asian origin populations in specific urban areas of the North West (for example, in 2021, over 30% of the population of Blackburn with Darwen was Pakistani or Bangladeshi), Yorkshire (the Pakistani community in Bradford made up over 25% of the population), and the Midlands (the proportion of the population identifying as Indian was nearly 35% in Leicester), dating from Commonwealth migration in the 1960s and 1970s. There are also notable Indian populations to the South and West of London in places like Slough, Hillingdon, Ealing, and Hounslow.

In contrast, Caribbean origin populations are most heavily concentrated in areas of London (especially South London) and Birmingham, while parts of Lincolnshire in the East of England have experienced high immigration from Eastern Europe in relative terms (compared to the size of the existing migrant population) since the 2000s. In the 2021 census, 19.4% of the population of Boston, Lincolnshire, identified as 'White: other'—capturing high levels of Eastern European migration to the area over the past twenty years. All major cities, but especially London, have experienced considerable inward migration from a range of groups over the past fifty years, increasing ethnic diversity but also clustering in often quite localized areas.

The impact of immigration has taken distinctive paths in different places not only in terms of its composition but also in the degree of mixing with other ethnic groups. In London, there is greater 'diversity of diversity' (Catney 2015, 2016; Catney et al. 2021), with a far wider range of migrant communities, whereas in towns in the North and Midlands the pattern is, generally, one of *relative* segregation, though *overall* the trend has been of increased mixing of populations. Much like other groups (i.e. graduates, younger people, service/gig workers), the spatial concentration of migrants in urban areas is strongly linked to Britain's path of economic development. Ethnic groups from earlier Commonwealth waves of immigration tended to move into areas with industrial employment (such as textiles and manufacturing), while those in later European waves were more centred on the demand for both high- and low-skill migrant labour in the service and knowledge economy in big cities, although there was also more localized demand for workers, such as in agriculture (e.g. fruit-picking) and ports (e.g. dockworkers).

Patterns of migration often overlap with social and economic deprivation. Compared to the white population in English cities, ethnically segregated communities are characterized by higher levels of unemployment, longer term illness, and exposure to pollution (Patias et al. 2023) It is also possible to identify ethnic-religious migration patterns from earlier time periods, such as the migration of Irish Catholic populations to the North West (especially around Liverpool) during the Industrial Revolution in the nineteenth century, and Jewish migration to the East End of London from Russia in the late nineteenth and early twentieth century, which have had lasting impact on local or regional identities and their political expression (e.g. Barclay 2020). Some of the migrant roots of electoral geography are therefore very old indeed, while others are newer in their origins. In most cases these migration flows are closely linked to distinct phases of Britain's economic development—and reflect a combination of demand for labour and chain migration processes. Importantly, the concentration of large ethnic and religious groups in particular areas can have significant consequences for voting behaviour, especially where those groups tend to lean heavily in the direction of one political party. At the same time, migration flows are claimed to, in certain circumstances, lead to a backlash from the native white British community in terms of its voting behaviour (e.g. Bowyer 2008; Kaufman 2017). Such dynamics are far less influential than the ethnic mix of the electorate, however.

The fifth mega-trend in Britain's social and economic structure, with substantial implications for the geographical distribution of party support, is its *ageing population*. Like many advanced industrial economies, improved medical care, lifestyles, and working conditions have contributed to increased life expectancy. This means that a greater proportion of the population is now in the retirement age band. In 1979, the average voter would spend a little over ten years out of the workforce after retirement (life expectancy 73.3 years, retirement age 65 for men and 60 for women). In 2019, this number was just over sixteen, with the average life expectancy having risen nearly eight years to 81.2 (and retirement ages for men and women being equalized at 65 years old in 2018). Additionally, the ageing of the post-war 'baby boom' and a significant fall in fertility rates during the 1970s has meant this group make up a disproportionately large part of the electorate—increasing from 14.8% in 1979 to 18.6% in 2019 (calculated as the respective share of men and women over the retirement age in 1979 and 2019 respectively).[5] Older voters also have a far greater propensity to turn out to vote, further increasing the size of this group (and its political clout). This 'greying of the vote' has had profound consequences for British politics, as older voters have distinct values and material interests (see Chrisp and Pearce 2019).

There is a distinct geography to ageing of Britain's population. Rural areas tend to have older populations than urban areas, as do declining urban areas which have experienced relative outflows of their populations. In 2019, the local authorities with the lowest median age (of around 30 years) were Oxford, Nottingham, Manchester, and Cambridge—all notable for their large student populations (Office for National Statistics 2020). Those with the highest median age (over 50 years on average) were all rural, coastal areas—North Norfolk, Rother, East Lindsey, and South Hams. Age is a strong predictor of internal migration within Britain, with London being a classic example. People in their twenties tend to move to the capital and those in their thirties to mid-forties are most likely to leave in search of space for a family, a quieter lifestyle, or more affordable house prices. Consequently, London and other larger cities have a much younger age structure than the rest of the country. In mid-2019, London's median age (35.6 years) was nearly five years lower than the national average and just 12.1% of its population was aged 65 years or older. Whether this process has peaked remains to be seen, as recent evidence suggests a turning of the demographic tide in London dating from 2017 that is linked to rising housing costs in the capital (Burn-Murdoch 2023), and potentially Brexit.

While the country has aged overall, this trend has been accentuated in areas that have seen relative outflows of native economic migrants (especially but not exclusively university graduates), and low inflows of foreign migrant populations. Peripheral, declining areas have experienced faster rates of ageing than their urban counterparts. This has even occurred in deprived areas that lag the national average in terms of life expectancy (such as the example

[5] In 1979, of a UK population of 56.2m, 8.3m were aged over 65 (3.3m men and 5.1m women). By 2019, over-65s made up 12.4m of a total population of 66.8m (5.7m men and 6.7m women).

of Blackpool discussed earlier, where the life expectancy is around six years below the national average). These have larger populations of old people now, despite those populations dying younger on average than their counterparts in more affluent areas. Up until 2019 at least, major cities and university towns have gone against the grain and their populations have got younger (although there is some evidence of a reversal since the Covid-19 pandemic). These population dynamics, intersecting with values divides between generations, have thus contributed to the growing political divides between places.

Together, these five mega-trends mean that over the past fifty years some areas have thrived while others have stagnated, seeing relative inflows or outflows of human and economic capital. The consequence is that the social and economic geography of England and Wales is now very different to how it looked in 1979. These processes of change, while deeply structural in many respects, have been significantly shaped by policy decisions taken by specific and multiple governments: through actions taken that have accelerated deindustrialization, expanded higher education, increased levels of immigration, and promoted agglomeration-based approaches of regional development. *All of these decisions have had spatial consequences that have shaped the geography of where particular voters live.* In the remainder of this chapter, we explore how the sociodemographic profile of parliamentary constituencies of England and Wales has changed, and how the policy appeals of political parties have changed over time—leading them to win or lose the support of different groups of voters in different places.

Left behind places: geographical consequences of the macro-level trends

A defining feature of contemporary British politics is the claim that, due to these social and economic forces, some places have prospered, while others have been left behind. But what does it mean for somewhere to be left behind? This term originally became a shorthand for places identified as ripe for the electoral advance of the UK Independence Party (Ford and Goodwin 2014), and later became inextricably linked to the Brexit vote in 2016 (Goodwin and Heath 2016) and to the 'levelling up' agenda of the Johnson government in the aftermath of its resounding victory in the 2019 general election (Jennings et al. 2021; McCann and Ortega-Argilés 2021). It has also become entangled with normatively loaded debates over 'Somewheres' vs 'Anywheres' (Goodhart 2017), acquiring a populist undertone that invokes a 'pure' people, pitted against an obstructive Westminster elite blocking their will over Brexit and other social, political, and economic changes. More broadly it has come to encapsulate a wide range of expressions of geographical inequalities (see Pike et al. 2023 for a review of the term).

Following Furlong (2019), we use the concept in an altogether different way. We distinguish between areas that can be characterized as left behind according to three different dimensions: economics (specifically areas with higher levels of deprivation and poor health as a proxy for poverty), demographics (based on their composition in terms of social class, education, and age—consistent with the group of voters identified in Ford and Goodwin's seminal *Revolt on the Right*), and precarious employment (typically younger workers in low-paid, insecure jobs—what might be called the 'new working class'). As we have argued, there is not a single category of left behind place, but rather a series of long-term trends that lead certain areas to lag others on particular social and economic dimensions. Of course, some places fall into all categories of left-behindedness and others none. There is also a difference between being left behind in a *static* sense (i.e. some places are worse off in absolute terms) and a *dynamic* one, with some places falling behind and others moving ahead (in relative terms). At a particular point in time, one place may be significantly less left behind than another, yet its direction of travel over time may be more negative. The political consequences tied to places *becoming* increasingly left behind, relative to other places, is explored in detail in Chapter 5.

These alternative varieties of left-behindedness are intrinsically linked to Britain's model of economic development—and reflect both successes and failures of deindustrialization. The first set of left behind places are the most deprived parts of the country, typically located in major urban areas, where multiple types of deprivation—e.g. high unemployment, low incomes, lack of education, high levels of crime, poor health—are concentrated together. Very often these *pockets of chronic poverty* are areas that historically *grew during periods of rapid urbanization* and suffer from poor social and economic outcomes. This deprivation tends to be highly persistent, reflecting the structural barriers to escaping poverty that exist in such contexts and limited progress that successive governments have made in tackling spatial inequalities. Such areas have tended to remain loyal to Labour (Furlong 2019), in contrast to the prevailing narrative about left behind places abandoning the party. In London, many of these economically left behind places are also extremely divided—inner-city constituencies where poverty and prosperity sit side by side.

The second set of places are areas that have experienced *relative decline during Britain's transition to a post-industrial economy*—especially during later waves of deindustrialization in towns and smaller cities. These are places that traditionally had a high share of manufacturing employment and large working-class populations with lower educational qualifications than the national average. Those populations also tend to be older and less ethnically diverse than other areas. This follows more conventional, demographic definitions of the left behind concept: older populations, typically white British, lower levels of educational attainment, drawn from routine and semi-routine occupations and formerly employed in manufacturing (consistent with the characterization of Ford and Goodwin 2014). These are the sorts of areas that swung towards UKIP in the 2010s and voted for Brexit in 2016 and for the Conservatives in 2019.

These demographically left behind places might best be understood as the counterpart to 'cosmopolitan' areas, such as London, Manchester, or Cambridge—all 'marked by their intellectual assets, cultural strength and the capacity of their infrastructure to attract people, ideas and skills' (Stoker and Jennings 2015, p. 3). While many bigger cities have areas of significant economic deprivation, they also have a more cosmopolitan urbanism characterized by high connectivity and an innovative environment that attracts skilled workers, thus encouraging inward migration and the establishment of a diverse population. This is in sharp contrast to the ageing, less qualified, older, white population dominating in demographically left behind areas. The idea is that this constitutes a new political cleavage: in the more demographically left behind areas, Jennings and Stoker (2016, p. 372) describe an England that is 'inward-looking, relatively negative about the EU and immigration, worried by the emergence of new rights for "minorities" and prone to embracing nostalgia'. Political attitudes and engagement are becoming increasingly polarized in left behind and cosmopolitan areas, as a result of location-based contextual, sorting, and self-selection effects. These two sorts of left behind areas—socio-economically and demographically—sometimes coexist, concentrated in particular in the North and the Midlands, though are found in other parts of the country as well.

The third and final set of places that might be considered left behind are those home to the *precarious service class* that support Britain's *shift to a service- and knowledge-based economy*. Core cities which serve as agglomerative engines of national growth are home to substantial pockets of deprivation and sizeable populations on low incomes and high rates of social and private renting. Substantial numbers of workers are employed in precariat occupations (e.g. the service and gig economy) in these places, which often are characterized by unaffordable housing and low rates of home ownership—but usually with access to greater cultural capital (Savage et al. 2013). These areas are distinct from those that have experienced long-term stagnation in terms of demography and industry (demographically left behind areas), but rather are at the forefront of Britain's contemporary economic model. They have to some extent adapted to the demands of the post-industrial economy but face their own challenges and deep-rooted inequalities.

All these left behind areas share a certain level of relative deprivation in terms of their social, economic, and human capital, and in different ways have been at the sharp end of Britain's economic model. They are in contrast to those places that have thrived under the UK's shift to a post-industrial, knowledge- and service-based economy that has relied on professional and financial services to drive growth. We understand these three categories as 'ideal types'—few constituencies match perfectly onto one classification of left-behindedness. Rather than mutually exclusive categories, some areas have characteristics of all three types of left-behindedness; others have none. Many larger urban constituencies characterized by sharp inequalities (e.g. Hornsey and Wood Green), are classed as simultaneously economically behind but also cosmopolitan, as they have high rates of deprivation and poor health but also a higher proportion of graduates and professional occupations (see Table 2.1).

Table 2.1 Varieties of left-behindedness

Type of left-behindedness	Characteristic
Demographically left behind[a]	**Deindustrialization:** areas with higher levels of manufacturing employment and routine/semi-routine ('working-class') occupations, with fewer 'cosmopolitan' industries
	Higher education: areas with lower qualification levels
	Migration: areas with low rates of gross migration and ethnic diversity
	Agglomeration: areas characterized by low population density, peripheral, and disconnected from 'cosmopolitan' cities and universities
	Age: areas with older (and ageing) populations
Economically left behind	**Poverty:** areas suffering from higher levels of poor health, unemployment, and household deprivation
	Housing: areas with higher-than-average rates of social renting and low rates of home ownership
Precariously left behind	**Employment:** areas with greater employment in insecure work and specifically in precariat occupations

[a]The demographically left behind category can be understand on a 'left behind–cosmopolitan' axis. As such, cosmopolitan areas are defined by the same characteristics but in the opposite direction (e.g. low levels of manufacturing employment, high qualification levels, etc).

Changing places: how the demographics of constituencies have changed

As a result of these trends, the electorates in many parliamentary constituencies have changed dramatically in the period since 1979—in both absolute and relative terms. Our harmonized data (detailed in Chapter 4) enables us to identify the constituencies with the greatest concentration of selected demographic variables and to compare these between data from the 1981 census (matched against the parliamentary boundaries for the 1983 general election) and the 2011 census (matched to the 2019 boundaries). This gives us some sense of how the populations of constituencies have changed over time, alongside these broader trends in the social and economic makeup of the country. In this section, we focus on the top-ten ranked constituencies at each time point, aiming to illustrate how the archetypal or 'ideal-type' constituency for each demographic variable (each of which make up one of the measures of left-behindedness) has changed, or remained stable, over this period.

We start by looking at constituencies with the highest share of manufacturing employment, routine/semi-routine occupations, over-65s, and social housing and home ownership, as shown in Table 2.2. Here we first see that, while there has been some change in the constituencies ranking most highly in terms of industrial employment, there is some overlap (Barrow & Furness and Leicester East appear in both 1981 and 2011 lists). There is also a noticeable fall in the presence of constituencies from the Midlands—with Warley West, Wolverhampton South East, West Bromwich West, Walsall North, Stoke-on-Trent North and South, and Dudley East all disappearing from the 2011 top ten. The pattern of change is much more distinct for areas with large working-class populations, i.e. those employed in routine and/or semi-routine occupations. In 1981, constituencies predominantly at the heart of major urban conurbations (London, Liverpool, Birmingham, Sheffield, and Manchester) had the highest share of population employed in routine, working-class occupations. By 2011, the profile of these places had changed substantially and that population was now in predominantly smaller, former industrial towns across the North and Midlands. By contrast, those constituencies with the highest share of over-65s have changed little over this thirty-year period, remaining heavily concentrated around coastal areas in the East and South (in towns like Christchurch and Worthing). Social housing remains most prevalent in constituencies in major cities, but these are now almost all found in London whereas previously they included areas in highly deprived parts of Manchester, Liverpool, and Sheffield. There has

Table 2.2 Constituencies with highest share of manufacturing, routine/semi-routine occupations, over-65s, and housing tenure, 1981–2011

| | INDUSTRY | | CLASS | | AGE | | HOUSING TENURE | | | |
| | *Industrial employment: manufacturing* | | *Routine/semi-routine occupations* | | *Age: 65+* | | *Social* | | *Owned* | |
Rank	1981	2011	1981	2011	1981	2011	1981	2011	1981	2011
1	Warley West	Scunthorpe	Liverpool Riverside	Blaenau Gwent	Windsor & Maidenhead	Christchurch	Bow & Poplar	Camberwell & Peckham	Castle Point	Sefton Central
2	West Bromwich West	Pendle	Birmingham Small Heath	Boston & Skegness	Bexhill & Battle	Clacton	Southwark & Bermondsey	Hackney South & Shoreditch	Cheadle	Rayleigh & Wickford
3	Barrow & Furness	Blaenau Gwent	Manchester Central	Great Grimsby	Worthing	North Norfolk	Bethnal Green & Stepney	Islington South & Finsbury	Rochford	Cheadle
4	Wolverhampton South East	Amber Valley	Knowsley North	Wolverhampton South East	Eastbourne	New Forest West	Peckham	Bermondsey & Old Southwark	Wokingham	Wyre & Preston North
5	Pendle	Leicester East	Birmingham Sparkbrook	Normanton, Pontefract & Castleford	Harwich	Bexhill & Battle	Manchester Wythenshawe	Bethnal Green & Bow	Bexleyheath	Castle Point
6	Walsall North	Alyn & Deeside	Bethnal Green & Stepney	Kingston Upon Hull East	Honiton	East Devon	Barking	Holborn & St Pancras	Crosby	Haltemprice & Howden

7	Leicester East	Barrow & Furness	Southwark & Bermondsey	Stoke-on-Trent North	Hove	West Dorset	Knowsley North	Vauxhall	Old Bexley & Sidcup	Charnwood
8	Stoke-on-Trent North	Islwyn	Sheffield Central	Nottingham North	Christchurch	Worthing West	Sheffield Brightside	Islington North	Wyre	York Outer
9	Dudley East	Wrexham	Bow and Poplar	West Bromwich West	Bournemouth East	Louth & Horncastle	Manchester Central	Greenwich & Woolwich	Croydon South	Mid Derbyshire
10	Stoke-on-Trent South	Corby	Preston	Walsall North	North Thanet	Totnes	Hackney South & Shoreditch	Birmingham Ladywood	Ribble Valley	Fareham

been some churn between 1981 and 2011 in terms of places with the highest rate of home ownership. Arguably the defining characteristic of most of these constituencies—scattered across different regions of England and Wales—is that they tend to be somewhat peripheral and characterized by low house prices relative to incomes.

Turning next to the share of employment in cosmopolitan sectors (i.e. creative, educational, and service industries) (see Table 2.3), these constituencies are even more dominated by London than they were in 1981—with only Sheffield Hallam now outside this group (where previously Gosport, Bristol, and Oxford had figured highly—thanks to employment in these areas being dominated by a large public sector and higher education presence). Similarly, the constituencies with the highest proportion of people in managerial-professional occupations has shifted away from the commuter belt south of London (in places such as Esher, Hendon, Cheadle, and Croydon) and north of London (Chesham, Beaconsfield, and Wokingham) and become concentrated towards inner London—in places like Battersea, Richmond, Wimbledon, Chelsea, Fulham, Twickenham, Westminster, Hampstead, Putney, and Kensington. Interestingly, at the same time, the constituencies with the highest number of young people (under-30s) have shifted slightly from central London to the centres of other major cities where there are notably large higher education presences—Sheffield, Cardiff, Liverpool, Newcastle, Manchester, Nottingham, Bristol, Leeds, and Oxford. The pattern for constituencies with the highest proportion of university graduates much more closely follows that for social class, with eight out of the top ten constituencies also featuring in that for managerial-professional occupations, again seeing a slight shift away from university towns (Sheffield, Bristol, Oxford) and outer London suburbia (Esher, St Albans, Cheadle) towards inner London. Lastly, while the most ethnically diverse constituencies have remained concentrated in Greater London there has been churn in those areas with the highest number of ethnic minorities (i.e. these are no longer the *same* London constituencies)—and the list no longer includes several constituencies from the Midlands, reflecting the growing dominance of London in terms of migration inflows over this period.

Of course, comparing the *top ten* highest ranked constituencies only tells part of the story about the demographic transformation of certain sorts of places over this period—missing out change and stability among those constituencies a little further down the list. What they do help illustrate is how much certain aspects of our social and economic geography have changed. For example, this highlights the shrinking of the working class and the growth of the younger, professional, graduate class in major cities, reflecting

Table 2.3 Constituencies with highest share of cosmopolitan industries, managerial-professional occupations, university graduates, under-30s, and ethnic minorities, 1981–2011

Rank	INDUSTRY *Industrial employment: cosmopolitan sectors*		CLASS *Managerial-professional occupations*		AGE *Age 16–29*		EDUCATION *University graduates*		ETHNICITY *Ethnic minorities*	
	1981	2011	1981	2011	1981	2011	1981	2011	1981	2011
1	The City of London & Westminster South	Cities of London & Westminster	Esher	Battersea	Brent East	Sheffield Central	Sheffield Hallam	Battersea	Ealing Southall	West Ham
2	Hampstead & Highgate	Chelsea & Fulham	Hendon South	Richmond Park	Vauxhall	Cardiff Central	Bristol West	Cities of London & Westminster	Brent South	Birmingham Ladywood
3	Gosport	Kensington	Cheadle	Wimbledon	Knowsley North	Liverpool Riverside	Richmond upon Thames & Barnes	Hampstead & Kilburn	Birmingham Ladywood	Brent Central
4	Chelsea	Islington South & Finsbury	Richmond upon Thames & Barnes	Chelsea & Fulham	Chelsea	Newcastle upon Tyne East	Hampstead & Highgate	Chelsea & Fulham	Brent East	Croydon North
5	Bristol West	Battersea	Croydon South	Twickenham	Fulham	Manchester Central	St Albans	Kensington	Birmingham Small Heath	Ealing, Southall

Continued

Table 2.3 *Continued*

Rank	INDUSTRY		CLASS		AGE		EDUCATION		ETHNICITY	
	Industrial employment: cosmopolitan sectors		*Managerial-professional occupations*		*Age 16–29*		*University graduates*		*Ethnic minorities*	
	1981	2011	1981	2011	1981	2011	1981	2011	1981	2011
6	Kensington	Dulwich & West Norwood	Chelsea	Cities of London & Westminster	Brent South	Nottingham South	Chelsea	Richmond Park	Birmingham Sparkbrook	Brent North
7	Oxford West & Abingdon	Wimbledon	Beaconsfield	Hampstead & Kilburn	Kensington	Bristol West	Hornsey & Wood Green	Wimbledon	Newham North East	Harrow West
8	Richmond upon Thames & Barnes	Hampstead & Kilburn	Chesham & Amersham	Putney	Streatham	Leeds Central	Oxford West & Abingdon	Hornsey & Wood Green	Newham North West	Hayes & Harlington
9	Epsom and Ewell	Sheffield Hallam	Sheffield Hallam	Kensington	Hornsey & Wood Green	Bethnal Green & Bow	Cheadle	Putney	Hackney	Walthamstow
10	Dulwich	Tooting	Wokingham	Esher & Walton	Lewisham Deptford	Oxford East	Esher	Tooting	Leicester East	East Ham

a dramatic shift in the post-industrial city (keeping in mind that major cities were the leaders of deindustrialization processes). But this lives alongside a high concentration of people living in social housing in those areas. Working-class voters now reside in greater numbers (relatively) in traditionally left behind towns than core cities, while older populations cluster in peripheral places.

The role of party strategies in changing electoral geography

Changes in demography are, of course, not the only driver of changing electoral geography. If voters' preferences and parties' strategies were held constant, these long-term trends in social and economic structure might alone have translated into very gradual shifts in electoral geography. Over this forty-year period, however, the political parties have moved significantly in terms of their appeals to particular groups of voters. It is the combination of changes in the geographical distribution of voters and changes in the parties' appeals to those voters (which has impacted changes in individual voting behaviour that we documented in the opening chapter), that has transformed the electoral geography of England and Wales. Here we briefly outline the key features of these dynamics of electoral competition, which have been extensively documented by other scholars (e.g. Fieldhouse et al. 2020; Sobolewska and Ford 2020; Hall et al. 2023).[6]

We can consider this broadly in the context of *two-dimensional* party competition. We use data from the Manifestos Project database (Lehmann et al. 2023), which codes the party manifestos published at election time. For the left–right ideological dimension we adapt the 'RILE' scale famously developed by Laver and Budge (1992), restricting it to socio-economic items (rather than left–right items generally), and for the liberal–authoritarian dimension we use an additive index of party emphasis of issues that correspond to social liberalism or social conservatism.[7] In broad terms, as we will see, the party strategies can be broken into two distinct phases, the 1979–97 and 1997–2019 periods.

---

[6] In our analysis, we set aside questions regarding the 'valence' or competence dimension (e.g. Green and Jennings 2017), since we assume that evaluations of party competence will primarily impact the frontier of electoral support, rather than shaping the geographical distribution of votes.

[7] Following Laver and Budge (1992), we subtract attention to topics associated with the economic left from attention to topics associated with the economic right, and similarly subtract attention to topics associated with social conservatism from attention to topics on issues associated with social liberalism. We centre the measure around zero and divide by the maximum absolute value so that the scale ranges from −1 to +1.

Starting with the left–right economic dimension (Figure 2.1), between 1979 and 1997 the Labour Party moved rightwards towards the centre (with shifts leftwards in 1983 and 1992). This enabled it to appeal to a wider cross-class coalition in the 1997 and 2001 landslide victories of Tony Blair (Evans and Tilley 2017), enhancing the appeal of the party to the professional classes and university graduates (as well as the party's traditional working-class base). Between 1997 and 2010 the party hovered around the economic middle ground. Since 2010, Labour has steadily moved left, eroding some of that appeal amongst the home-owning, suburban and small-town middle class. The Conservatives, in contrast, took a position firmly on the economic right under Margaret Thatcher in 1979, standing on a platform of less state intervention in the economy. Nevertheless, the party drifted towards the economic centre over the period up until 2001, before moving to the right again in 2005 and 2010. In 2015, however, the party moved sharply leftwards on the economy (in a similar move to Labour), and it has since retained its position near the economic centre ground—supporting increased spending on the NHS and pensions (e.g. the 'triple lock'). This has enabled it to attract more working-class voters, and increasingly older voters, culminating in the 'realigning' 2019 general election victory and the significant demographic shift in the party's support (see Ford et al. 2021).

On the liberal–authoritarian dimension (Figure 2.2), the Conservative Party moved slightly in a socially conservative direction between 1987 and 1997 but overall has remained fairly close to the centre. In contrast, Labour steadily moved in a socially conservative direction over the period up to 2005, notably on issues such as crime (Newburn 2001, 2007) and defence (Daddow 2013), which helped maintain its support among more socially conservative voters, but has since moved dramatically in a socially liberal direction. The party's adoption of increasingly permissive positions on social issues has reinforced its appeal to younger voters, university graduates, and ethnic minorities—at the expense of support among its older, white, working-class base. While the Conservative Party has adopted more liberal positions on certain issues (such as same-sex marriage), it has in relative terms tended to promote a more socially conservative agenda, most notably on issues such as immigration and lately Brexit, and consequently has attracted a growing support among white, working-class, and older voters. It is not our goal here to pass judgement on whether these trends represent a *complete* realignment of the class basis of British politics. Labour still secures a substantial share of its support from working-class and poorer voters, while the Conservatives continue to be backed by many affluent, educated

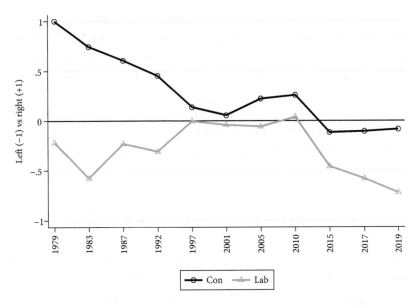

Figure 2.1 Party positions on the left–right economic dimension, 1979–2019

Left–right economic index = *(Free market economy + incentives + anti-protectionism + economic orthodoxy + anti-welfare + anti-labour groups)* minus *(Market regulation + economic planning + protectionism + controlled economy + nationalization + pro-welfare + pro-labour groups)*

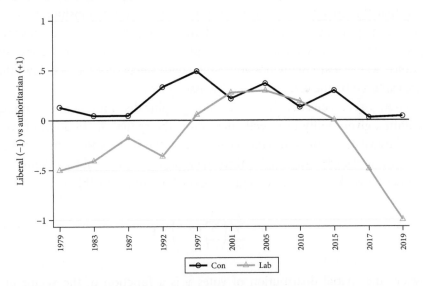

Figure 2.2 Party positions on the liberal–authoritarian dimension, 1979–2019

Liberal–authoritarian index = *(Pro-military + pro-national way of life + traditional morality + pro-law and order + anti-multi-culturalism)* minus *(Peace + freedom and human rights + pro-democracy + pro-environmentalism + pro-equality + pro-multiculturalism)* professionals with economically conservative views. What is crucial, however, is that as a result of the changing strategies of the parties, Labour's support has been bolstered among those demographic groups increasingly found in major cities and urban centres, while Conservative support has grown among groups found in post-industrial towns and other peripheral places that are characterised by their left-behindedness. As we have noted, the trends that we document here are a product of the changing behaviour of individuals and the prevalence of certain types of individuals in certain places.

Towards a general model of electoral geography

In the remainder of this book, we explore how the electoral geography of England and Wales has changed as a function of these demographic trends and the changing preferences of voters—reacting to the strategies and performance of parties themselves. Before doing so, it is helpful to formally elucidate the mechanisms that we consider drive these patterns of electoral geography (both relating to stability and change), even if we do not offer direct tests of them empirically. We should perhaps begin by emphasizing that this model explains the way in which the relationships between sociodemographic characteristics and voting behaviour influence electoral geography. It is not an attempt to capture every factor that shapes vote choice, as there are many possible contextual effects (discussed below) that are captured by the error term, as discussed below.

First, we can consider the spatial demographic distribution of individuals within a given polity to directly determine the spatial distribution of votes (and translation into seat winner), given that the social and economic characteristics of each individual within an electoral district will lead them to be more or less likely to vote for a given party. We can define this as follows:

$$\gamma = \sum_{i=1}^{n} \left(\sum_{j=1}^{k} (v_{ij}) \right) + \varepsilon_i$$

where the spatial distribution of votes γ is a function of the vector of k sociodemographic characteristics of a population across n electoral units, where each of these sociodemographic characteristics is associated with a given propensity v to vote for each party p, and the final vote outcome for a particular party is a function of the sum of vote propensities across k sociodemographic characteristics.

The error term ε captures unexplained variance, that is, patterns of voting that are not accounted for the composition of electoral districts and their predicted propensity to vote for a given party. These are the contextual factors that include everything from the effects associated with the household or the workplace to those that might operate across a wider geography, such as city or region (which is essentially what Chapter 7 of this book considers). Changes in electoral geography can thus occur through changes in the sociodemographic composition of an area φ or through changes in the propensity of different sociodemographic groups to vote for parties v. What we show in the ecological analysis in the remainder of this book is a combination of these dynamics.

Building upon this model, one might next consider how those sociodemographic factors are spatially distributed and the degree to which they lead to particular geographical unevenness in electoral outcomes. As we will show in the next chapter, this has significant consequences for the electoral inefficiency of the political parties.

3

Electoral change in England and Wales

How has the electoral geography of England and Wales changed over time? A long line of research has investigated regional variations in voting at parliamentary elections since 1945. Curtice and Steed (1982) noted the emergence of a North–South and urban–rural cleavage dating from the 1950s, while Johnston et al. (1988) observed a growing North–South divide in the 1980s, with the North and major cities tending towards Labour, and Southern, suburban, and rural areas trending towards the Conservatives. These divides have prompted much debate over whether regional variation simply reflects the demographic composition of various parts of the country (with a focus on whether occupational class alone explained the North–South divide in voting) or if there were contextual factors peculiar to particular areas (such as over-performance of the Labour vote in coalfield areas). Analysis by Crewe (1973) suggested that the Conservatives performed better in areas with more 'affluent workers' employed in boom sectors of the economy, while Labour retained an electoral grip on areas with 'traditional workers' employed in industry and manufacturing. The role of demography was considered further through the role of migration flows between North and South. Drawing on individual-level survey data from the 1987 British Election Study (contrasted with data from 1964, February 1974, and 1979), McMahon et al. (1992) found that southerly migration led individuals to trend away from Labour and northerly migration led them towards the party, further reinforcing this geographical cleavage. Also drawing on BES data, Fieldhouse (1995) found a growing divide between North and South in attitudes towards economic issues over the period between 1964 and 1987. Later evidence suggested that the North–South divide in voting behaviour had closed over the period 1987 to 1997 (Curtice and Park 1999), attributed to ideological moderation of the Labour Party. Beyond the two main parties, researchers noted the growing electoral strength of the Liberal Democrats since the 1970s in South West England and Wessex, rural Scotland and Wales, and outer London (MacAllister et al. 2002). The party's electoral map had echoes of historical strongholds of their predecessor, the Liberal Party, in the 'Celtic fringe', dating back more than a century.

The Changing Electoral Map of England and Wales. Jamie Furlong and Will Jennings, Oxford University Press.
© Jamie Furlong and Will Jennings (2024). DOI: 10.1093/9780191943331.003.0003

Regional divides in election outcomes tell us a lot about geographical cleavages in voting behaviour but they give only a partial picture of spatial variation. Stability of voting behaviour at the regional level may conceal considerable divergence at lower levels of geography. In this chapter we first present an overview of long-term trends in regional support for the parties between 1945 and 2019, before exploring how within-region support has changed over time, and specifically consider the growing electoral divide related to population density. Clustering of support for the Labour Party in densely populated urban centres, and the relative concentration of the Conservative vote in smaller towns and rural areas, is a product of the demographic processes married to shifting party appeals we outlined in Chapter 2. We further show how this has significant consequences for the *distributional efficiency* of each party's vote. The regional and urban–rural trends that we describe here form the general context of our analysis in later chapters, and importantly highlight the value of examining change in electoral geography with a fine-grained spatial lens. Our later analysis also speaks to how the demographic composition of certain areas translates into patterns of party support, but how even at these local levels there remains residual unexplained variation that merits further investigation (and this is what the remainder of the book sets out to do).

Regional trends in party support

How has the regional geography of support for the parties changed over time? Drawing on historical data back to 1945,[1] in Figure 3.1 we plot the share of the vote received by each party in every region of England and in the nations of Scotland and Wales.[2] This suggests there have been some notable long-term shifts in the regional concentration of the parties' votes. Labour in particular has won a declining share of the vote in Wales, Scotland, the Midlands, the East, the South, and parts of the North. These downward trends are somewhat accentuated due to the fact that the time series starts in 1945,

---

[1] For our analysis of regional trends and electoral inefficiency, we use data from the House of Commons Library (2020) that draws on a range of valuable historical sources, including W. Field (1918–49) [UK Data Service, SN: 5673], F. W. S. Craig (1950–1), D. Dorling (1955–92) [UK Data Service: SN 3061], and its own House of Commons Library elections data (1997–2019). For our analysis of population density, we use data from I. Crewe (1955–74) [UK Data Service: SN 661], W. L. Miller (1918–79) (UK Data Service: SN 1383) and the Electoral Calculus historical election data archive (1955–2010) (https://www. electoralcalculus.co.uk/).

[2] Of course, Scotland and Wales have their own distinctive political histories, identities, cultures, and party systems, but we include them in our analysis of regional trends as they are comparable to English regions in terms of the size of population and number of parliamentary seats.

a high electoral tide for the Labour Party in modern British history thanks to Clement Attlee's post-war landslide, after which the party has only achieved similarly large victories in 1997 and 2001, under Tony Blair. Likewise, the resurgence of the Liberal Party and later the Liberal Democrats has put pressure on the Labour and Conservative vote in different regions at different times, or at the very least made electoral competition more complicated. Labour has retained electoral strength in London and the North West and has seen a positive trend in both regions since 1979. For the Conservatives, rising electoral strength in a lot of regions since 1997 represents a reversal of long-term decline. London and, to a lesser extent, the North West are the relative exceptions, where there has not been a comparable recovery in support. In these two regions, Labour's support has fluctuated but not declined—the trend in the North West is driven by Labour's dominance in Merseyside and Greater Manchester.

While many regions simply follow the national trend in party support, some diverge more substantially from the national level of support than others. In Figures 3.2 and 3.3 we plot the Labour and Conservative vote respectively in each region *relative to* the party's national vote share. This tells us whether a party is under- or over-performing in a region relative to its national performance. It is helpful because there are elections where a party's vote was universally higher or lower than average. For example, Labour's vote was relatively high everywhere in 1945 and 1997 and relatively low everywhere or in most regions in 1983 and 2010. In this sense, we can disentangle national swing from regional swing. These charts are arguably much more revealing than the *absolute* vote share and suggest that trends are much more stable than implied by fluctuation of the national swing. For Labour there is relative stability in a number of the regions (Wales, the West and East Midlands, Yorkshire and the Humber, and the South East) where vote shares are consistently higher than the national average. London has rapidly seen a strengthening of the Labour vote since 2005, while the party has steadily done better in the North West (and was on a similar trajectory in the North East up until 1997, after which the trend reversed). The trend for Scotland is something of a rollercoaster, becoming one of Labour's best regions between February 1974 and 1987, falling away between 1992 and 2005, strengthening sharply in 2010 under a Scottish Prime Minister, Gordon Brown, but collapsing in the realigning election of 2015. The Conservatives, on the other hand, have enjoyed relative improvement in their electoral performance in Wales, the East of England, the East Midlands, and (more recently) the West Midlands, as well the South West. The party has done steadily worse in the North West and Scotland

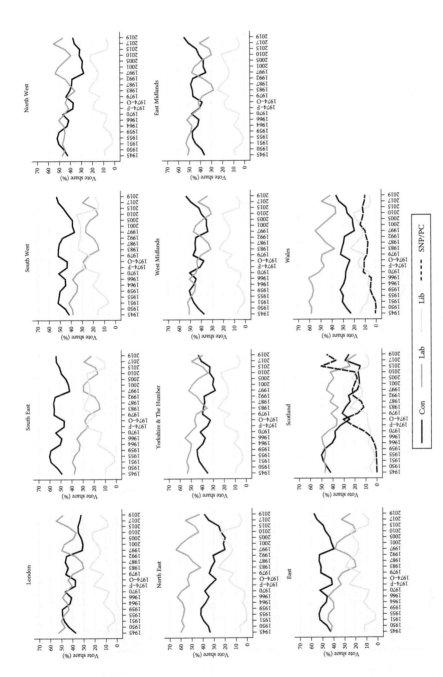

Figure 3.1 Party vote share by region, 1945–2019

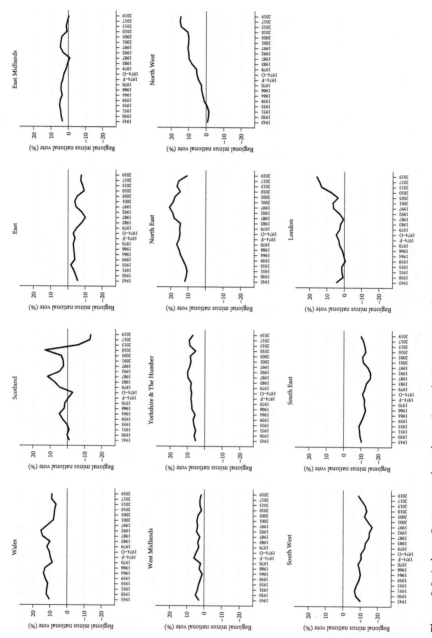

Figure 3.2 Labour Party vote share by region relative to national vote share, 1945–2019

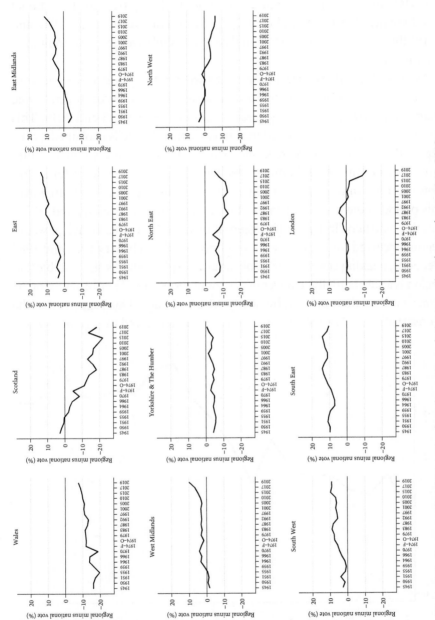

Figure 3.3 Conservative Party vote share by region relative to national vote share, 1945–2019

over the entire post-war period. Indeed, compared to other regions in the North of England and the Midlands where there has been either longer term or recent improvement, the North West stands out as an exception. It is also notable that, up until 2015, London closely tracked the national trend for the Conservatives but in the most recent two elections (2017 and 2019) the party has seen a substantial drop in its relative electoral strength in the capital.

As an additional exercise, in Figure 3.4 we plot the adjusted R-squared of a linear regression of region on Conservative and Labour constituency vote share, respectively, for each general election between 1945 and 2019. This simply captures how much variance in each party's vote is explained by the region that constituencies are located within. These summary statistics offer a number of important illuminations. First, there is a significant long-term upward trend in the extent to which region predicts patterns of voting over this period (note that our data for this analysis include Scotland and Wales, but not Northern Ireland). The steepest increase in the predictive power of region occurred for the Conservatives between the February 1974 and 1987 elections, peaking at around 50% of variance explained. It is also notable that region is a substantially stronger predictor of the electoral performance of the Conservatives than Labour, by nearly 0.1 on average. This suggests that the Conservative Party's vote is consistently more structured in regional terms.

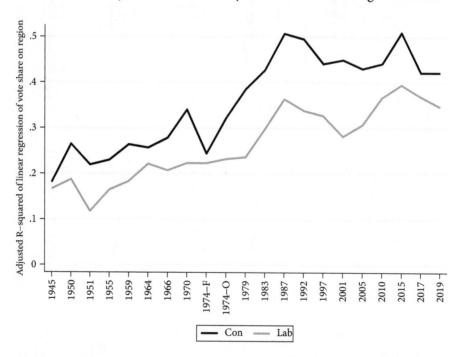

Figure 3.4 Region as a predictor of party constituency vote share, 1945–2019

Varieties of geographical polarization

These regional trends do not, however, tell the whole story about the changing electoral geography of England and Wales. Just as there are *between* region trends, there are political divergences *within* regions that reflect divisions between urban and rural areas, inner cities and their suburbs, and larger cities and smaller towns. Of course, regions are not uniform; rather, they are demographically and politically heterogeneous, made up of cities, towns, and rural areas with varied and sometimes diverging characteristics. Recent studies have suggested a growing geographical polarization between major cities (and university towns) and rural, small-town Britain (Jennings and Stoker 2017, 2019)—the former becoming Labour strongholds whilst the latter have been shifting towards the Conservatives. Others have focused more specifically on the decline of Labour support in former industrial towns (Cutts et al. 2020) and coastal areas (Jennings and Stoker 2016). There is also significant long-term evidence of an urban–suburban divide in British politics in which inner-city areas have favoured Labour and more suburban areas the Conservatives (Walks 2005)—a divide that may have been a factor in the Conservative victory in 2019 (*The Economist* 2021). Together, these studies make clear that there are other geographical divides that result in significant *within-region* variation in demographic and electoral trajectories.

One clear example of this within-region political heterogeneity is in the North West. Labour's relative gains in the region are underpinned by the party's dominance in the two major cities: the inner cities and suburban parts of Manchester and Liverpool have been a focus of growing Labour strength and Conservative decline in recent decades (e.g. Wilks-Heeg 2019; Jeffery 2023a, 2023b). The regional trend conceals the reverse dynamic found in outlying towns where Labour has increasingly struggled and the Conservatives have gained support, in places such as Copeland, Barrow and Furness, Carlisle, Fylde, and Rossendale and Darwen. Even between 2017 and 2019, this divergence was clear: contrast the swings of just 1.1 and 3.8 points from Labour to the Conservatives in Liverpool Walton and Manchester Central respectively with the swings of 6.5 and 6.4 points in Barrow and Furness and Stalybridge and Hyde. Beyond regional variations, sharp divides have emerged in the voting behaviour of parts of major cities, and smaller, outlying towns, and rural areas. These in part reflect the demographic processes described in the previous chapter, as well as the changing appeal of the parties to these electorates.

Boundary changes make it difficult to go far back in time with a great deal of precision at the national level, but it is possible to track how electoral support has changed between city, industrial town and rural constituencies where boundary changes have been relatively limited. For this we use historical data of party vote shares for a subset of around forty archetypal city/industrial town/rural constituencies over the period from 1950 to 2019, eleven of which are drawn from the most middle-class and professional areas of core cities, fifteen of which are constituencies covering smaller towns that have experienced relative industrial decline, and fourteen of which are rural constituencies with a high level of agricultural employment.

The city constituencies are shown in Figure 3.5,[3] revealing two distinct trends. First, the Conservative Party has experienced a steady decline in support in these city seats from a high point in 1955. This reflects both the changing demographic makeup of these types of constituencies—which are increasingly home to younger, more educated, more ethnically diverse, professional populations, even if there is significant entrenched poverty—and changes in the voting behaviour of these groups, such as observed at the 2017 and 2019 elections (Sturgis and Jennings 2020; Ford et al. 2021; also see Chapter 1). Secondly, Labour started to make inroads in these core cities in the mid-1980s. Over three decades Labour has seen its support in these seats in major cities nearly double from around 30% in 1983 to just under 60% in 2019 (an election in which the party otherwise performed poorly).

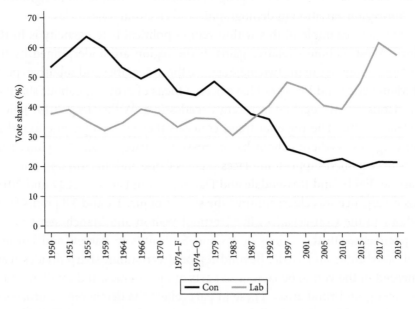

Figure 3.5 Labour and Conservative vote share in selected core city constituencies, 1950–2019

[3] The core city constituencies are Birmingham Edgbaston, Birmingham Selly Oak, Bristol West, Cardiff Central (North 1955–83), Leeds North East, Leeds North West, Liverpool Wavertree (Broadgreen 1983–97), Manchester Blackley, Manchester Withington, Newcastle upon Tyne Central (North 1955–83), and Sheffield Hallam.

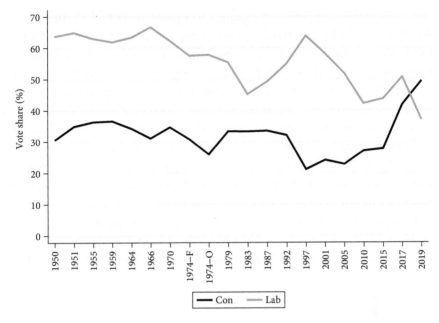

Figure 3.6 Labour and Conservative vote share in selected industrial town constituencies, 1950–2019

In contrast, voting patterns in our industrial town constituencies[4]—which are drawn from across the North of England, Midlands, and Wales—have trended in the opposite direction. This is plotted in Figure 3.6. These seats have seen a long-term decline in Labour's share of the vote, temporarily interrupted by the party's recovery from its devastating 1983 defeat and the height of popularity of the New Labour project. Notably, the trajectory of Conservative support is not a mirror image of the Labour experience. Between 1950 and 1992 the party largely stood still in these sorts of area, with the average level of support fluctuating a little over 30%. Since the low of 1997, the Conservatives have more than doubled their vote in industrial towns, taking the lead from Labour in 2019.

Next, we consider a set of rural constituencies[5]—the sorts of seats traditionally held by the Conservatives. We plot the vote share for the parties over time in Figure 3.7. Here it is notable that both parties experienced a period of decline in their rural vote, but the Conservatives have managed to

[4] The industrial town constituencies are Barrow and Furness Bassetlaw, Bishop Auckland, Blyth Valley, Bolsover, Don Valley, North West Durham, Leigh, Great Grimsby, Mansfield, Rotherham, Stoke-on-Trent Central, Stoke-on-Trent North, Stoke-on-Trent South, Wakefield, Workington, and Wrexham.

[5] The rural constituencies are Berwick-upon-Tweed, Brecon and Radnorshire (Brecon and Radnor, 1950–97), Gainsborough (Gainsborough and Horncastle, 1983–97), Hexham, Ludlow, North Cornwall, North Devon, North Shropshire (Oswestry, 1950–83), Penrith and The Border, Preseli Pembrokeshire (Pembroke, 1950–97), Richmond (Yorks), South West Norfolk, Thirsk and Malton (Ryedale, 1983–2010), and West Dorset.

steadily rebuild support since hitting a low point in 1997. Labour's decline was briefly halted as the party rebuilt its popularity in the 1980s and 1990s, but has been more sustained by comparison. This reflects in particular the revival of the Liberal Democrats as a challenger in certain parts of the country (MacAllister et al. 2002). There are some important regional and national variations to these patterns. In a few Welsh rural constituencies[6]—shown in Figure 3.8—there has been a long-term decline of the Labour (and the Liberal) vote, as electoral support for the Conservatives and Welsh nationalist party, Plaid Cymru, has risen steadily. It is apparent, then, that the long-term electoral fortunes of the parties are defined—in part—by geography, in the divergent trends of cities, towns, and rural areas.

This pattern of divergence between less populous peripheral areas and more populous urban areas fits with cross-national evidence of growing *urban–rural divides* in voting behaviour (Rodden 2019; Taylor et al. 2023).

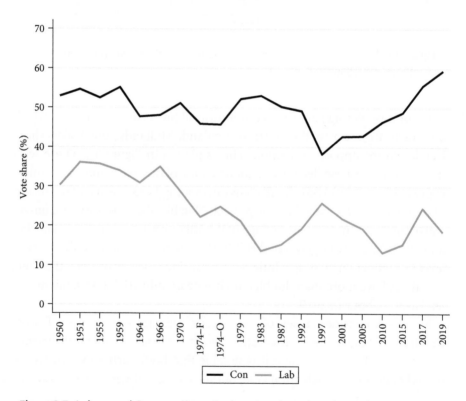

Figure 3.7 Labour and Conservative vote share in selected rural constituencies, 1950–2019

[6] The Welsh rural constituencies are Montgomeryshire (Montgomery 1950–97), Ceredigion (Cardigan, 1950–79; Ceredigion and Pembroke North, 1983–92), Carmarthen East and Dinefwr (Carmarthen, 1950–92), and Dwyfor Meirionnydd (Merioneth, 1950–83; Meirionnydd Nant Conwy, 1983–2005).

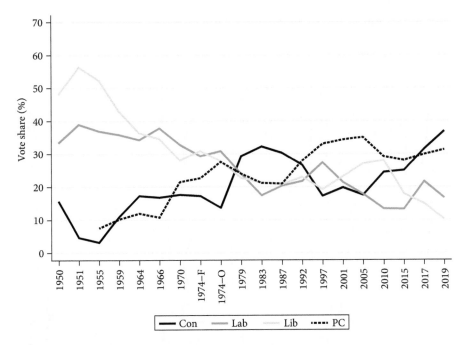

Figure 3.8 Labour and Conservative vote share in selected Welsh rural constituencies, 1950–2019

Earlier analysis of UK parliamentary elections by Curtice and Steed (1982) identified the emergence of an urban–rural cleavage at the 1955 election. Similarly, Walks (2005) showed that, between 1950 and 2001, there was significant polarization between the suburbs (where Conservative support was increasingly located) and inner cities (where Labour's vote strengthened over time). Importantly, Walks noted considerable heterogeneity as to *when* this city–suburban polarization occurred in different settings—starting earlier in London and much later in Edinburgh, for example. While the dichotomy between towns and cities we present above is useful for highlighting extreme cases of geographical polarization, the relationship between voting and population density enables a more continuous measurement (and allows us to look beyond constituencies with minimal boundary changes) that ranges from sprawling, low-density, suburban seats to more compact urban centres. Specifically, it takes into account the *whole* of the constituency, including those that have sizeable rural peripheries.

Figure 3.9 plots the Labour-Conservative margin (lead) in each constituency on the y-axis and the number of people per hectare (the measure of population density) on the x-axis by election. In each panel of the chart the data are fitted with Locally Weighted Scatterplot Smoothing (LOWESS) to determine if there is clear structure in the relationship between population

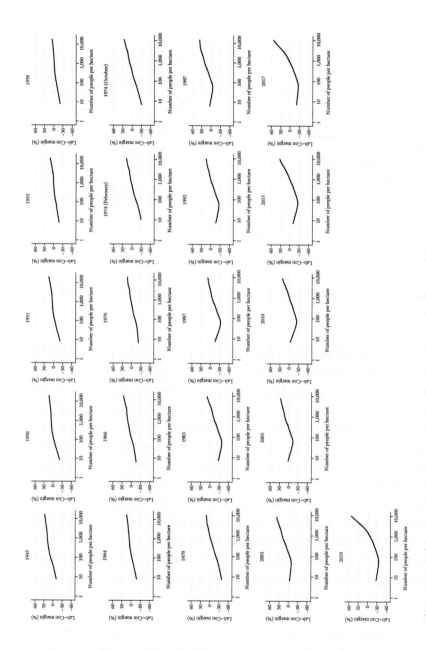

Figure 3.9 Labour-Conservative vote margin by population density, 1945–2019

Note: the boundary maps used to calculate the land area for estimates of population density for the 1974–79 and 1997–2005 general elections were obtained from parlconst.org

density and the relative Labour-Conservative vote. The line-of-best fit plotted in the figure reveals limited structure by density in the period from 1945 to 1979, with a gentle upward slope indicating that Labour receives greater support in densely populated urban areas. The trajectory of this relationship becomes considerably steeper from 1983 onwards. The emergence of a curvilinear pattern over the same period is attributable to the divergence of voting behaviour in Scotland, in particular sparsely populated Highland and Island constituencies. By the end of the period Labour's average lead in the areas with the highest population density was on average 50 points, and in the areas with the lowest its average deficit was around 30 points. This encapsulated the huge divergence in Labour's performance—winning by a large margin in a relatively small number of densely populated seats and losing by smaller margins across a much wider range of seats.

Electoral (in)efficiency of the Labour and Conservative votes

The combination of securing a high level of support from demographic groups who are spatially clustered in cities, and a lower level of support with groups who are more evenly distributed across the country, has profound electoral consequences for Labour. Specifically, the distribution of Labour's vote has become increasingly inefficient over time, with the party winning disproportionately large majorities in a number of city seats while becoming less competitive in more marginal constituencies, many of which are former industrial heartlands (and notably those which voted Leave in the 2016 EU referendum). The Conservatives, in contrast have seen their vote share decline in affluent suburbs of major cities and university towns where the party once was more successful, and those places where the local economy or culture attracts a higher proportion of younger, educated, and professional voters (such as some, but not all, suburban areas). It has made steady gains, though, in former industrial areas and peripheral coastal areas characterized by ageing, predominantly white populations and dwindling local economies. Part of the story may simply be that there are more of the kinds of places where the Conservatives have gained support: Labour's vote has become increasingly concentrated in larger cities and university towns at the expense of almost all other types of constituency, from their post-industrial heartlands to smaller, market towns and rural areas. The Conservatives have increased their vote in post-industrial towns whilst simultaneously holding on to their wealthier small-town, suburban, and rural heartlands.

We can explore long-term trends in electoral efficiency more precisely by plotting (by party) the majority won for each constituency in Great Britain against the constituency's rank of marginality. This is shown in Figure 3.10, for all elections between 1945 and 2019. The seats won by each party are ordered in decreasing rank of marginality on the x-axis (where 1 denotes the most marginal seat), with the size of the majority (measured by difference in vote share between the winning and second placed party) shown on the y-axis. A line with a shallow, near linear gradient indicates that there is a gradual, incremental increase in the size of the party's constituency majorities, implying that it translates its support into seats in a relatively proportional fashion. A line with a steeper and/or exponential component, on the other hand, indicates that a party's vote is disproportionately concentrated in safe constituencies (leading votes to be 'wasted' in uncompetitive seats). The length of the line is indicative of the number of seats won by the party at that election.

In both 1997 and 2001, both parties saw a very steady linear increase in majority for each additional seat gained. This was also interestingly true, for the most part, in 2010—though the tail of Labour's vote distribution revealed a few constituencies where the party's majority rose sharply—as well as in elections in 1950 and 1951. The gradual slope indicates *relative* electoral efficiency since it means that each additional seat is won with a relatively even increase in electoral support. There are many other instances where one party (often the Conservatives) has won constituencies with gradually rising majorities, against an opponent whose majority size has risen (over a smaller number of seats) at a faster (less efficient) rate. Perhaps the most obvious example of this is the 2019 election, where the size of Labour majorities rose much more sharply than for the Conservatives, such that in Labour's least marginal seat (202 out of 202) they had a majority of over 70 percentage points whereas in the equivalent seat for the Conservatives (202 of 365) they had a majority of around 30 points. This pattern became more noticeable in 2015 and 2017, and previously had been evident between 1979 and 1987 (although the pattern was slightly less pronounced). In these two time periods where Labour have been out of power, the party has gained a smaller number of seats but with disproportionately large majorities, implying that their support was too heavily concentrated in a small number of 'stronghold' seats (mining areas in the 1980s and large urban centres between 2015 and 2019) rather than across a wider range of seats. The Conservative Party has never suffered from the same degree of electoral inefficiency in the tail of its vote distribution.

We can also calculate, based on the same data, the average majority size for seats won by each party at each election (in terms of both raw votes and

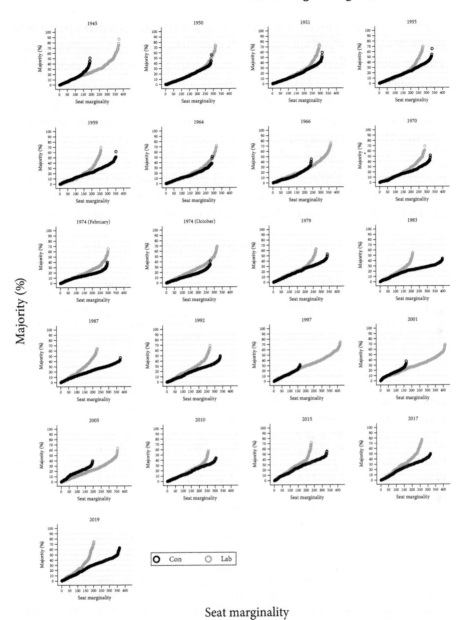

Figure 3.10 Size of constituency majority by marginality, Great Britain, 1945–2019

percentage vote share), and the marginal increase in the average number of votes (and average vote share) required to win each additional seat. These summary statistics are reported in Table 3.1 for all elections between 1945 and 2019. To take an example, in 1945, for each additional seat won by the Conservatives, their average number of votes increased by 30 and average vote share increased by 0.077. An 'efficient' vote distribution is one where there is a very small increment between each seat won, such that a party only needs to secure a small increase in its vote share to win an additional seat. The obvious corollary to this is that a party with a highly efficient vote might experience a large number of losses due to a relatively small decrease in its vote share. Nonetheless, since the Conservative landslide of 1979, the party with the most efficient vote (or the smallest mean increase in vote share per seat won) has won most seats.

Figure 3.11 shows that between 1945 and 2019, there was only one time period in which Labour's vote was more efficient than the Conservatives— between 1997 and 2005. There is also a striking, growing gap between the parties in terms of electoral efficiency. This had previously peaked in 1987, at

Table 3.1 Majority size and electoral efficiency, Great Britain, 1945–2019

	Conservative					Labour			
		Average majority					*Average majority*		
	Number of seats	*Votes*	*Vote share*	*Votes per seat gain*	*Share per seat gain*	*Number of seats*	*Votes*	*Vote share*	*Votes per seat gain*	*Share per seat gain*
1945	192	5,824	14.8	30	0.077	373	9,103	25.7	24	0.069
1950	288	7,734	17.1	27	0.059	315	10,262	22.2	33	0.070
1951	312	8,430	19.0	27	0.061	295	9,993	21.8	34	0.074
1955	334	8,616	21.0	26	0.063	277	8,436	20.5	30	0.074
1959	353	9,313	21.2	26	0.060	258	8,357	19.8	32	0.077
1964	291	7,238	16.0	25	0.055	317	8,683	21.9	27	0.069
1966	242	6,143	13.6	25	0.056	363	9,722	25.4	27	0.070
1970	322	8,851	18.1	27	0.056	287	7,947	21.3	28	0.074
1974–F	296	7,592	14.5	26	0.049	301	9,207	20.9	31	0.070
1974–O	276	6,739	13.8	24	0.050	319	9,804	24.1	31	0.076
1979	339	11,663	21.7	34	0.064	268	8,713	21.0	33	0.079
1983	397	10,187	20.4	26	0.051	209	7,722	18.4	37	0.088
1987	375	11,406	21.1	30	0.056	229	10,621	24.3	46	0.106
1992	336	11,721	20.3	35	0.060	271	10,373	23.8	38	0.088
1997	165	6,593	12.6	40	0.076	418	13,245	30.6	32	0.073
2001	166	6,925	15.3	42	0.092	412	9,616	27.5	23	0.067
2005	198	8,286	17.5	42	0.089	355	7,786	21.5	22	0.060
2010	306	9,459	19.0	31	0.062	258	7,902	19.3	31	0.075
2015	330	12,955	25.3	39	0.077	232	10,484	24.5	45	0.106
2017	317	12,480	23.2	39	0.073	262	13,424	28.3	51	0.108
2019	365	13,960	26.7	38	0.073	202	11,956	25.2	59	0.125

Note: National Liberals are counted as Conservative for all elections (the National Liberals stood against the Conservatives in just four seats in 1945). Speakers of the House of Commons are excluded, even where their constituencies were contested. Multi-member seats are excluded from the data for the 1945 general election.

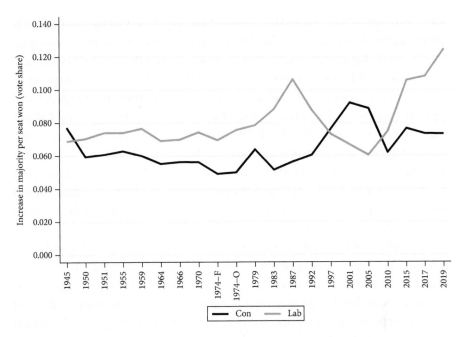

Figure 3.11 Increments of majority increase by marginality, 1945–2019

a time when the landslide victory of the Thatcher Government forced Labour to retreat into its heartlands. Since a low in 2005, the size of the average incremental rise in vote share per Labour seat won doubled from 0.06 to 0.13 points in 2019. So in 2005, moving from the most marginal seat to the 10th most marginal seat saw a 0.6 point increase in the size of Labour's vote share majority. In 2019, this same move led to a 1.3 point increase.

Reflecting on long-term trends in electoral geography

Since 1945, there have been profound changes in the electoral geography of England and Wales (and Britain more generally). Many of these shifts have occurred gradually but also relentlessly, as the steady march of demographic change has navigated the ebb and flow of political fortunes, and the changing appeals to the electorate of the two main parties—the Conservatives and Labour—and their challengers. With the benefit of hindsight, it is clear how long-term trends in support for the parties have resulted from the accumulation of small, incremental gains (and losses) over extended periods of time in particular parts of the country. In terms of the regional picture, we have shown a mixture of stability and change. In some regions, parties' electoral support has tracked the national average closely or has been steadily above/below it for much of this seventy-year period. In others, substantial shocks or realignments have seen a divergence from the national trend (e.g. the collapse of Labour's support in Scotland in 2015, and the sharp fall in Conservative support in London in 2017–19), and others have experienced gradual change in the balance of electoral competition (e.g. rising Labour support over time in the North West, rising Conservative support in the East Midlands and East of England). We have also shown that region has become an increasingly strong predictor of electoral outcomes over time, but to understand this requires further investigation as the spatial distribution of demographic trends we outlined in Chapter 2 may be behind the growing variation between regions.

Beyond these regional patterns, the evidence points to growing polarization of the electoral geography of England and Wales. The Conservative Party has suffered a sustained long-term decline in its vote in major cities, while Labour have seen a similar decline in its vote in many industrial towns—representing a substantial part (but not all) of the party's historical strongholds. Labour's recovery in those towns between 1983 and 1997 (and the partial revival in 2017) suggests that the party's fate may not yet be completely terminal in those places, but there clearly has been a structural shift with the surge in Conservative support in industrial towns between 2015 and 2019 clearly linked to Brexit. The long-term decline in Labour's vote in rural constituencies suggests that this geographical divide goes beyond towns and cities to a broader core–periphery dimension. Accordingly, we find that population density is strongly correlated with higher levels of support for Labour than for the Conservatives. As we have discussed, these geographies do not align cleanly with economically left behind areas of high deprivation that are found in pockets inside major cities as well as in more peripheral towns and urban areas.

A crucial insight from these geographical divides, confirming the argument of Rodden (2019), is that the clustering of electoral support for the left (i.e. Labour) in densely populated urban areas leads to the inefficient distribution of its vote, putting it at an electoral disadvantage. This inefficiency has become more pronounced relatively recently, reinforced by Labour's relative decline in support in its industrial heartlands in England and Wales in part due to Brexit and in Scotland due to rise of the SNP. As we will show in the remainder of the book for England and Wales specifically, these regional, city–town and urban–rural divides are a product of the changing relationship between the demographic profile of places and support for the parties.

Appendix

Table A3.1 Labour vote share (%) by region, 1945–2019

Election	North East	North West	Yorkshire & The Humber	East Mid-lands	West Mid-lands	East	South East	South West	London	Wales	Scotland
1945	60.2	47.6	53.5	51.8	51.2	42.7	38.0	38.3	53.0	58.6	47.2
1950	57.1	44.8	52.2	50.3	51.0	41.5	36.7	38.8	46.9	58.1	46.3
1951	59.3	47.2	53.9	53.2	52.5	45.4	39.5	42.1	50.2	60.5	47.9
1955	57.7	45.8	52.5	51.4	49.4	44.6	37.5	38.6	47.8	57.6	46.7
1959	56.7	44.9	50.4	48.6	45.9	39.9	33.5	34.7	43.3	56.4	46.7
1964	58.4	45.9	49.7	47.6	45.2	40.4	32.5	34.1	44.5	57.7	48.7
1966	63.1	50.4	55.3	52.2	50.7	44.6	35.3	38.4	49.0	60.7	49.9
1970	59.6	45.7	50.5	47.1	45.0	39.9	31.1	34.3	45.7	51.6	44.5
1974 Feb	52.4	41.5	45.1	40.3	43.1	33.1	25.1	26.6	40.4	46.8	36.7
1974 Oct	53.9	44.5	46.8	41.8	43.9	36.2	28.4	28.9	43.9	49.5	36.3
1979	51.8	42.5	45.0	38.2	40.1	31.9	24.8	24.6	39.6	48.6	41.5
1983	42.0	35.6	35.3	28.0	31.2	19.6	14.5	14.7	29.8	37.5	35.1
1987	49.0	40.6	40.6	30.0	33.3	20.7	15.5	15.9	31.5	45.1	42.4
1992	53.4	44.3	44.3	37.4	38.8	26.4	18.9	19.2	37.1	49.5	39.0
1997	64.0	53.6	51.9	47.8	47.0	38.6	29.1	26.4	49.5	54.7	45.6
2001	59.4	50.7	48.6	45.1	44.8	36.8	29.4	26.3	47.4	48.6	43.3
2005	52.9	45.1	43.6	39.0	38.7	29.8	24.4	22.8	38.9	42.7	38.9
2010	43.6	39.4	34.4	29.8	30.6	19.6	16.2	15.4	36.6	36.2	42.0
2015	46.9	44.6	39.1	31.6	32.9	22.0	18.3	17.7	43.7	36.9	24.3
2017	55.4	54.9	49.0	40.5	42.5	32.7	28.6	29.1	54.5	48.9	27.1
2019	42.6	46.5	38.9	31.7	33.9	24.4	22.1	23.4	48.1	40.9	18.6

Table A3.2 Conservative vote share (%) by region, 1945–2019

Election	North East	North West	Yorkshire & The Humber	East Mid-lands	West Mid-lands	East	South East	South West	London	Wales	Scotland
1945	33.8	42.4	34.8	36.4	37.4	42.8	48.9	41.7	37.1	23.0	42.0
1950	35.3	45.4	38.6	38.9	42.8	46.1	53.2	45.0	43.4	27.4	45.4
1951	39.5	50.6	42.5	44.5	46.8	52.4	59.0	51.9	47.4	30.8	48.6
1955	41.9	52.0	44.1	47.2	49.2	53.2	60.2	51.0	49.2	29.9	50.1
1959	41.9	50.3	44.5	47.4	50.7	51.5	59.0	50.2	49.3	32.6	47.2
1964	37.6	43.1	39.2	42.5	46.8	46.6	50.5	45.0	42.3	29.5	40.6
1966	34.5	41.5	37.1	41.4	44.7	45.8	49.1	45.3	40.9	27.9	37.6
1970	38.2	46.7	41.5	47.8	50.5	52.3	54.5	51.1	46.6	27.7	38.0
1974 Feb	33.4	37.5	35.0	40.9	40.8	41.2	46.9	43.5	37.6	25.9	32.9
1974 Oct	28.1	37.2	32.5	38.5	37.5	42.1	46.8	43.4	37.4	23.9	24.7
1979	34.2	43.9	39.3	46.7	47.1	51.5	56.0	51.6	46.0	32.2	31.4
1983	32.3	40.5	38.7	47.2	45.0	51.1	55.9	51.4	43.9	31.0	28.4
1987	29.2	38.7	37.4	48.6	45.5	52.9	56.5	50.6	46.5	29.5	24.0
1992	30.8	38.4	37.9	46.6	44.8	52.6	54.9	47.6	45.4	28.6	25.7
1997	19.8	27.6	28.0	34.9	33.7	39.5	41.9	36.7	31.2	19.6	17.5
2001	21.3	29.3	30.2	37.3	35.0	41.8	42.9	38.5	30.5	21.0	15.6
2005	19.5	28.7	29.1	37.1	35.0	43.3	45.0	38.6	31.9	21.4	15.8
2010	23.7	31.7	32.8	41.2	39.5	47.1	49.3	42.8	34.5	26.1	16.7
2015	25.3	31.2	32.6	43.5	41.8	49.0	50.8	46.5	34.9	27.2	14.9
2017	34.4	36.2	40.5	50.7	49.0	54.6	53.8	51.4	33.1	33.6	28.6
2019	38.3	37.5	43.1	54.8	53.4	57.2	54.0	52.8	32.0	36.1	25.1

Table A3.3 Liberal/Alliance/Liberal Democrat vote share (%) by region, 1945–2019

Election	North East	North West	Yorkshire & The Humber	East Mid-lands	West Mid-lands	East	South East	South West	London	Wales	Scotland
1945	5.7	8.7	10.0	8.2	7.7	11.9	9.9	16.6	7.8	14.9	4.5
1950	6.8	8.9	8.9	10.0	5.8	12.1	9.9	15.2	8.6	12.6	6.6
1951	0.7	2.2	3.5	2.3	0.7	2.1	1.5	6.0	1.9	7.6	2.7
1955	0.4	2.1	3.4	1.3	1.2	2.2	2.0	8.3	2.6	7.3	1.9
1959	1.5	4.6	5.0	4.0	3.2	8.5	7.5	15.0	7.0	5.3	4.1
1964	3.9	10.6	10.9	9.8	7.8	12.9	16.9	20.4	12.5	7.3	7.6
1966	2.0	7.6	7.3	6.4	4.1	9.5	14.4	16.1	9.3	6.3	6.8
1970	2.2	7.2	7.7	4.6	4.2	7.6	12.9	14.5	7.0	6.8	5.5
1974 Feb	12.4	19.3	19.3	17.1	14.9	25.5	27.6	29.5	20.8	16.0	7.9
1974 Oct	16.4	17.9	19.9	18.3	17.8	21.6	24.3	27.4	17.0	15.5	8.3
1979	12.2	13.0	14.7	14.2	11.5	15.8	18.2	22.6	11.9	10.6	9.0
1983	25.6	23.3	25.5	24.1	23.4	28.9	28.9	33.2	24.7	23.2	24.5
1987	21.5	20.4	21.7	21.0	20.8	26.0	27.6	33.0	21.3	17.9	19.2
1992	15.5	15.8	16.8	15.3	15.0	19.8	24.7	31.4	15.9	12.4	13.1
1997	12.6	14.5	16.0	13.6	13.8	17.1	23.3	31.3	14.6	12.3	13.0
2001	16.7	16.7	17.1	15.4	14.7	17.5	23.7	31.2	17.5	13.8	16.3
2005	23.3	21.4	20.7	18.5	18.6	21.8	25.4	32.6	21.9	18.4	22.6
2010	23.6	21.6	22.9	20.8	20.5	24.1	26.2	34.7	22.1	20.1	18.9
2015	6.5	6.5	7.1	5.6	5.5	8.2	9.4	15.1	7.7	6.5	7.5
2017	4.6	5.4	5.0	4.3	4.4	7.9	10.5	14.9	8.8	4.5	6.8
2019	6.8	7.9	8.1	7.8	7.9	13.4	18.2	18.2	14.9	6.0	9.5

Table A3.4   Nationalist party vote share (%) in Scotland and Wales, 1945–2019

Election	Plaid Cymru, Wales	SNP, Scotland
1945	0.8	0.0
1950	0.1	0.1
1951	0.7	0.3
1955	3.1	0.5
1959	5.2	0.8
1964	4.8	2.4
1966	4.3	5.0
1970	11.5	11.4
1974 Feb	10.8	21.9
1974 Oct	10.8	30.4
1979	8.1	17.3
1983	7.8	11.8
1987	7.3	14.0
1992	9.0	21.5
1997	9.9	22.1
2001	14.3	20.1
2005	12.6	17.7
2010	11.3	19.9
2015	12.1	50.0
2017	10.4	36.9

4

How places vote

To this point, we have sought to trace long-term change and stability in the broad contours of the electoral geography of Britain since 1945. In this chapter we seek to understand in more detail the demographic underpinnings of those trends in England and Wales specifically over the period from 1979 to 2019. This forty-year period is notable for covering three extended terms of party control of government—the Thatcher and Major governments (1979–97), the Blair and Brown governments (1997–2010) and the Cameron, May, and Johnson governments (2010–19). This arguably entailed four *critical elections* that saw substantial swings that to some extent, at least, redrew the electoral map—1979, 1997, 2010, and 2019.[1] The 2019 election is arguably the anomaly of the four since it was a *realigning* election in favour of a party that had already been in power for nine years. Nevertheless, each of these elections represented a significant shift in the sentiment of voters—producing distinct geographical expressions of support.

Using a new, harmonized data source, we explore the changing relationships between the compositional characteristics of parliamentary constituencies and the Labour and Conservative vote between 1979 and 2019. In so doing, we shed light on the kinds of constituencies that have returned high (and low) votes shares for each of the two main parties at each general election over this period. Most importantly, we consider how particular types of constituencies have become more or less likely to return a Labour or Conservative Member of Parliament over time. The extended timeframe of our analysis enables a detailed exploration of both long-term trends and short-term fluctuations in this process—as electoral fortunes of the parties have ebbed and flowed nationally. In the chapter, the claim that older, dominantly white, working-class areas have swung from Labour to the Conservatives is examined in detail. These areas—often termed 'left behind'—are typically the primary focus of the debate over geographical polarization and a growing divide between left behind and cosmopolitan areas more precisely (see Furlong 2019; Jennings and Stoker 2019). However, we are

---

[1] The Labour to Conservative swings at these elections were +5.2, −10.0, +5.0, and +4.6 points respectively.

The Changing Electoral Map of England and Wales. Jamie Furlong and Will Jennings, Oxford University Press.
© Jamie Furlong and Will Jennings (2024). DOI: 10.1093/9780191943331.003.0004

also interested in electoral trends in other areas that might also be characterized as left behind, in terms of socio-economics or precarity, as outlined in
Chapters 1 and 2. This enables us to demonstrate how broader economic and
demographic trends are resulting in fundamental changes in the electoral
geography of England and Wales. Specifically, we consider socio-economic
and sociodemographic indicators that are associated with constituencies that
are: (a) *demographically left behind* (older, whiter, more working-class, lower
educational levels, more isolated; Table 4.1);[2] (b) *economically left behind*
(high rates of unemployment, social housing, and poor health; Table 4.2);
(c) *precariously left behind* (high proportions of insecure employment;
Table 4.3).

Importantly, these place-types are not necessarily mutually exclusive.
Demographically left behind areas may also be economically left behind (suf-
fering from both sociodemographic decline and high levels of deprivation),
while precariously left behind areas may also be 'cosmopolitan' (with high
levels of insecure employment but also more diverse, more educated, and
younger populations). In Table 4.1, we summarize the measures that are associated with these alternative types of left behind areas (Furlong 2019). The
final column indicates whether a high or low value of the variable contributes
to the left behind measure in question. The data sources used to create these
measures, alongside the election results data, are outlined in Table 4.4 later
in the chapter.

Table 4.1 Classification and measurement of demographically left behind areas

Measure	Description (proportion of population unless otherwise stated)	High or low value?
Employed in manufacturing	Of the economically active population (post-2001) or employed population (pre-2001), the proportion employed in manufacturing.	High
Routine/semi-routine occupations	For elections since 2001, the NS-SEC categories of 'routine/semi-routine occupations' are used. Prior to this, the Registrar General's Social Class (RGSC) measure of 'semi-skilled/unskilled occupations' is used—the percentage of the head of households whose occupations are coded as IV or V in the RGSC.	High
Degree-level qualifications	Population with a level four qualification or higher (post-2001), higher degree, degree or diploma (1992 and 1997) or the proportion in employment with degrees or professional vocational qualifications (pre-1992).	Low

[2] Demographically left behind areas are understood as the opposite of 'cosmopolitan' areas. Cosmopolitan constituencies are ethnically diverse, typically close to a major city or university, with high proportions
of younger residents and graduates.

Table 4.1 *Continued*

Measure	Description (proportion of population unless otherwise stated)	High or low value?
Age: 16–29	Population aged 16 to 29.	Low
Age: 65+	Population aged 65 and over.	High
Ethnic diversity	The Herfindahl concentration index is used (Hirschman 1964) to calculate the probability that two randomly selected residents of the same parliamentary constituency are of a different ethnicity (Sturgis et al. 2014). This is well-suited to the quasi-monoethnic composition of the UK (Schaeffer 2014).	Low
Gross migration	A proxy for geographical mobility. From 1997 onwards, those that have migrated into the area from the UK or out of the area to anywhere in the previous year. Prior to 1997, this includes only those with a different address to one year previously.	Low
'Urban-ness'	Not employed in 'agriculture' (1981 and 2011 censuses), 'agriculture, hunting or forestry' (2001 census), or 'managers in farming, horticulture, forestry and fishing' and not employed in 'other occupations in agriculture, forestry and fishing' (1991 census).	Low
Distance: 'cosmopolitan' local authority	Distance (decimal degrees) from centroid of the constituency to centroid of the nearest 'cosmopolitan' local authority. An index of 'cosmopolitan-ness' for each local authority in 2011 was calculated from four standardized variables: percentage of population aged 18 to 29, with a level four qualification, living in an urban environment, and the ethnic diversity (Herfindahl index) of the local authority.	High
Distance: university	The distance in decimal degrees from the centroid of each constituency to the closest university, based on designation of universities in that particular year.	High
'Cosmopolitan' industries	See appendix for outline of the industries comprising this measure.	Low

Table 4.2 Classification and measurement of economically left behind areas

Measure	Description (proportion of population unless otherwise stated)	High or low value?
Poor health	A proxy for poverty (Benzeval et al. 2014). Population who described their health as 'bad' or 'very bad' (2010 onwards), 'not good' (2001 and 2005), population with a long-term illness (1992 and 1997) or those permanently sick (pre-1992).	High

Continued

Table 4.2 *Continued*

Measure	Description (proportion of population unless otherwise stated)	High or low value?
Social renters	Proportion of households that live in social (council/local authority/housing association) housing.	High
Unemployment rate	Economically active population aged 16–74 (post-2001) or aged 16 and over (pre-2001) that were unemployed.	High
Household deprivation	The proportion of households deprived on three or more of four dimensions: employment, education, health, and housing (Office for National Statistics, 2017b). This is only used in exploratory analysis for elections from 2001 onwards because of multicollinearity and a lack of data prior to 2001.	High

Table 4.3 Classification and measurement of precariously left behind areas

Measure	Description (proportion of population unless otherwise stated)	High or low value?
'Precariat' occupations	See appendix for outline of the occupations compromising this measure.	High
Secure employment (residual)	See appendix for explanation of this measure	Low

Untangling the electoral geography of left behind (and cosmopolitan) places

Based on this framework, in this chapter we consider the degree to which different types of left behind places have become more or less positively associated with Conservative and Labour support between 1979 and 2019. By assembling analysis across a range of sociodemographic and socio-economic measures, we can conclude how the relationship between left behind places and Labour and Conservative support varies depending upon the particular definition of left-behindedness adopted. While recent evidence has shown that 'left behind' places—typically based on a demographic understanding of older, white, post-industrial towns, often in the Red Wall—have swung from Labour to the Conservatives—to what extent does this depend on the definition of left-behindedness that is used?

The methodological approach of this chapter begins with an exploratory examination of the bivariate, constituency-level relationships between variables associated with the three alternative definitions of left-behindedness and Labour and Conservative vote shares at each election between 1979 and

2019. These graphs show, for each unit increase in a particular variable (e.g. percentage of population unemployed), the average change in Labour and Conservative vote share. Simultaneously, constituencies have been ranked into deciles according to distinctive characteristics that fall under the alternative definitions of left behind places. For example, in Figure 4.2 there are ten deciles of either fifty-seven or fifty-eight constituencies each, ranked according to the ratio of working-class to middle-class occupations. Within each decile, the mean vote shares for each party in 1979 and 2019 are displayed, allowing us to understand in more detail how the demographics of Labour and Conservative seats have changed over time. Finally, the results of multiple linear regression models are analysed with reference to the three left behind types—an approach which allows us to better understand not just how vote shares vary across different measures, but which specific constituency characteristics drive support for Labour and the Conservatives at each election.[3]

Overall, the results presented in this chapter reveal that there has been a significant shift away from Labour to the Conservatives in areas with dominantly white, working-class populations with lower educational levels. While it accelerated at the 2017 and 2019 general elections, this political dealignment has been occurring since 1979 with notable fluctuations, such as in 1997. In contrast, Labour's electoral dominance in areas with high levels of economic deprivation and higher proportions of the insecurely and precariously employed (groups that are relatively poor in capital and which have been called the 'new working class')[4] has remained mostly stable. It is important to pull apart these three types of left behind area: in the former are many post-industrial towns in the 'Red Wall' (e.g. Stoke-on-Trent North), seaside towns (e.g. Blackpool South), and less well-off rural areas (e.g. North East Cambridgeshire). In contrast, the poorest constituencies are predominantly (though not solely) located in larger cities. Indeed, Labour's dominance in the relatively small number of large city-based constituencies has come at a price, as they have lost ground to the Conservatives across swathes of England and Wales that fall under the traditional definition of being left behind, whilst making no progress in Conservative heartlands—smaller towns with high levels of home ownership. The chapter concludes by emphasizing how these

---

[3] The results from these OLS models were validated with additional Generalized Least Squares (GLM) and Seemingly Unrelated Regression (SUR) models. Each model type had different specifications that had no significant impact on the findings from the OLS models.

[4] Savage et al. (2013) develop categories of 'emergent service workers' and 'precariat' that correspond to this economically vulnerable group. Ainsley (2018) similarly identifies a 'new working class' consisting of lower- and middle-income voters working in the service and hospitality industries (such as teaching assistants, cleaners, admin staff). This new working class is younger, more diverse, and more likely to have qualifications than those in traditional routine occupations.

trends have contributed to the redrawing of the map of Britain's electoral geography and changing electoral fortunes for the two main parties.

Data and methods: a brief overview

Creating three consistent conceptualizations of left-behindedness across time and analysing associations with party vote shares across both changing electoral boundaries and census questionnaires has required an innovative and careful methodological approach. In this overview, we explain how census data across ten general elections is utilized to provide conclusive evidence of long-term changes in the association between the sociodemographic characteristics of places and support for different political parties. Careful harmonization and areal interpolation of this census data has overcome issues of changing parliamentary constituency boundaries that have restricted most other geographical research to analysis of much shorter time periods. This fits with the broader contribution of this study—to provide an authoritative account of the changing electoral geography of England and Wales between 1979 and 2019.

The data used in this research come from a range of sources: the 1981, 1991, 2001, and 2011 censuses (Office of Population Censuses and Surveys 1997, 2000; Office for National Statistics 2003, 2013) alongside other data sets containing merged constituency-level demographic information and general election results (Electoral Calculus n.d.; McAllister and Rose 1988; Norris 2001, 2005, 2010; Crewe and Fox 2011; Fieldhouse et al. 2017; House of Commons Library 2020). We have, for each general election between 1979 and 2019, created a data set of constituency-level demographics, geographical and socio-economic characteristics merged with party votes and vote shares. While changes in census questions across time have led to some limitations (e.g. due to changes to country of birth and ethnic group classifications, we have had to use an aggregated and simplified classification), careful harmonization has ensured that at each election the variables are either identical or very closely matched.

For elections that fall within three years of the nearest census (e.g. the 2010 general election), the election data have been matched to data from the closest census. For 1987 and 1997—years in which the elections were more than three years from the closest census—linear interpolation of sociodemographic data has created estimates for the election year alongside existing notional electoral results. To account for boundary changes, the spatial unit of the start and end point of the interpolation is always matched to the constituency boundaries used in the election. For 2005, due to the lack of 2011 census data notional to 2005 constituency boundaries, areal interpolation has been used. This interpolation process involves overlaying output areas (the smallest census geography) onto parliamentary constituencies and distributing the population (and their census characteristics) according to the spatial fit between the output areas and constituencies. Once the 2011 data set had been created notional to 2005 constituency boundaries, the same linear interpolation method used in 1987 and 1997 was subsequently used to create census data as accurate as possible to the 2005 general election. For the election years since the 2011 census, only extrapolation is possible, which would raise far greater concerns about errors in the estimations. As a result,

Table 4.4 Pre-existing census and electoral data sets used for this research

Data Set Name	Publisher/author	Electoral data[a]	Demographic data
General Election 2019: full results and analysis	House of Commons Library (2020)	2019 general election	2011 census
BES 2017 Constituency Results with Census and Candidate Data	Fieldhouse et al. (2017)	2017, 2015, and 2010 general election	2011 census
May 6th 2010 British General Election Constituency Results Release 5.0	Norris (2010)	2017, 2015, and 2010 general election	2011 census
The British Parliamentary Constituency Database 1992–2005 Release 1.3	Norris (2005)	1992, 1997, 2001, 2005 general election	1991 and 2001 census
The British Parliamentary Constituency Database 1992–2001 Release 1.2	Norris (2001)	1992, 1997, 2001 general election	1991 and 2001 census
(Actual) Election Result	Electoral Calculus (ND)	1992 general election	n/a
United Kingdom Ecological Data, 1981–1987	McAllister and Rose (1988)	1979, 1983, and 1987 general elections	1981 census
British Parliamentary Constituencies, 1979–1983	Crewe and Fox (2011)	1979 and 1983 General Elections	1981 census

[a]2005 election results in the BES data set are notional to 2010 constituency boundaries. 1992 election results in the dataset by Pippa Norris are notional to the constituency boundaries that were first implemented in 1997. Both sets of 1979 election results are notional to the boundaries implemented in 1983.

2011 census data are used in the analysis of the 2015, 2017, and 2019 general elections.

Using areal interpolation to create census data notional to different constituency boundaries offers a clear benefit to this analysis in that we can compare demographic characteristics for constituencies across elections where there are boundary changes. Some additional data sets—not relating to election results—have been used at various points in the analysis that follows. These are all referenced accordingly when there is discussion of the data that are used from each. The only constituencies that have been omitted from the data sets above and thereby any subsequent analyses are the Speaker's seat at each election and any cases where Labour or the Conservatives did not stand. In addition, for the 1979 general election, due to lack of available data, all variables including vote shares are notional to the 1983 constituency boundaries.

The changing relationships between place characteristics and vote shares

In order to understand the changing relationships between some key explanatory variables and Labour and Conservative vote shares, we present in this chapter a series of graphs. The *line graphs* show the correlation coefficient between each indicated explanatory variable and Labour and Conservative vote shares at constituency level at each election from 1979 to 2019. The idea is to be able to track changes over time in the bivariate relationship between a particular variable, such as proportion with a university degree, and the Labour and Conservative vote shares across constituencies in England and Wales. The *bar graphs* contrast the 1979 and 2019 elections by showing the mean Labour and Conservative vote shares across different constituency types grouped into and ordered by deciles (e.g. top 10% of constituencies by proportion with degree). The idea here is to contrast the distribution of Conservative and Labour support across constituencies at the start and end of this time period, in two elections where the vote shares of both parties were quite similar (Table 4.5). Indeed, as a helpful reference, in

Table 4.5 Party vote share in England and Wales, 1979 vs 2019 general elections

Party	1979 Share	2019 Share	Change in vote share
Conservatives	46.3	46.6	0.3
Labour	37.4	34.4	−3.0

1979, the Conservatives acquired 46.3% of the vote in England and Wales compared to 46.6% in 2019. Labour's vote share across the same time period fell from 37.4% to 34.3%.

Demographically left behind (and cosmopolitan) constituencies

The current Labour Party has been described as a fractured coalition consisting of predominantly young, 'middle-class liberals' living in urban, cosmopolitan, ethnically diverse areas of the country and 'working-class social conservatives' living in post-industrial, economically stagnant, largely white and demographically left behind communities (Pearce 2016). At the same time, the party's support amongst the working class has been shown to be diminishing with the socio-economic class cleavage over time (Evans and Tilley 2012, 2017). For Labour, we would therefore expect to see, over time, increasingly negative correlations with demographic measures of left-behindedness such as manufacturing employment, routine and semi-routine occupations, and older people, and increasingly positive associations with measures such as ethnic diversity and employment in cosmopolitan industries. Where a high value of the variable in the demographically left behind definition in Table 4.1 contributes to being left behind, the expectation is of

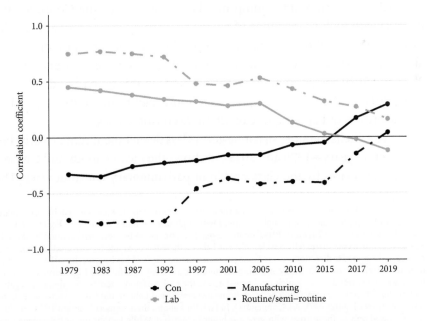

Figure 4.1 Correlation between traditional working-class occupations and Labour and Conservative vote share, 1979–2019

an increasingly negative correlation and vice versa. In theory, the opposite should be the case for the Conservatives, who at the same time should see an increasingly negative correlation with those employed in cosmopolitan industries as areas with higher proportions of these types of employment move towards the Labour Party.

Figure 4.1 shows a gradual weakening of the negative association between manufacturing employment and Conservative vote shares, such that, by 2017, it had been eliminated altogether. For Labour, the reverse is true, and for the first time in 2017 the Labour vote share was, albeit very weakly, negatively correlated with the proportion of a constituency employed in manufacturing—a trend that continued in 2019. The same pattern can be seen with the proportion of the population in semi-routine and routine occupations, to which the Conservative vote share became markedly less negatively associated in 1997 and 2017 (representing something of a structural shift in voting patterns). By 2019, there was no longer a negative correlation between routine and semi-routine occupations and the Conservative vote share. For Labour, there has been a slow, long-term weakening in the once strong positive association of its vote with routine and semi-routine employment, with the most noticeable decline in 1997—a result of the broadening of electoral support in more typically middle-class areas under Tony Blair.

In fact, despite significant differences in the political positioning of the Labour Party in the 1997 and 2017 general elections, they both mark a point at which there was a small jump in relative support for the Conservatives in areas with high proportions of people in working-class occupations. The increasing gradient of the routine/semi-routine correlation lines for Labour and Conservatives in 1997 and for both measures for the Conservatives in 2017 and 2019 suggest that, of all the elections in this time period, it was in 1997, 2017, and 2019 where there were more significant shifts in the class characteristics of Labour and Conservative constituencies.[5]

Figure 4.2 tells the story of a long-term class dealignment more clearly. For two election years—1979 and 2019—it shows the mean Labour and Conservative vote shares by the class profile of parliamentary constituencies. The

---

[5] This acceleration of the Conservative expansion into more working-class areas is matched by changes in areas with middle-class jobs, though not areas with high rates of home ownership. Figure A4.3 (see appendix) shows that, in 2017 and 2019, the strong positive association between typical middle-class jobs and Conservative vote shares fell considerably. For Labour, there has been much more gradual, long-term change in the opposite direction—a strong negative correlation of −0.74 has become, by 2019, a moderate negative correlation of −0.43. This contrasts with middle-class areas as defined by high home-ownership levels, where the trend is very much unchanged across the entire period: there is a moderately negative and moderately positive association between home ownership and Labour and Conservative vote shares respectively (see Figures A4.3–A4.4, appendix). In fact, for Labour, their support between 1979 and 2019 has increased only in those areas with very low home ownership. While Labour might have made *some* progress in areas with more middle-class occupations, they continue to lose ground to the Conservatives in areas with above average home ownership.

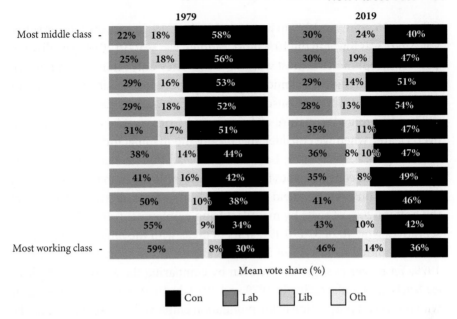

Figure 4.2 Mean party vote share (1979 and 2019) by social class[a]

[a] Note that this measure is based on a ratio of professional and managerial occupations/routine and semi-routine occupations.

constituencies at each election are ordered into deciles, from the 10% most working class to the 10% most middle class. Note that the constituencies in each bar can be quite different in 1979 compared to 2019, as some places become, relatively speaking, more or less working or middle class. In 1979, moving from bottom to top (from most working class to most middle class) on the graph, the Labour vote share consistently decreases and the Conservative vote share consistently increases. In fact, despite losing the 1979 election to a Conservative landslide, Labour secured significant leads in the top 30% most working-class constituencies overall. In the most working-class decile, their vote share (59%) was almost double that of the Conservatives (30%). In contrast, the Conservatives had large average leads over Labour in the top 50% most middle-class constituencies. By 2019, the picture is much messier— no longer is there a clear pattern in party support by the class character of parliamentary constituencies. In fact, of all the deciles, Labour only retained a substantial lead in the most working-class constituencies, albeit one that had fallen from 29 points to just 10 points across this time period.

Across the same period, the average Conservative vote share increased across the top 50% most working-class constituencies. In contrast, in the top 20% most middle-class seats, the Conservatives have seen a massive fall in support. Much like Labour's ever-decreasing lead in the most working-class seats, the Conservatives lead in the top 10% most middle-class constituencies fell from 36 points in 1979 to just 10 points in 2019. In fact, the Conservative vote share was lower in the 10% most middle-class seats in 2019 than all other deciles, except the 10% most working-class. They only retain an overall lead over Labour in these most middle-class seats because the Liberal Democrats have benefited from the Conservative demise as much as Labour.

The changing class nature of Labour and Conservative constituencies is even clearer when we consider specifically the manufacturing profile of the areas (Figure 4.3). In 1979, Labour held a lead in each decile representing the top 40% of constituencies by proportion employed in manufacturing; by 2019, the Conservatives held significant leads across all seat types, except the bottom 20% of seats by manufacturing employment. In 2019, the Conservatives won 40 of 57 (70.2%) seats in areas with the most manufacturing jobs, compared to just 15 of 56 (26.8%) seats in the same type of areas in 1979. Yet bigger changes can be seen by comparing the areas with the lowest levels of manufacturing in 1979 and 2019. In 1979, in the top 10% of seats with the lowest proportion of the population employed in manufacturing, the Conservatives had a lead of 19 points over Labour. By 2019, this is the only manufacturing decile in which Labour have a lead over the Conservatives— of some 20 points. This points to an obvious conclusion: Labour's support has become much more heavily concentrated in areas with very low levels of manufacturing.

The correlation coefficients reported in Figure 4.4 support the idea that an age cleavage has developed at the constituency level in British politics, but rather than 2017 or 2019 representing anything exceptional, this process has been strengthening since 1997. Labour's relative support has decreased in areas with higher proportions of older people, and since 2010, has increased in areas with higher proportions of young people.[6] By 2019, Labour's vote share association with the proportion aged 16 to 29 was at its highest level (0.64) and with the proportion aged 65 and over was at its lowest level (−0.65) in this time period. An almost identical inverse trend has occurred for the Conservatives, whose equivalent correlation coefficients in 2017 were −0.64 and 0.62. The implication is that, for each 1% increase in the proportion aged 16 to 29, the Labour vote share increases and the Conservative vote share decreases by 0.64 percentage points. The relationship is almost identically opposite for the proportion aged 65 and over.

When we examine the average party vote share by seat age profile, the pattern is startling. In 2019, Labour's vote share increases at every decile, from

---

[6] This is consistent with individual-level evidence which shows an increasing age gradient in the vote between 2010 and 2017 (see Sturgis and Jennings 2020).

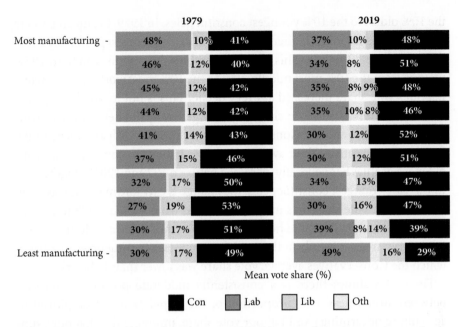

Figure 4.3 Mean party vote share (1979 and 2019) by manufacturing employment

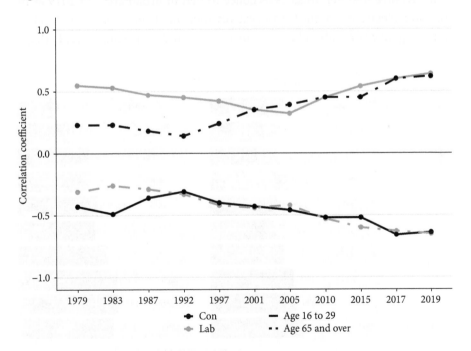

Figure 4.4 Correlation between age and Labour and Conservative vote share, 1979–2019

the 10% oldest to the 10% youngest constituencies. In 1979, the mean Labour vote share was 23 points higher in the seats with the youngest profile; by 2019, this was some 40 points. This closely resembles the way in which, in 1979, moving from the 10% most middle-class to the 10% most working-class seats, Labour's vote share increased at every decile. This is not to say that age was not important back in 1979: clearly Labour generally did better in seats with a younger profile and the Conservatives better in seats with an older profile. For the Conservatives, their average lead over Labour in constituencies with older age profiles has generally increased between 1979 and 2019 (Figure 4.5). In the 10% youngest constituencies, the change is extraordinary: the average Conservative vote share has more than halved from 44% in 1979 to 21% in 2019. In fact, showing quite how narrowly confined Labour's dominance is in younger areas, it is only in the top 20% youngest constituencies in 2019 in which the Conservatives average vote share was lower than Labour's.

Figure 4.6 shows there is a consistently moderate positive correlation between 'urban-ness' (the proportion of the population not employed in agriculture or farming) and Labour vote share, implying that Labour's support, relative to other areas, is as concentrated in urban areas in 2019 as in previous elections. For the Conservatives, there has been a consistent moderately negative correlation between urban-ness and their vote share. Perhaps

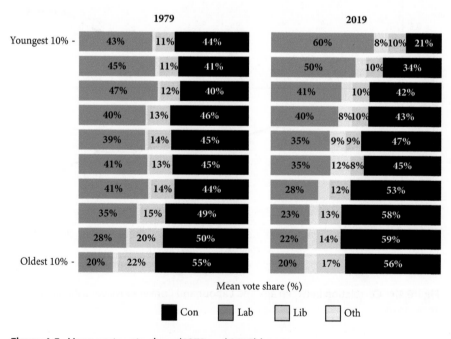

Figure 4.5 Mean party vote share (1979 and 2019) by age

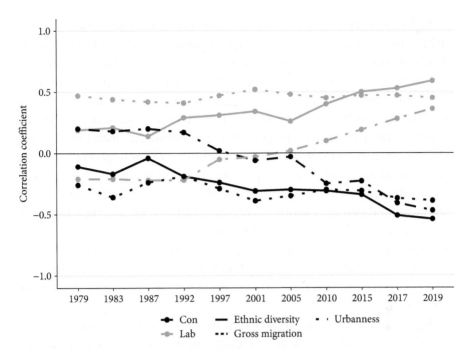

Figure 4.6 Correlation between urban-ness, ethnic diversity, gross migration, and Labour and Conservative vote share, 1979–2019

unsurprisingly given that larger, urban areas are more ethnically diverse, an increase in Labour's vote share has been positively associated with an increase in ethnic diversity and for the Conservatives the opposite trend is true. Most notable is that these associations have been increasing over time, indicating that Labour's vote share is likely to be higher, relative to their mean vote at each election, in 2019 than at previous elections in areas that are more ethnically diverse. However, some caution should be advised: the weak correlation coefficients between ethnic diversity and vote shares in the earlier elections in this time period may result from a lack of variability in the ethnic diversity index variable—an idea that statisticians refer to as 'range restriction' or 'truncated range' (Goodwin and Leech 2006).

Alongside an increasingly positive association between ethnic diversity and Labour vote shares, the same trend can be observed between levels of gross migration and Labour support. This suggests that Labour's vote share has become more positively associated with areas in which there is greater geographical mobility and where populations are more transient, and the Conservative vote share with areas that are 'stickier' with less transient populations. In fact, in 1979, Labour's vote share was, on average, higher in areas with *less* transient populations; the Conservative vote share was higher in areas with *more* geographically mobile populations. Since 1997, this pattern has been steadily reversed, such that the trend is now the exact opposite.

Figure 4.7 shows the mean party vote share by ethnic diversity. In 1979, there was little pattern to the Conservative vote share, except that (remarkably when compared to 2019), their mean vote share was in fact higher in the 10% most ethnically diverse constituencies than the 10% least diverse constituencies. Labour's vote share in 1979 was generally highest in the most and least diverse constituencies, with much lower vote shares in constituencies in the centre of the distribution. By 2019, the pattern looks quite different: Labour's vote share in the least diverse constituencies has dropped from 51% in 1979 to 28% in 2019. At the same time, the Conservative mean vote share has increased by 19 points to 51% in an almost exact reversal. In the most ethnically diverse constituencies, Labour's vote share has increased to 61% in 2019 compared to just 24% for the Conservatives.

Figure 4.8 portrays the relationship between the 'cosmopolitan-ness' of constituencies and vote shares for both parties. We can see that the proportion employed in cosmopolitan industries has gradually become more positively correlated with Labour support and more negatively correlated with Conservative support over time. In fact, in 1979, the cosmopolitan-ness

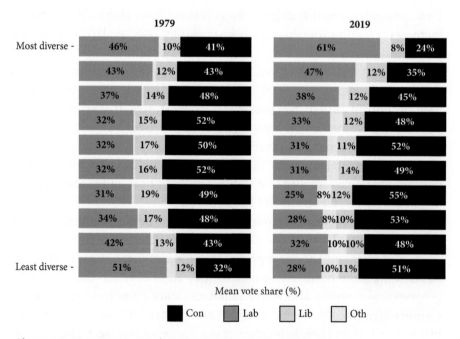

Figure 4.7 Mean party vote share (1979 and 2019) by ethnic diversity

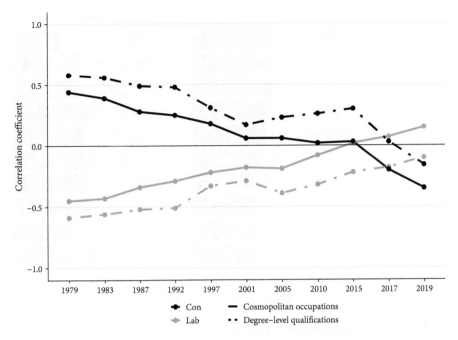

Figure 4.8 Correlation between cosmopolitan occupations, degree-level qualifications, and Labour and Conservative vote share, 1979–2019

of a constituency was moderately positively associated with the Conservative vote share and moderately negatively associated with Labour vote share. While there was a gradual erasing of the positive Conservative association with cosmopolitan-ness prior to 2005, the most substantial changes happened in 2017 and 2019. By 2017, there was in fact a weak negative correlation of −0.20 between cosmopolitan industries and the Conservative vote share. This strengthened further in 2019 to −0.35. For Labour, the opposite trend has occurred, though consistently gradually, such that there is now a weak positive association between constituency cosmopolitan-ness and Labour's vote share. Labour are no longer the weaker party in areas with high levels of cosmopolitan employment. This matches Figure A4.1 in the appendix, where one can see that Labour's relative support has increased (largely because of a marked shift at the 1997 election) in areas closer to cosmopolitan local authorities, with the opposite trend true for the Conservatives. Similarly, Labour's relative support increased significantly in 1997 in areas with high levels of gross migration, high proportions of university-educated residents, and low proportions of routine/semi-routine employment.

Figure 4.9 displays the average party vote share by the relative cosmopolitan-ness of constituencies in 1979 and 2019. In 1979, the pattern is clear: generally, the more cosmopolitan a constituency, the lower the Labour

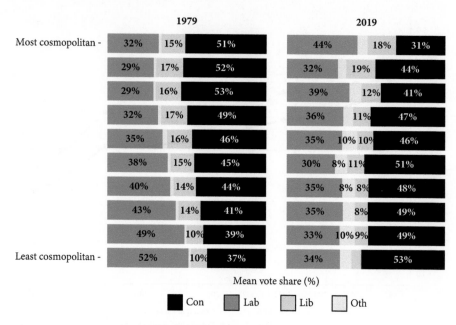

Figure 4.9 Mean party vote share (1979 and 2019) by cosmopolitan-ness

vote share and the higher the Conservative vote share. While there is no longer an obvious trend by 2019, the most significant changes have taken place at either end of the scale. The Conservatives now hold a substantial average lead of 19 points in the least cosmopolitan seats and Labour a lead of 13 points in the most cosmopolitan.

The changing association between the proportion of the population with university degrees and Conservative and Labour vote shares is just as remarkable (see Figure 4.8). Before 1997, there was a strong or moderate positive correlation between the proportion of the constituency population with degree-level qualifications and Conservative vote share. Since then, there have been two periods of significant decline: the first in 1997 and 2001 and the second in 2017 and 2019. The result is that, by 2019, there was, for the first time, a negative correlation coefficient (−0.16) between proportion of graduates and Conservative vote share. The association with degree-level education remains negative for Labour, although this has increased steadily from −0.59 in 1979 to −0.10 in 2019, indicating that it is now a very weak negative correlation. Whereas in 2015, the Conservative coefficient for degree-level qualification was 0.52 higher than Labour's vote share coefficient, in 2019 this was 0.06 lower. Labour's vote share was, for the first time, slightly more positively associated with the proportion of degree-holders than the Conservative vote share.

The correlation coefficients are matched by the extraordinary changes in the mean vote shares by the educational profile of the seats, as shown in Figure 4.10. In 1979, Labour's average vote share was some 2.3 times higher in areas with the lowest proportion of degree-holders than areas with the highest proportion of degree-holders. In fact, in the former, Labour's average vote share was 23 points higher than the Conservatives' and in the latter it was 33 points lower. By 2019, the Conservatives held a marginal average vote share lead over Labour in areas with the lowest proportion of degree-holders. In areas with the highest proportion of degree holders, the Conservatives mean vote share has fallen dramatically from 57% in 1979 to just 29% in 2019. While Labour now secure higher levels of support in these areas, their lead over the Conservatives is muted by Liberal Democrat support.

Economically left behind constituencies

While the previous section presented evidence of a clear long-term decline in Labour support and an increase in Conservative support in areas that are left behind according to the demographic definition of the concept, a rather different trend emerges when looking at indicators capturing economic deprivation. Figure 4.11 points to a clear and defined socio-economic cleavage: areas that have higher proportions of deprivation, unemployment, poor health,

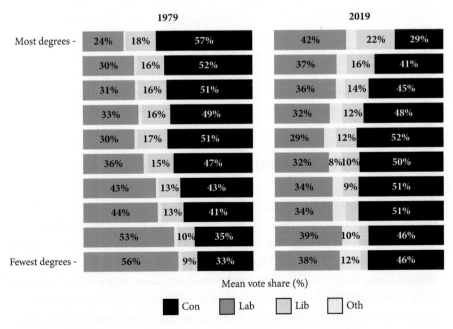

Figure 4.10 Mean party vote share (1979 and 2019) by degree-holders

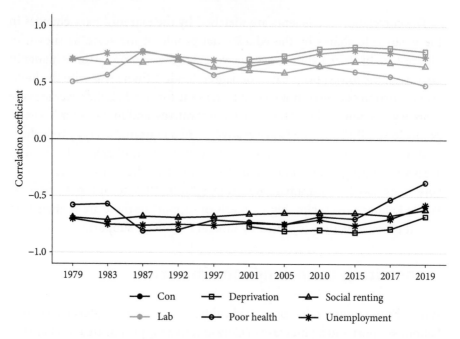

Figure 4.11 Correlation between economic deprivation and Labour and Conservative vote share, 1979–2019

and social housing have favoured Labour strongly across all years and have particularly low vote shares for the Conservative Party. Labour's electoral support in the most disadvantaged areas has been high for some time, and while there may be sign of some weakening in 2017 and 2019, particularly in the association with poor health, there is little evidence of significant changes. The same largely unmoving trend is evident in Figure A4.2 (see appendix), where one can see that, in both 1979 and 2019 (and, in fact, at every election in between), Labour's vote shares were consistently higher and the Conservatives' consistently lower in seats with higher unemployment.

Precariously left behind constituencies

Figure 4.12 presents the relationship between the proportion of the population in 'precariat' occupations and secure employment and Labour and Conservative vote shares. According to this measure of left-behindedness, one would conclude that Labour remain relatively strong in precariously left behind areas, despite the Conservatives making some gains in such areas in both 2017 and 2019. Indeed, between 1979 and 2015, there was a stable moderate negative correlation between the proportion employed in precarious

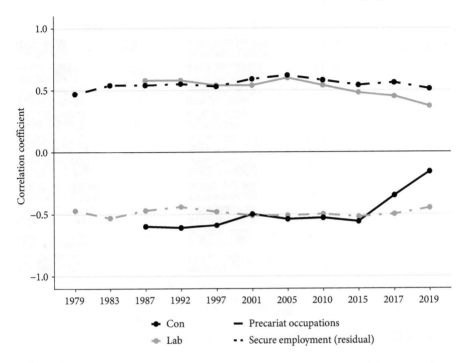

Figure 4.12 Correlation between precarious occupations, secure employment, and Labour and Conservative vote share, 1979–2019

forms of employment and the Conservative vote share. Between 2015 and 2019, this figure increased from –0.56 to just –0.16. Relative to previous elections, in 2017 and 2019 the Conservatives gained support in areas with higher levels of precarious employment. For secure employment, the consistently moderate negative correlation with Labour's vote share indicates that the party is electorally weaker in areas with higher levels of employment security. In contrast, there is a consistent positive association between Conservative vote shares and the proportion of the population in secure employment.

Figure 4.13 shows the mean party vote shares distributed across seats ranked by precariousness of employment in 1987[7] and 2019. This confirms the findings from Figure 4.12. For Labour, in both time periods, vote shares increased with increasing precariousness of work, although the gap in mean shares between the most and least precarious seats has decreased from 35 points to 25 points between 1987 and 2019. For the Conservatives, in 1987 there was a clear trend—the lower the seat precarity, the higher the vote share. By 2019, as a result of some disproportionate changes at the two extremes

---

[7] The 1987 general election is used rather than 1979 because there was no comparable way to measure precarious occupations using data from the 1981 census.

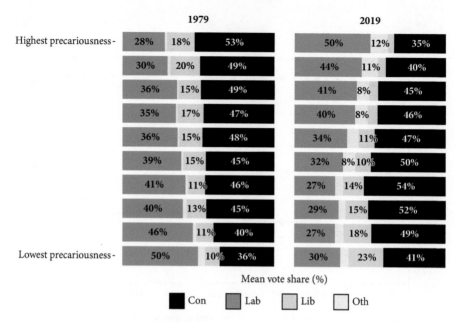

Figure 4.13 Mean party vote share (1987 and 2019) by occupational precariousness

(a 7-point increase in the most precarious seats and a 14-point fall in the least precarious), the pattern is much more subtle. In fact, the most substantial Conservative leads over Labour are found in seats with above average precarity, but not in the most precarious, where their mean vote share lead was only 11 points.

Summary of bivariate relationships

Table 4.6 presents a summary of the bivariate relationships between key variables in the left behind conceptualizations and Labour and Conservative vote shares at four key general elections: 1979, 1997, 2010, and 2019. This table shows even more clearly that almost all of the change in relationships has occurred in the constituency characteristics that fall under the demographically left behind definition, rather than the economically left behind or precariously left behind characteristics.

Alongside analysis of the bivariate relationships between left behind characteristics and vote shares, we have created various statistical models to test, when we account for the relationships between all variables and Labour/Conservative vote shares, which characteristics have a statistically significant positive or negative association. Separate models have been estimated for each election year, first with the dependent variable as Labour vote share,

Table 4.6 Summary of bivariate correlations between constituency characteristics of left-behindedness and Labour and Conservative vote shares

Demographically left behind		Labour				Conservatives			
Variable	High or low value?	1979	1997	2010	2019	1979	1997	2010	2019
Employed in manufacturing	High	+	+	±	±	-	-	±	+
Routine/semi-routine occupations	High	+	+	+	+	-	-	-	±
Degree-level qualifications	Low	-	-	-	±	+	+	+	-
Age 16 to 29	Low	+	+	+	+	-	-	-	-
Age 65 plus	High	-	-	-	-	+	+	+	+
Ethnic diversity	Low	+	+	+	+	±	-	-	-
Gross migration	Low	-	±	±	+	+	±	-	-
'Urban-ness'	Low	+	+	+	+	-	-	-	-
Distance: 'cosmopolitan' local authority	High	±	-	-	-	±	+	±	+
Distance: university	High	-	-	-	-	+	+	+	+
'Cosmopolitan' industries	Low	-	-	±	+	+	+	±	-

Economically left behind		Labour				Conservatives			
Variable	High or low value?	1979	1997	2010	2019	1979	1997	2010	2019
Poor health	High	+	+	+	+	-	-	-	-
Social renters	High	+	+	+	+	-	-	-	-
Unemployment rate	High	+	+	+	+	-	-	-	-
Household deprivation	High			+	+			-	-

Precariously left behind		Labour				Conservatives			
Variable	High or low value?	1979	1997	2010	2019	1979	1997	2010	2019
'Precariat' occupations	High		+	+	+		-	-	-
Secure employment (residual)	Low	-	-	-	-	+	+	+	+

and second with the dependent variable as Conservative vote share. The aim of these regression models is to compare the relationships between variables that constitute different definitions of left-behindedness and vote shares for the two main parties at each general election. Therefore, each model at each election uses almost identical harmonized explanatory variables. Interpreting the regression coefficients will allow an understanding of the extent to which variables have statistically significant changing associations with Conservative or Labour vote shares across elections.

In Figures 4.14 and 4.15 respectively, the standardized coefficients predicting the Labour and Conservative vote shares are presented from the models at each general election. Standardized coefficients allow us to assess the importance of each variable relative to all other variables. On the Labour graph (Figure 4.14), the darker the shade of red, the more important the variable as a positive predictor of Labour's vote share; the darker the shade of blue, the more important the variable as a negative predictor. The opposite is the case on the Conservative graph (Figure 4.15). If the variable is greyed out, it was not a statistically significant predictor of the party's vote share in that election. It is important to remember that the unit of measurement of the standardized coefficient should only be used in order to assess the relative impact of each explanatory variable on the Labour or Conservative vote shares for a particular election. For instance, at the general election in 1979, poor health was the most important positive predictor of Labour's vote share followed by the proportion of social renters, the proportion aged 16 to 29, and so on.

From the standardized coefficients predicting Labour vote shares presented in Figure 4.14, the clearest finding is the consistently critical importance of the poor health variable. At every election between 1979 and 2019, poor health—a proxy for poverty in an area (Benzeval et al. 2014)—had the most substantial positive impact upon Labour's vote share. The opposite association can be observed in Figure 4.15, where poor health has been by far the most important variable negatively associated with the Conservative vote share at every election. For both parties, there is a broad trend in which the relative importance of poor health in shaping vote shares was lowest in 1979 and 1983 and then generally highest between 1992 and 2017. As poor health captures the level of socio-economic disadvantage in an area, this offers further evidence that economic left-behindedness, at the constituency level, remains a dominant structuring force upon Labour and Conservative vote shares.

The importance of secure employment is similarly consistent from 1979 to 2019: it is a negative predictor of Labour vote shares and a positive predictor of Conservative vote shares. This matches the previous finding that

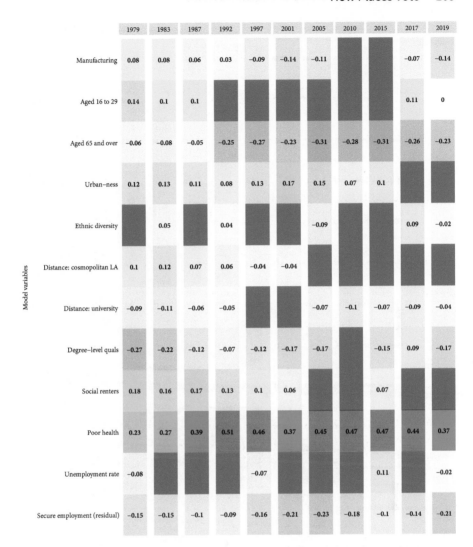

Figure 4.14 Standardized coefficients predicting Labour vote share, 1979–2019

Note: grey shading indicates the variable was not a significant predictor of party vote share

Labour's vote share is generally higher in seats with higher levels of precarious forms of employment. On both the economic (poor health) and the precarity measure of left-behindedness, there is limited evidence here for the idea that left behind characteristics are increasingly positively associated with Conservative vote shares.

However, while there is significant continuity in the relative importance of variables that account for socio-economic disadvantage, there is an enormous change seen in other variables, particularly some of those captured

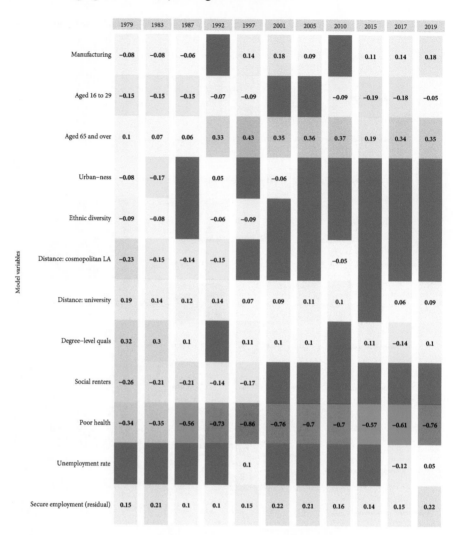

Model variables	1979	1983	1987	1992	1997	2001	2005	2010	2015	2017	2019
Manufacturing	−0.08	−0.08	−0.06		0.14	0.18	0.09		0.11	0.14	0.18
Aged 16 to 29	−0.15	−0.15	−0.15	−0.07	−0.09			−0.09	−0.19	−0.18	−0.05
Aged 65 and over	0.1	0.07	0.06	0.33	0.43	0.35	0.36	0.37	0.19	0.34	0.35
Urban−ness	−0.08	−0.17		0.05		−0.06					
Ethnic diversity	−0.09	−0.08		−0.06	−0.09						
Distance: cosmopolitan LA	−0.23	−0.15	−0.14	−0.15				−0.05			
Distance: university	0.19	0.14	0.12	0.14	0.07	0.09	0.11	0.1		0.06	0.09
Degree−level quals	0.32	0.3	0.1		0.11	0.1	0.1		0.11	−0.14	0.1
Social renters	−0.26	−0.21	−0.21	−0.14	−0.17						
Poor health	−0.34	−0.35	−0.56	−0.73	−0.86	−0.76	−0.7	−0.7	−0.57	−0.61	−0.76
Unemployment rate					0.1					−0.12	0.05
Secure employment (residual)	0.15	0.21	0.1	0.1	0.15	0.22	0.21	0.16	0.14	0.15	0.22

Figure 4.15 Standardized coefficients predicting Conservative vote share, 1979–2019

Note: grey shading indicates the variable was not a significant predictor of party vote share

under the demographically left behind definition. Remarkably, in 1979, the proportion of the population with degree-level qualifications had a greater negative effect on Labour vote shares than any other variable. Yet, by 2019, the degree-level qualifications variable had, after poor health, the strongest relative positive impact on Labour vote shares. The exact reverse process can be seen in the relative importance of educational qualifications on the Conservative vote share. In 1979 and 1983, degree-level educational qualifications were the most important positive predictor of Conservative vote share; by 2019, it was the second most important negative variable.

The opposite trend can be seen with the proportion employed in manufacturing, though the change has been slower and less extreme. Between 1979 and 1992, manufacturing was, relative to other variables, a weakly positive predictor of Labour vote share, and between 1979 and 1987 a weakly negative predictor of Conservative vote share. At most elections since, the trend has reversed: manufacturing has been a statistically significant, though weak, positive predictor of Conservative vote share and a weak negative predictor of Labour's vote share.

There are also significant changes in the relative importance of the proportion of residents at retirement age or older. While in 1979, relative to other variables, there was a weak positive effect on Conservative vote share and a weak negative impact on Labour's vote share, this has strengthened over time. In fact, at every election since 1992, the proportion of residents aged 65 plus and over had the strongest positive impact on Conservative vote shares and the strongest negative impact on Labour vote shares relative to the other variables in the model.

Are left behind areas leaving an increasingly 'cosmopolitan' Labour Party behind?

The findings here suggest a long-term trend in which demographically left behind areas have been gradually moving from the Labour Party towards the Conservatives. In particular, areas in which manufacturing industries are prevalent have shown a marked shift towards the Conservatives over this time period, with the level of manufacturing becoming an important positive predictor of the level of Conservative support. Constituencies such as Amber Valley, Scunthorpe, and Telford are archetypal—significant manufacturing industries and the Conservative Party building substantial majorities by 2019. Many of these areas are also characterized by ageing populations and low levels of educational qualifications. Back in 1979, areas with relatively fewer degree-holders were far more likely than other areas to elect a Labour MP than a Conservative MP. By 2019, this had completely shifted and Labour only held an average lead over the Conservatives in the top decile of constituencies ranked by degree-holders. In fact, once other variables are accounted for, the greater the proportion of the population with degree-level qualifications, the more likely there is an increased vote share for Labour in 2019. Again, if we understand left behind areas as those with low numbers of university graduates, on this characteristic, Labour have been losing ground to the Conservatives. Most worrying for Labour is that their relative support has been falling in all but the most educated areas—this is not a problem for the party unique to the areas with the lowest levels of education.

This might all be evidence of a Labour Party with its appeal inefficiently centred on the most ethnically diverse, urban areas that are home to large numbers of middle-class graduates who are typically employed in the service sector and renting their homes. It is undoubtedly the case that Labour have been piling up votes in a relatively small number of city and university seats whilst the Conservatives have been achieving widespread support in the suburbs, towns, and rural areas that make up the majority of seats in England and Wales. Yet it is also true that many of these urban areas where Labour have been dominating are also home to some of the most economically disadvantaged communities in the country. If a definition of left behind is adopted that captures areas with the most pronounced economic deprivation—many of which are in large urban centres—there is limited evidence to suggest that left behind areas are moving from Labour to the Conservatives. In fact, the extent of poor health in an area—a proxy for poverty levels—remains the most important constituency-level characteristic that results in increased Labour and decreased Conservative vote shares. The problem, of course, for Labour lies in the fact that the two types of constituencies in which they are dominant—university areas and seats with high levels of economic deprivation combined with ethnic diversity and a young population—are not numerous enough to win an election without regaining ground in either the demographically left behind areas lost to the Conservatives more recently or in the rural, small town, and suburban Conservative heartlands.

Indeed, the Conservatives remain largely dominant in towns and suburbs with high proportions of older, largely white, home-owning middle-class residents who are employed in secure, managerial, and professional jobs. While question marks remain over the extent to which a Brexit-delivering Conservative Party that extends its reach in the 'Red Wall' can hold off any potential resurgence of the Liberal Democrats, in 2019 the Conservatives held onto places such as Wokingham and Windsor. However, the evidence presented here is somewhat suggestive of a long-term split in the political mood of the middle class. While Conservative support in older, whiter, middle-class areas has held firm enough, they have witnessed a collapse in areas characterized by younger graduates, particularly where home ownership rates are relatively low. Once cosmopolitan Conservative strongholds such as Hove, Bristol West, and Canterbury have witnessed huge swings to Labour.

Whilst there is evidence of an increasingly cosmopolitan Labour Party losing ground to the Conservatives amongst demographically left behind constituencies, this is only one part of the story. If the economic deprivation definition of left behind is adopted, it seems premature to suggest that they have even begun abandoning Labour for the Conservatives. That is, of course, if we recognize that those living in deprivation in ethnically diverse cities can be 'left behind' and not simply cast as 'cosmopolitans' or 'Anywheres' (Goodhart 2017). Labour's superiority over the Conservatives was, for the most part, as strong in the most deprived areas of England and Wales in 2019 as it was when Margaret Thatcher came to power. In fact, this research shows that poverty itself is a stronger predictor of returning a Labour MP today than it was back in 1979.

The Conservatives have also failed to make significant inroads into Labour support in constituencies with high levels of insecure labour, confirming the null hypothesis for the precarious employment definition of left behind. This confirms Jennings and Stoker's (2017) findings that Labour's support 'shored up' in areas with high proportions of precariats and increased slightly in more cosmopolitan areas between 2005 and 2017. Nonetheless, caution should be urged in assuming that the anger and anxiety of the increasing numbers of 'precariats' described by Standing (2011) will automatically generate a new class cleavage or mass support for Labour. While places they inhabit may be, as Standing (2015) suggests, firmly on Labour's side, further analysis of the data shows that they have—with exceptions—had disproportionately decreasing levels of turnout between 1979 and 2015. This reflects long-standing evidence of a negative association between turnout and economic insecurity (Dempsey and Johnston 2018; Heath 2018; Wolfinger and Rosenstone 1980).

This detailed statistical analysis of each election between 1979 and 2019 has shown that the 'left behind' thesis is far too simplistic. Ultimately, understanding whether so-called 'left behind' places have left Labour behind for the Conservatives is determined by the definition of 'left behind' that is adopted. If we understand left behind areas to be those with large proportions of old, low-skilled, white, working-class people living far enough from cosmopolitan cities, then there is significant supporting evidence presented here. However, if a conceptualization of left behind is adopted which describes constituencies that are the most economically disadvantaged—often ethnically diverse, urban areas—then there is no evidence of any shift away from Labour to the Conservatives. In fact, this research suggests that Labour's support remains particularly strong in those areas of the country with not only the most significant levels of poverty but also those with the greatest proportion of insecure employment. The problem, of course, for the Labour Party is that its support has become increasingly concentrated in the most urban, ethnically diverse, and most deprived areas as well as the most educated at the expense of not only the more numerous demographically left behind constituencies, but also the more demographically middle-of-the road seats.

Appendix

'Cosmopolitan' industries: The industries that have been grouped together at the 2001 and 2011 census to create a percentage employed in cosmopolitan industries are outlined below. Note that the final two categories in Table A4.1 in both censuses have only been included because at the output area level in 2011 (in order to perform areal interpolation to the 2005 constituency level), they were inseparable from the previous two industries (Human health and social work activities; Arts, entertainment and recreation/Other service activities).

The 1991 census relied upon the 1981 SIC (Standard Industrial Classification) UK for industrial measures, which had very little detailed classification of service-sector employment. Almost all of the industries identified as cosmopolitan in the 2001 census are, according to the Office for National Statistics (2002), captured by just two less granular industrial categories

Table A4.1 'Cosmopolitan industries': 2001 and 2011 harmonization

Industrial classifications: the harmonization of 'cosmopolitan' industries	
2001 census	2011 census
Financial intermediation	Financial and insurance activities
Real estate, renting, and business activities	Real estate activities Professional, scientific and technical activities Administrative and support service activities
Public administration and defence; compulsory social security	Public administration and defence; compulsory social security
Education	Education
Health and social work	Human health and social work activities
Other community, social, and personal services activities	Arts, entertainment and recreation Other service activities
Activities of private households as employers and undifferentiated production activities of private households	Activities of households as employers; undifferentiated goods and services producing activities of households for own use
Extraterritorial organizations and bodies	Activities of extraterritorial organizations and bodies

in 1991: 'banking and finance etc.' and 'Other services'. Therefore, these employment categories have been used in the measure. Similarly, in 1981, the variable combined the proportion of the employed population who were employed in 'finance' and 'public administration and other services'.

'Precariat' occupations: A recent data set shows a clear association between zero-hour contracts (precarious employment) and different occupational groups: between October and December 2017, 69.9% of those employed on zero-hour contracts fell into four occupational categories: 'Caring, leisure and other service occupations', 'Sales and customer service occupations', 'Process, plant and machine operatives', 'Elementary occupations' (Office for National Statistics 2018b). Therefore, from the 2011 census, the proportion of the population in each constituency that are employed in these occupations has been used to create a measure of 'precariat' occupations. For elections using 2001 census data, the four corresponding groups from the SOC (Standard Occupation Classification) 2000 classification are: 'Personal Service Occupations', 'Sales and customer service occupations', 'Process; plant and machine operatives', 'Elementary occupations'. At the 1991 census, the closest match using the SOC90 is as follows: 'Personal and protective service occupations'; 'Sales occupations'; 'Plant and machine operatives'; 'Other occupations'. In 1981, because these occupational classifications were unavailable and a more complex measure incorporating part-time labour did not appear to be capturing precariousness, we do not use this variable for corresponding elections (1979 and 1983).

Secure employment: This is an inverted measure of 'insecure employment': the standardized proportion of the population in precarious employment (see 'precariat' occupations) combined with the standardized proportion in routine/semi-routine employment (2001 onwards) or semi-skilled/unskilled employment (pre-2001).

In many election years, secure employment was strongly positively correlated with degree-level qualifications. In order to retain these two conceptually important variables without creating invalidated coefficients as a result of collinearity, a method of sequential regression has been used. This involved first executing a constituency-level regression model with degree-level qualifications as the only explanatory variable and secure employment as the dependent variable. The residual from this regression model represents the part of the secure employment variable that is not correlated with degree-level qualifications. The regular measure of degree-level qualifications has then been included in the election regression models, whereas secure employment has been replaced by the aforementioned residual. Accordingly, the degree-level qualification coefficients in the following models can be interpreted normally whereas the secure employment residual coefficients can be interpreted as the independent contribution of secure employment once its shared explanatory contribution with degree-level qualifications has been accounted for (Graham, 2003; Dormann et al. 2013). To summarize, the secure employment variable is created as follows:

If x_1 is the percentage with a degree and x_2 is the index of secure employment, one first estimates:

$$x_2 = a_0 + a_1 x_1 + e_1$$

In this initial simple linear regression, a_0 refers to the constant and e_1 the error term. Once this regression is completed, the residual is used in the static models as follows:

$$Y = b_0 + b_1 x_1 + b_2 e_1 + b_3 x_3 + \cdots + e_y$$

Where Y refers to Labour or Conservative vote share, b_0 is the constant, $b_n x_n$ the regression parameters, $b_2 e_1$ the regression parameter taking the residual from the previous model and e_y the error term.

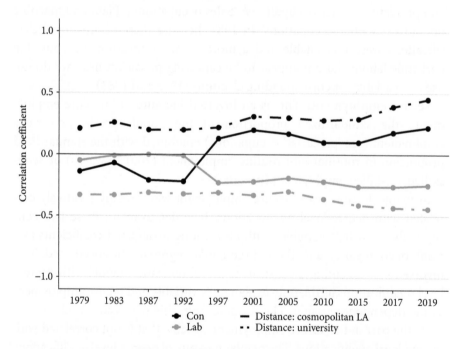

Figure A4.1 Correlation between distance from nearest cosmopolitan place and distance from the nearest university and Labour and Conservative vote share, 1979–2019

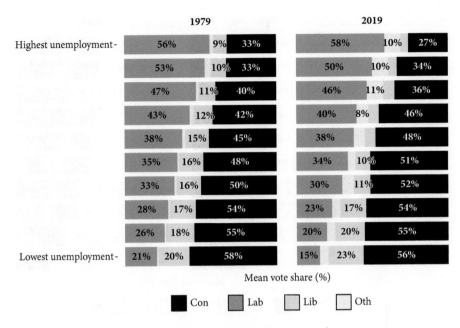

Figure A4.2 Mean party vote share (1979 and 2019) by unemployment

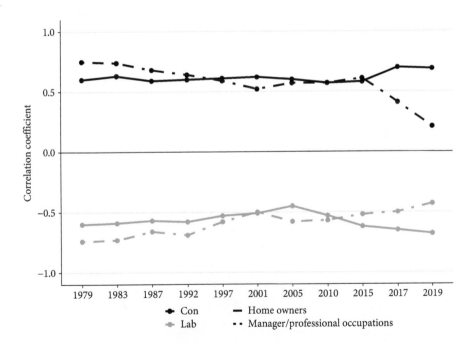

Figure A4.3 Correlation between home ownership, professional occupations, and Labour and Conservative vote share, 1979–2019

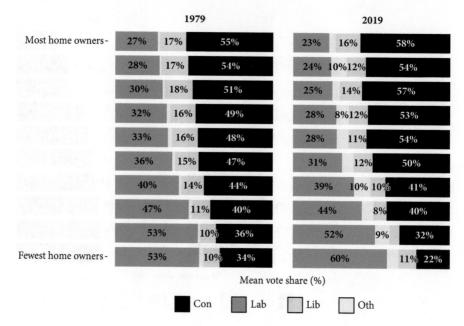

Figure A4.4 Mean party vote share (1979 and 2019) by home ownership

5

Relative decline (and growth) and the changing electoral geography of England and Wales

As we emphasized in the discussion in Chapter 2, there have been considerable changes to Britain's social structure since the Conservative landslide of 1979, most notably deindustrialization and the associated decline in the size of the working class, the growth in higher education, the expansion of jobs connected to a global knowledge economy, increased occupational and housing precarity, greater ethnic diversity, and an ageing population. These changes are not geographically uniform—with some exceptions, larger cities have tended to see the biggest growth in younger graduates and increased ethnic diversity, while rural areas and smaller towns have seen their populations become much older and, relatively speaking, less ethnically diverse. These changes in the spatial distribution of voters across the country can impact on party competition by creating, or reinforcing, geographical cleavages (Ford and Jennings 2020). This is most profound in first-past-the-post systems like the UK since where voters are located can have significant, disproportionate effects.

While the previous chapter considered the relationship between the social and economic characteristics of constituencies and party support in terms of *levels* (i.e. determining where Labour or Conservative vote shares were higher or lower based on the composition of an area), we here explore how *change* in those characteristics is associated with shifts in electoral support for the two parties between 1979 and 2019. This is premised on the idea that electoral trends may differ in places that have experienced relative decline (or relative growth) compared to those areas that have not experienced the same degree of social or economic change. Some places may not appear left behind in absolute terms but have experienced a sustained and noticeable relative deterioration in their social and economic fabric compared to the past or as other places have overtaken them. Numerous studies suggest that

The Changing Electoral Map of England and Wales. Jamie Furlong and Will Jennings, Oxford University Press.
© Jamie Furlong and Will Jennings (2024). DOI: 10.1093/9780191943331.003.0005

feelings of resentment, nostalgic deprivation, and status loss are contributing to electoral shifts towards the populist right (see Gest et al. 2017; Gidron and Hall 2017; 2019). This focus on change in the social and economic characteristics of places adds to understanding of how their relative trajectory is influencing patterns of party support. People living in areas that might not have the highest levels of deprivation or low-skilled, precarious employment may still feel as though their local area has fallen behind relative to other areas. In many cases this may indeed be an accurate assessment of change in objective social and economic conditions (Green et al. 2023). The fact that some areas are experiencing *relative* outflows of human and economic capital, while others are relatively thriving (Martinez-Fernandez et al. 2012), is central to the divergent political trajectories of different places (Jennings and Stoker 2019).

Some parliamentary constituencies may appear rather average in terms of their economic prosperity, yet this can conceal quite significant decline over time. For example, Gravesham in Kent is a constituency incorporating most of Gravesend and the associated countryside to the south. At the 2011 census, the area had levels of home ownership, social renting, deprivation, and semi-routine and routine forms of employment that were very typical of England and Wales more widely, as Table 5.1 shows.

However, this rather average profile in 2011 conceals the fact that on many measures the constituency experienced a period of relative decline between 1981 and 2011. As Table 5.2 shows, between 1981 and 2011, Gravesham experienced a slower growth in the proportion of households that were owner occupied than England and Wales as a whole. At the same time, it saw an above average increase in semi-skilled and unskilled occupations and a smaller than average decrease in unemployment. In 2011, Gravesham might not be considered left behind, but on these measures, we could argue that it has become more left behind relative to other places. The word *relative* is key

Table 5.1 Socio-economic profile of Gravesham vs England and Wales

Variable	Gravesham (2011)	England & Wales (2011)
Households that are owner occupied	64.6%	64.3%
Households that are socially renting	17.3%	17.4%
Residents living in deprivation on 3 or 4 measures	5.8%	5.7%
Employees in semi-routine or routine employment	29.0%	25.5%

here: becoming more left behind *does not imply absolute decline*. On many measures, there may have been an improvement in living standards, such as the fall in unemployment (see Table 5.2). But, if such improvements are less than observed across most constituencies, then we can argue Gravesham is *becoming* increasingly left behind. In other words, it might be improving more slowly, or potentially declining more quickly, than other areas of the country.

Table 5.2 Change in the socio-economic profile of Gravesham vs England and Wales

Variable	Gravesham (1981–2011)	England & Wales (1981–2011)
Change in % of households that are owner occupied	+1.8	+5.5
Change in % of unemployed economically active residents	−1.7	−3.2
Change in % of employees in unskilled or semi-skilled employment	+12.3	+7.4

Measuring this change should encompass a sufficiently wide timeframe that can uncover any entrenched rather than short-lived processes—a point emphasized by Watson (2018, p. 20): 'The "left behind" are not so much those that sense they have fallen behind most recently as those that have fallen furthest over a more sustained period of time'. By using the method of spatial overlaying (explained in more detail in 'A methodology for analysing relative change and electoral trends') to generate data for the 1979 general election year against the constituency boundaries used in the 2019 general election, we are able in this chapter to offer a long-term assessment of the relationship between socio-economic decline (and growth) and changes in party vote shares between 1979 and 2019. This allows us to address the question of how electoral support has changed for Labour and the Conservatives between 1979 and 2019 in places that are, relatively speaking, improving or declining. Are Labour's electoral heartlands to be found in relatively improving urban areas? Are Conservative strongholds increasingly located in declining left behind suburbs and smaller towns?

Following a brief description of the methodological approach, this chapter begins with an examination of the constituency-level relationships between change in the characteristics associated with the three definitions used in Chapter 4 (demographically left behind, economically left behind, precariously left behind) and change in Labour and Conservative Party vote shares at each election between 1979 and 2019. It then expands upon these definitions to create an over-arching index of relative decline and explores the relationship with party support. A more specific focus on deindustrialized areas follows, separating out the analysis into those areas that have, socio-economically speaking, recovered and those that have continued to experience a more prolonged relative decline. The findings in 'improving areas' are especially clear: these places are associated with a growing Labour vote and declining support for the Conservatives. The problem for the Labour Party is that these areas are largely found in cities—which have become more attractive places to live for younger graduates and professionals in particular—but the party is already a dominant electoral force in these densely populated urban areas. Under Britain's first-past-the-post system, there are few gains to be had in places that are already electoral strongholds. This puts the electoral geography of England and Wales in the same situation as identified by Rodden (2019), and also as we observed in Chapter 3, with an inefficient clustering of electoral support for the left in major urban centres.

A methodology for analysing relative change and electoral trends

The aim in this chapter is to explore the relationships between demographic and vote share changes across constituencies between 1979 and 2019—constituencies that, for the most part, have had significant boundary changes. To enable a like-for-like comparison of change across the two elections, it is essential that the same constituency boundaries are used. Therefore, we have used the same method (as used in Chapter 4) of areal interpolation (or spatial overlaying) to estimate demographic characteristics and vote shares in 1979 notional to the boundaries used in 2019. Data from the 1981 census at the enumeration district level have been overlaid onto the constituency boundaries used at the 2019 general election to calculate demographic values as if these were the constituencies used in the 1979 general election. This meant we were able to calculate key changes in the population characteristics of the constituencies used at the 2019 general election between these two elections.

Calculating changes in party vote shares across two elections with rather different constituency boundaries was more challenging. There was not a publicly available data set that includes 1979 general election results notional to the constituency boundaries used in 2019, which would allow an easy comparison between the two elections. One possible solution—overlaying 1979 constituencies onto the constituencies used in 2019—would rely on assumptions of an equal distribution of party voters across entire constituencies and would therefore be far too imprecise. Instead, we built a statistical model[1] to predict, using 1981 census data, the vote shares for Labour and the Conservatives at the 1979 general election, but on the boundaries used in the 2019 general election. Therefore, where a constituency has significant boundary changes between 1979 and 2019, the vote share change is calculated using the actual 2019 results and the predicted 1979 results for the boundaries used in 2019.

The demographic variables used in this analysis are largely similar to the variables used in the previous chapter, but here we use percentage point changes (increase or decrease) across different time periods rather than levels at a particular point in time. The chapter is again structured around our conceptualization of places becoming more or less: (i) demographically left behind (versus more or less cosmopolitan), (ii) economically left behind, or (iii) precariously left behind. The precarious measure of left-behindedness employed in the last chapter has been extended beyond a more distinctly occupational measure to also encompass change in the levels of housing precarity. Indeed, precarity is hardly restricted to work, with clear evidence that, particularly since the financial crisis in 2007–8, housing tenure has been increasingly characterized by insecure, short-term tenancies—the decreasing (though highly spatialized) access to affordable home ownership being a more recent addition to the 'precariat' concept (McKee et al. 2017). Housing affordability—a relatively low salience issue in the 1980s—has increasingly become an issue of public concern, especially in London, due to significant inflation of rents and house prices (Ansell and Adler 2019; Waldron 2021). To reflect this, the measure of precarious left behindedness includes home ownership and changes in housing affordability[2] as additional variables.

Some variables used in Chapter 4 have also been removed from the analysis here: (a) manufacturing, gross migration, and urban-ness, because it is unclear whether a change (increase or decrease) would constitute becoming

---

[1] The linear regression model used was refined until it achieved a high level of accuracy in predicting Labour and Conservative vote shares. When testing the model on the actual 1979 general election results (using 1983 boundaries), there was a correlation of 0.913 between Labour predictions and results and for the Conservatives there was a correlation of 0.892.

[2] Housing unaffordability is calculated as a ratio—the median house price (Office for National Statistics 2015a) divided by median annual earnings (Office for National Statistics 2018a) in the constituency. The change is subsequently the change in this ratio between two points in time. An increase in the value of the index means a decrease in affordability. Due to data availability, this change value has only been created for the time period between the 2010 and 2014. Subsequently, the measure has only been used with change between the 2005 and 2017 elections. Due to a small number of constituencies—all in London—with extremely large increases in the ratio value, a logarithmic scale is used in this analysis.

more or less demographically left behind; (b) distance from the nearest cosmopolitan local authority and distance from the nearest university because they are subject to very little change; and (c) household deprivation, as this variable was not a feature of the 1981 census.

The measures described in Table 5.3 constitute the percentage point change in the value between the closest census year or the election year when data have been interpolated. For example, when our analysis considers change between the 1979 and 2019 general elections,[3] while the election results are taken from these elections, the change in sociodemographic characteristics of parliamentary constituencies is measured between 1981 and 2011. For the ethnic diversity variable, the change refers to the change in the Herfindahl index[4] value, in which an increase in the value implies increasing ethnic diversity.

Table 5.3 Measurement of whether an area is becoming left behind for each classification

Measure	Left behind = above or below mean change?
Demographically left behind	
Routine/semi-routine occupations (semi-skilled and unskilled)	Above
Degree-level qualifications	Below
Age: 16–29	Below
Age: 65+	Above
Ethnic diversity	Below
Employed in 'cosmopolitan' industries	Below
Economically left behind	
Poor health	Above
Social renters	Above
Unemployment rate	Above
Precariously left behind	
'Precariat' occupations	Above
Housing unaffordability	Above
Homeowners	Below

[3] While most of the focus in this chapter is on change between 1979 and 2019, we have also completed the same analysis of change across shorter time periods: 1979–92, 1992–2005, and 2005–19. This analysis is occasionally referred to where the trends across the shorter time period do not match those seen across the wider 1979–2019 period.

[4] The Herfindahl concentration index is used (Hirschman 1964) to calculate the probability that two randomly selected residents of the same parliamentary constituency are of a different ethnicity (Sturgis et al. 2014).

The relationships between changing demography and change in vote shares

Change in demographically left behind (and cosmopolitan) places

Our expectation with regard to the demographic definition of left behind places is that areas that have become *increasingly left behind* against these criteria have generally seen declining Labour support and increasing Conservative support over time. This idea is tested by exploring bivariate associations between changes in our defined characteristics of left behind constituencies and changes in Labour and Conservative vote shares. In areas that are becoming more demographically left behind, we would expect to see an *above average* change in the proportion of low-skilled jobs and a *below average* change in the proportion employed in cosmopolitan industries. This is because these tend to be former industrial areas that have struggled to make the transition to the modern, globalized knowledge economy. Likewise, these are areas that have (relative to other areas) ageing populations, lower growth in the number of university graduates living in the area, and lower growth in ethnic diversity. These characteristics are expected to be associated with falling support for Labour and rising support for the Conservative Party.

Consistent with those expectations, Figure 5.1 reveals a remarkable shift over time: generally, the larger the (relative) increase in semi-skilled or unskilled occupations, the greater the swing from Labour to the Conservatives between 1979 and 2019. In the top 10% of seats that have seen the largest relative growth in semi-skilled and unskilled labour, there has been a swing from Labour to the Conservatives of some 8.6 points between 1979 and 2019. This includes seats such as Mansfield (24.4 point swing), Stoke-on-Trent North (23.2 point swing), and Boston and Skegness (18.7 point swing). In contrast, the 10% of seats that have seen a fall in the proportion of low-skilled occupations have actually seen a 13.1 point swing from the Conservatives to Labour. Almost all of these seats are in London or other large cities: constituencies such as Walthamstow (32.6 point swing to Labour), Bristol West (31.9 point swing to Labour), and Manchester Withington (31.7 point swing to Labour). The evidence is clear: Labour have been losing ground to the Conservatives in areas with growing low-skilled employment and gaining ground in areas with shrinking low-skilled employment.

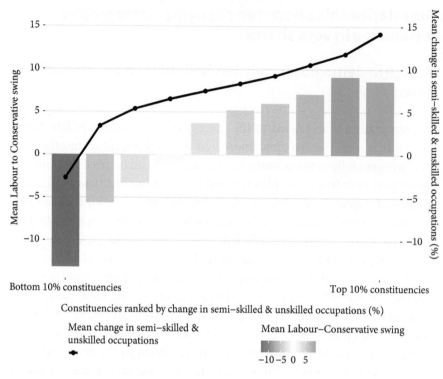

Figure 5.1 Labour to Conservative swing (1979–2019) by change in semi-skilled and unskilled[a] occupations (1981–2011)

[a] As discussed in Chapter 4, the 1981 census variable used here is proportion employed in semi-skilled/unskilled occupations and in 2011 the proportion employed in routine/semi-routine occupations. While the measures are somewhat similar, caution should be exercised in interpreting in particular the mean change in semi-skilled and unskilled occupations, which we know is unlikely to be positive in this time period in 90% of constituencies.

For change in the age profile of constituencies, the associated electoral shift is striking (Figure 5.2). When constituencies are ranked by change in the proportion of young people (aged 16 to 29), only the top two deciles (or top 20% of constituencies) have seen an actual increase in the proportion of the population made up by this group. It is only in this top 20% of seats that there has been a swing from the Conservatives to Labour between 1979 and 2019. Yet this swing is substantial: a 9.9 point swing in the top decile and a 7.7 point swing in the second highest decile. Most of these seats are urban and many have large universities: Leeds North West (26.3 point swing to Labour), Cambridge (23.5 point swing to Labour), and Oxford East (18.4 point swing to Labour). The remaining 70% of constituencies that have experienced a relative decline in their younger populations have seen consistent but less extreme swings to the Conservatives. Seats with the most

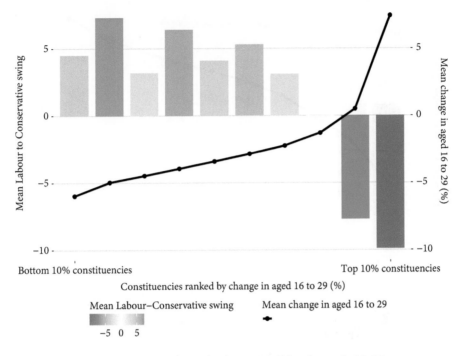

Figure 5.2 Labour to Conservative swing (1979–2019) by change in 16–29 age group (1981–2011)

substantial declines are a mix of smaller market towns, post-industrial towns, and largely rural areas, from Harlow (26.4 point swing to the Conservatives) to Tamworth (20.8 point swing to the Conservatives) and New Forest East (13.3 point swing to the Conservatives). In contrast to Labour, whose support has increased markedly in just a small minority of urban/university constituencies with growing populations of young people, the Conservatives have gained ground across a much wider range of constituencies by their changing age profile.

The same pattern is evident when we consider seats by the change in the proportion of their population aged 65 and over (Figure 5.3). Again, Labour's mean vote share has increased between 1979 and 2019 in the 30% of seats that have experienced *relative* declines in their older population while the Conservative mean vote share has increased in the other 70% of seats. At one end of the spectrum, constituencies such as Hove (34.4 point swing to Labour) and Hornsey and Wood Green (26.8 point swing to Labour) have seen falling older populations and big swings to Labour. At the opposite extreme are suburban smaller towns and post-industrial areas, such as

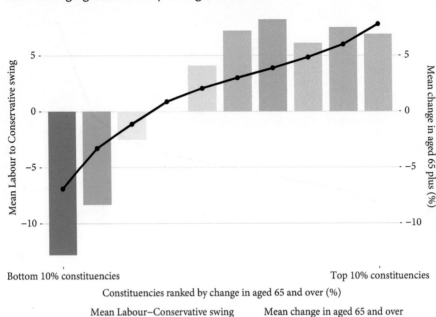

Figure 5.3 Labour to Conservative swing (1979–2019) by change in over-65 age group (1981–2011)

Havant (21.1 point swing to the Conservatives) and Washington and Sunderland West (21.9 point swing to the Conservatives). For Labour, it would not be so electorally damaging if these trends simply counterbalanced each other, but they have lost ground to the Conservatives in the most average of places in terms of their changing age profile. Seats with fairly 'average' changes in the age profile of their population, such as Morley and Outwood (14.6 point swing to the Conservatives), Amber Valley (21.8 point swing to the Conservatives), and North Swindon (14.1 point swing to the Conservatives) have all been won (or won back) by the Conservatives from Labour in recent elections.

In terms of change in ethnic diversity, Figure 5.4 shows that in the 70% of seats that have seen less than a 14-point increase in the Herfindahl ethnic diversity index score,[5] there have been consistent swings to the Conservatives. In contrast, Labour's support has grown only in the 20% of seats that have experienced the most substantial increases in ethnic diversity. This includes

---

[5] The Herfindahl index refers to the probability that two randomly selected residents of the same parliamentary constituency are of a different ethnicity. Therefore, a 14-point increase implies that the probability of two residents being of a different ethnicity has increased by 0.14.

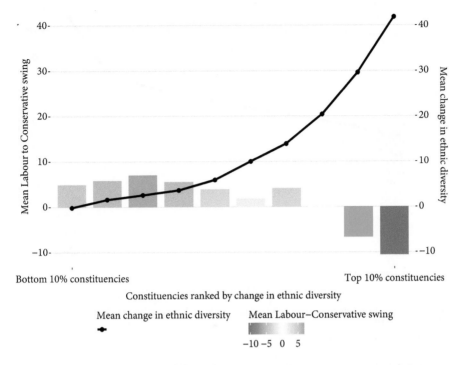

Figure 5.4 Labour to Conservative swing (1979–2019) by change in ethnic diversity (1981–2011)

almost every inner-city seat of every large city in England and Wales, but most notably seats in London, Birmingham, and Manchester. One interesting exception is West Bromwich East, which is in the top 10% of constituencies ranked by increase in ethnic diversity yet has seen a swing from Labour to the Conservatives of some 18.5 points. This reflects a wider success story for the Conservatives in the towns of the West Midlands: Walsall North (32.7 point swing to the party), Dudley North (27.7 point swing), Wolverhampton North East (26.9 point swing), West Bromwich West (25.7 point swing), Wolverhampton South East (19.3 point swing), and Stoke-on-Trent Central (17.2 point swing) are all constituencies that have experienced above average increases in ethnic diversity and yet have swung from Labour to the Conservatives. In most seats across England and Wales that have become much more ethnically diverse, Labour have gained support, yet in the West Midlands—outside of Birmingham itself—their vote has fallen sharply.

There is not a single constituency in England and Wales where there has been a negative change in the proportion of the adult population holding degree-level qualifications between 1981 and 2011. As Figure 5.5 shows, even the bottom 10% of constituencies ranked by change in the share of university

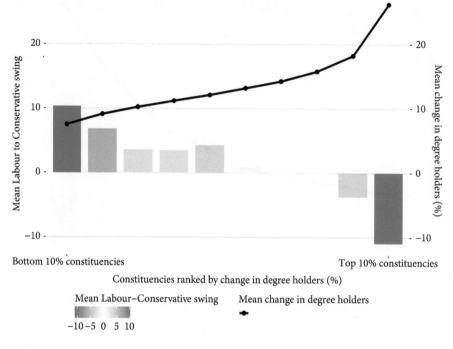

Figure 5.5 Labour to Conservative swing (1979–2019) by change in university graduates (1981–2011)

graduates have seen a mean increase of some 7.5 percentage points. There is a similar pattern (to the trends described in relation to ethnic diversity) in terms of Labour's electoral inefficiency: in only the top 20% of seats that have seen the most substantial growth in degree-holders has there been an overall swing from the Conservatives to Labour. In the other remaining 80% of seats, the Conservatives have gained on Labour. Once again, Labour has secured large swings towards them in a small number of largely urban seats that have seen big increases in degree-holders, such as Walthamstow (32.7 point swing to Labour), Ilford South (29.4 point swing to Labour), and East Ham (23.3 point swing to Labour). Many of these seats are also home to large student populations: Bristol West (31.8 point swing to Labour), Manchester Withington (31.7 point swing to Labour), and Sheffield Hallam (28.6 point swing to Labour). The Conservatives have seen substantial swings in seats with the smallest growth in graduates, many of which are in the West Midlands, such as Walsall North (32.7 point swing to the Conservatives), Dudley South (27.8 point swing to the Conservatives), and Stoke-on-Trent South (27.2 point swing to the Conservatives). The key, however, is that the Conservatives have also gained in constituencies that have experienced closer to average levels of graduate growth—Portsmouth North (12.4 point swing to the Conservatives) and Telford (24.3 point swing to the Conservatives).

To summarize, between 1979 and 2019 swings from Labour to the Conservatives have been larger in constituencies that, using a demographic definition, we understand as *becoming* more left behind. That is, those areas with the most substantially ageing populations, the largest relative increases in working-class occupations, the lowest increases in ethnic diversity, and the lowest increases in the proportion of university graduates. Labour's gains from the Conservatives have been limited to a more defined set of constituencies: only areas with very high growth in ethnic diversity and where the population profile has become younger, and only those with, relatively speaking, smaller increases in working-class occupations. These trends are consistent with claims made previously (often for shorter timeframes) regarding the electoral inroads made by the Conservatives in areas that are becoming demographically left behind (e.g. Ford and Goodwin 2014; Furlong 2019; Cutts et al. 2020) and the growing electoral strength of Labour in increasingly 'cosmopolitan' areas (Jennings and Stoker 2016, 2017, 2019).

Change in economically left behind places

While we have shown a swing from Labour to the Conservatives in areas becoming more demographically left behind, to what extent do we observe the same pattern amongst areas that have become more left behind in recent decades in socioeconomic terms? In Chapter 4, we showed that measures of economic left-behindedness (poor health, social housing, unemployment, and deprivation) remained consistently positively associated with Labour's vote shares over time. This concluded that the most economically left behind areas continue to overwhelmingly elect Labour MPs. Here we use the same measures (except deprivation as there are no data back to 1981) to understand whether becoming more economically left behind, compared to other areas, is associated with changes in vote shares for either party. We begin by looking at social housing, which as a proportion of all housing tenure has fallen in every constituency in England and Wales between 1981 and 2011, except two (Ilford South and Bournemouth East).

There is a clear relationship between change in social housing and change in vote share: moving left-to-right on the x-axis from constituencies with the largest declines to those with the smallest declines in social housing, we see a decrease in the swing from Labour to the Conservatives (Figure 5.6). It is only in the 20% of constituencies that have seen the smallest reduction in

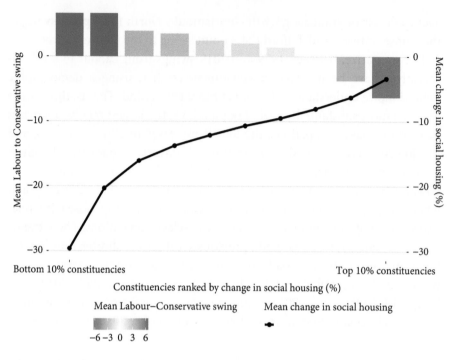

Figure 5.6 Labour to Conservative swing (1979–2019) by change in social housing (1981–2011)

the proportion of social tenants that Labour have gained relative to the Conservatives overall. Many of these seats are in urban areas of London and the North West, such as Ilford South (29.4 point swing to Labour), Brent Central (13.6 point swing to Labour), and Manchester Gorton (26.6 point swing to Labour) In addition, we might note that, while the pattern is consistent, the vote share changes are relatively small compared to those associated with the more demographically left behind measures explored in the previous section.

The vast majority of constituencies have also seen a fall in unemployment between 1979 and 2019. The relationship between change in unemployment and swing from Labour to the Conservatives is less clear cut than for many other measures. In the 10% of constituencies that have, on average, seen a 0.4-point increase in the proportion of unemployed adults, there has actually been a small swing of 3.3 points from the Conservatives to Labour. Yet, aside from the 20% of constituencies that have seen the biggest falls in the unemployed, where Labour have also made slight (relative) gains, the Conservatives have gained in most other deciles. Once again, it is a case of a swing from Labour to the Conservatives in most areas and those areas with most average change—those constituencies in the middle of the distribution (Figure 5.7).

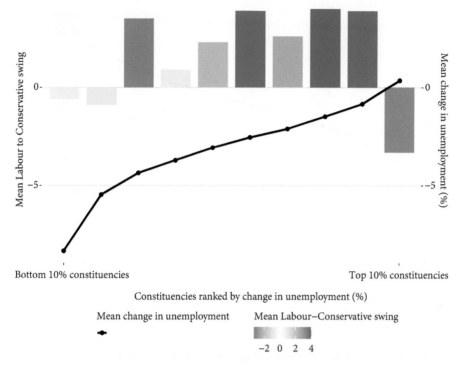

Figure 5.7 Labour to Conservative swing (1979–2019) by change in unemployment rate (1981–2011)

Perhaps unsurprisingly given the significantly ageing population of England and Wales, the proportion of the population in poor health has increased across most constituencies between 1981 and 2011. However, poor health is also a clear indicator of the relative poverty of an area (Benzeval et al., 2014). In areas that have seen the biggest increase in poor health, there have been substantial swings from Labour to the Conservatives (Figure 5.8). Indeed, the top 10% of constituencies by change in poor health have a mean swing from Labour to the Conservatives of 6.1 points. Constituencies such as Mansfield (24 point swing to the Conservatives), West Bromwich West (25.7 point swing to the Conservatives), and Wolverhampton South East (19.3 point swing to the Conservatives) are driving this trend. This contrasts with the finding for the absolute level of poor health in the previous chapter, where poor health being high overall is strongly associated with a high Labour vote share.

Overall, the findings from this analysis suggest that, compared to changing measures of demographic left-behindedness, the relationship between socio-economic change and changing relative support for both parties is unclear. On the one hand, areas where health has worsened most significantly

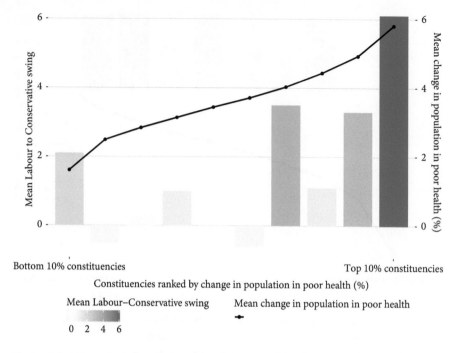

Figure 5.8 Labour to Conservative swing (1979–2019) by change in poor health (1981–2011)

have swung to the Conservatives, yet constituencies in which the proportion of social housing has fallen the least have swung to Labour. In areas with increasing unemployment, Labour have gained ground, yet in most other seats where the decline in unemployment has been below average, there has been a swing to the Conservatives. The picture regarding socio-economic change and change in party support over the last forty years is evidently quite messy.

Change in precariously left behind places

Alongside deindustrialization, an ageing population, the growth in higher education, and increasing diversity, perhaps some of the most significant changes to British society have been in housing tenure. The 'Right to Buy' policy implemented in 1980 led to a decreasing supply of social housing and widespread home ownership. More recently, there has been a fall in home ownership and a growth in private renting. Here we interpret areas with the most substantial falls in home ownership as those with increasingly precarious populations who lack this level of housing security. Between

1981 and 2011, in most constituencies there was growth in home owner-ship, despite more recent falls. In the small proportion of seats that have experienced a decline in home ownership, there has been a swing to Labour (see Figure 5.9). Once again, these are predominantly seats in London and other large urban areas. Examples include East Ham (23.3 point swing to Labour), Ilford South (29.4 point swing to Labour), and Bristol West (31.9 point swing to Labour). In contrast, in most seats where home ownership has grown, so has the Conservative vote share. Constituencies that have seen big increases in homeowners, from Harlow (26.4 point swing to the Con-servatives) to Tony Blair's former seat of Sedgefield (25.3 point swing to the Conservatives), have turned sharply towards the Conservatives.

Urban areas have seen enormous increases in the proportion of residents that privately rent properties (Jefferys 2013). This is not a simple result of the 'studentification' of areas of large cities and towns but reflects the increasing inability of many young families to buy a home. While in some gentrifying areas of larger cities, an increase in renting may reflect an influx of younger, highly educated residents, it is also indicative of an inability to access the

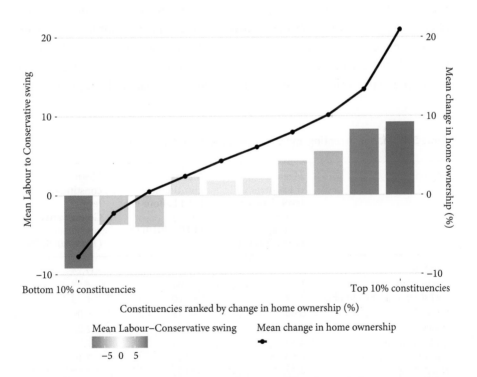

Figure 5.9 Labour to Conservative swing (1979–2019) by change in home ownership (1981–2011)

housing market—a kind of left-behindedness that disproportionately affects younger people. Private rental contracts are also more likely to lead to precarious living arrangements than owning or socially renting (Corlett and Judge 2017).

Perhaps unsurprisingly, given the association with younger residents living in urban environments, Table 5.4 shows that in London and the North West, where the proportion of rented households has increased most significantly, Labour have improved across the time period relative to the Conservatives. In the North West, these trends are driven by largely urban constituencies such as Liverpool Riverside, Preston, Manchester Central, Manchester Withington, and Chester—all have had significant growth in private renting and a swing to Labour. The problem, of course, for Labour is that outside of these areas, where growth in private renting has been a little less pronounced, the Conservatives have gained ground. It is important to note that, even in completely different types of election, where the tide might move in and out in favour of one particular party, the same underlying trends are occurring.

Due to the lack of historical, fine-grained occupational classifications and the lack of constituency-level house price data, we can only measure the change in precarious forms of employment and housing affordability across more recent time periods (between 2005 and 2011 and 2005 and 2014 respectively). Figure 5.10 shows the relationship between the change in proportion employed in precarious forms of employment (jobs that might be poorly paid

Table 5.4 Change in renting and change in vote share, by region

Region	Mean constituency-level change in households renting (1981–2011) (%)	Mean constituency-level Labour vote change (1979–2019) (%)	Mean constituency-level Conservative vote change (1979–2019) (%)
London	8.33	7.45	−12.24
North West	6.17	4.94	−6.34
Yorkshire and The Humber	5.72	−2.40	−0.35
West Midlands	5.60	−7.13	9.09
Wales	4.88	−6.29	2.02
East Midlands	4.64	−5.64	7.73
East of England	4.60	−7.05	7.10
North East	4.57	−10.01	4.57
South West	4.35	−4.91	1.60
South East	4.17	−5.59	0.85

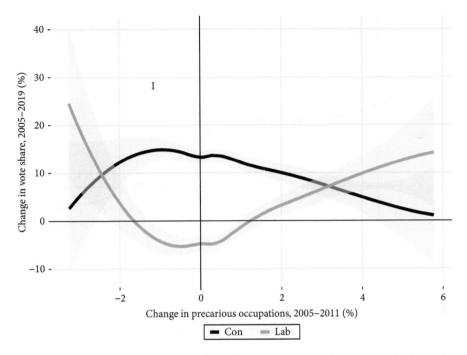

Figure 5.10 Change in Labour and Conservative vote share (2005–19) by change in employment in precarious occupations (2005–11)

or insecure) and change in Labour and Conservative vote share across constituencies between the 2005 and 2019 general elections. While there is an unclear trend in constituencies that have seen the largest increases or largest falls in precarious employment, overall, there is a weak to moderate positive association (0.29) between the change in precarious employment and Labour vote share, with the opposite pattern for the Conservatives (−0.22). On the whole, areas that have seen a recent growth in precarious forms of employment have, relative to the average trend, become more favourable to Labour than the Conservatives.

A similar trend can be seen in Figure 5.11, which plots the association between the logged change of house price/income ratio and the change in Labour and Conservative vote shares. In most areas, house price increases between 2010 and 2014 exceeded income increases. However, in those areas where house prices have risen *much* faster than incomes, there has been a small swing from the Conservatives to Labour. Perhaps unsurprisingly, almost all these seats are in London or the South East of England. In constituencies that have seen house prices increase a little less drastically compared to incomes—the more average constituencies—the trend has been a swing to the Conservatives.

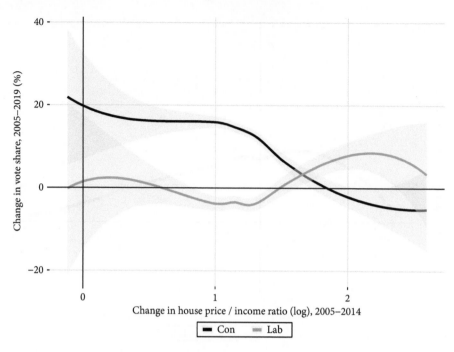

Figure 5.11 Change in Labour vote share (2005–19) by change in employment in house price to logged income ratio (2005–14)

Relative economic decline and changes in electoral support

Having explored change in terms of individual measures, our interest here is in how a broader, area-based measure of socio-economic decline is associated with wider electoral trends. An index of relative decline has been created by adapting measures constructed by Pike et al. (2016) and Jennings et al. (2017). These measures combine demographic and employment change variables into one index that determines the relative rate of decline of each area. Because of difficulties related to boundary changes and data availability, Jennings et al. (2017) do not provide a long-term picture of relative decline. By using the data generated from overlaying 1981 census data onto 2019 constituencies and by predicting 1979 vote shares at 2019 boundaries, the index of decline used here allows for a longer term analysis of the association between socio-economic decline and change in vote shares for Labour and the Conservatives.

Any index of area-level decline must reflect its multi-faceted nature rather than being based on a single indicator. The index used here incorporates widely accepted measures of socio-economic decline. To calculate the index, different indicators are first calculated for each constituency in England and Wales at the boundaries used in 2019:

1. Change in proportion of the population with degree-level qualifications, 1979–2019
2. Change in total population, 1979–2019
3. Change in unemployment rate, 1979–2019
4. Change in proportion of households deprived on three or four measures, 2001–11
5. Change in median weekly income (£), 2010–19
6. Change in proportion of professional jobs (calculated by adding together the change in managerial and professional employment with the change in 'cosmopolitan' employment), 1979–2019
7. Change in number of businesses, 2010–19

These indicators give a broad measure of the economic course that parliamentary constituencies have been on over this period. Although due to data availability there is some variation in the time periods across the indicators, most are still in the 1979–2019 period and, where they are not, the periods are of sufficient length to indicate some meaningful change rather than simply fluctuation. After calculating these indicators, they were standardized by calculating the 'z-scores' for each—that is, how many standard deviations above or below the mean the value is. For some of the variables—unemployment and household deprivation—the standardized score was reversed so that a negative score indicated decline. For all of the other variables, a positive standardized score contributed to the overall decline. The standardized scores were subsequently added together and divided by the total number of indicators to create an overall relative decline score for each constituency.

The constituencies were subsequently ranked by their relative decline score so that the constituency ranked 1st (Cities of London and Westminster) has experienced the least rate of decline and the constituency ranked 572nd (Cheadle)[6] the most. Considering the reader's likely surprise that Cheadle is ranked bottom, it is worth emphasizing that this is not a measure that captures the area that is poorest or most economically deprived in 2019, but rather, a measure of relative change across this time period. Less surprisingly, in the ranking positions 1st to 20th, there are only three constituencies outside of London (Birmingham Ladywood, Manchester Central, and Milton

---

[6] 572 constituencies are included rather than 573 because the Speaker's seat is omitted from the data.

Keynes South). It should also be noted that while some places are moving ahead and others are treading water, no constituency is economically collapsing. In this sense, this measure of decline is a reflection that they are falling behind *relative* to other areas, not that economic conditions are becoming objectively worse.

More relative decline, more Conservative support?

In Figure 5.12, along the x-axis is the decline ranking of each constituency from 1 to 572 and on the y-axis is the change in vote share between 1979 and 2019 for Labour and the Conservatives. The line showing the smoothed conditional mean presents a clear, albeit relatively weak pattern: there is a slight negative correlation between decline and Labour vote share change and a slight positive correlation between decline and Conservative vote share change. In a small number of areas where the socio-economic change has been the most positive, Labour's vote share has tended to increase and the Conservative vote share decrease. For the Conservatives, their vote shares have, on average, improved in most areas. However, they have tended to see the largest vote share increases and swings from Labour in areas that have experienced the most relative decline. The slightly stronger correlation between Conservative vote share change and decline rank (0.29) than for Labour vote change (−0.16) indicates that, for the Conservatives, compared to Labour, there is a more significant difference in their vote share change between constituencies that have declined the most and those that have declined the least.

In Table 5.5, constituencies have been sorted into five categories according to the level of positive or negative relative change that they have experienced: most positive change, above average relative positive change, average change, above average decline, and the highest decline. Each category represents an equal number (114 or 115) or 20% of constituencies. For the Conservatives, the most substantial changes have taken place in the constituencies that have seen the most positive change, many of which are located in inner-city areas of large cities such as London, Leeds, Liverpool, Manchester, Cardiff, Bristol, and Brighton. In these areas that have experienced the highest relative positive change, Labour's vote share has increased by a mean 2.6 percentage points and the Conservatives' vote share has decreased by a mean 7.9 percentage points. For the Conservatives, this represents a marked difference from the other categories, for which the mean vote share change is always above zero. For Labour, their mean vote share change is negative across all categories except in the areas that have experienced the most positive relative change. Labour have not fallen away more in only the most declining areas; rather they have fallen away in all areas except those with the most positive socio-economic change. However, the Conservatives have gained most substantially in areas that we can understand to be becoming more left behind—those that are declining most significantly. The Conservative vote increase in these areas is larger than in any other category.

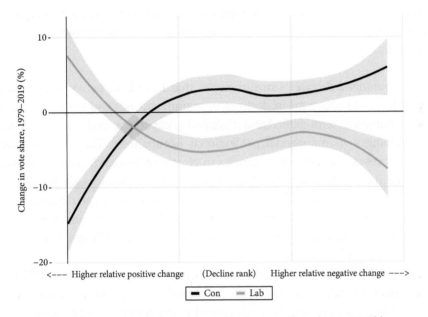

Figure 5.12 Change in Labour and Conservative vote share (1979–2019) by ranking of socio-economic decline (1981–2011)

Table 5.5 Mean vote share changes (1979–2019) across constituencies by categories of socio-economic change

Socio-economic change categories	Mean Labour vote share change	Mean Conservative vote share change
Most positive (top 20%)	2.60	−7.91
Above average change	−4.47	1.24
Average change	−5.33	3.15
Above average decline	−1.60	1.26
Highest decline (bottom 20%)	−5.04	4.82

Deindustrializing areas: continued decline or recovery?

One specific type of decline that has been well documented in the UK is associated with deindustrialization. Where manufacturing industries have diminished, some areas of the UK have replaced them with low-skilled, typically insecure, low-paid work. These areas that have not recovered well from deindustrialization are referred to here as areas of 'prolonged decline'. Other areas that have seen more successful regeneration and economic recovery have had significant rises in the proportion of the population employed in largely well-paid, managerial, and professional roles. These areas are characterized by some degree of embourgeoisement. To capture these two types of contrasting deindustrializing areas, two groups of constituencies have been created:

- *'Prolonged decline'*: Constituencies that have had, between 1979 and 2019: (1) above mean declines in manufacturing; and (2) above mean changes in semi-skilled and unskilled occupations; and (3) below mean changes in managerial/professional occupations. There is an over-representation of constituencies in Northern England, Wales, the Midlands, Essex, and Kent in this category. Examples include Batley and Spen in West Yorkshire, Denton and Reddish in Greater Manchester, Hartlepool in the North East, all three Stoke-on-Trent constituencies in the West Midlands, Merthyr Tydfil and Rhymney in Wales, Romford in Essex, and Gillingham and Rainham in Kent.
- *'Embourgeoisement'*: Constituencies that have had, between 1979 and 2019: (1) above mean declines in manufacturing; and (2) above mean changes in managerial/professional occupations and (3) below mean changes in semi-skilled and unskilled occupations. This includes a wide range of constituencies, from Shipley and Calder Valley in West Yorkshire to High Peak and Derbyshire Dales in the Midlands and Hackney South and Shoreditch in London.

By grouping constituencies in this way, clear findings emerge that are otherwise obscured when exploring manufacturing decline and the change in managerial and professional employment alone. Table 5.6 shows the mean vote share changes by each constituency type. There are stark findings from constituencies that have deindustrialized and experienced prolonged decline: the Conservatives have a mean vote share increase of 10.5 points and Labour a mean fall of 11.6 points. Note that the change in these deindustrializing prolonged decline areas is even more substantial than the previous analysis of the most declining areas. The Conservatives have made huge progress at Labour's expense in areas where manufacturing has fallen and where there has been limited growth in typical middle-class jobs. Even within this group of constituencies, there is some regional variation. There is, for example, a host of constituencies in the West Midlands where Labour's vote has fallen and the Conservatives' vote had increased by more than 20 points respectively. Walsall North, Wolverhampton North East, West Bromwich West, Dudley North, Dudley South, and Stoke-on-Trent North have all seen extreme swings from Labour to the Conservatives. Labour have a serious problem identified later in this book of electoral under-performance in these areas of the West Midlands.

In contrast, in areas that, simultaneously to deindustrializing, have seen a growth in middle-class forms of employment, Labour's mean vote share has fallen slightly less than that of the Conservatives between 1979 and 2019.

Table 5.6 Mean vote share changes (1979–2019) across deindustrialized constituencies compared to all constituencies

Constituency type	Mean Labour vote share change	Mean Conservative vote share change
Embourgeoisement	−1.12	−2.91
Prolonged decline	−11.60	10.50
All constituencies	−2.76	0.50

Until now, we have understood in which kinds of places—characterized by changing characteristics—Labour and Conservative vote shares have changed. However, it is important to pinpoint which characteristics are driving this change. This can only be done using more complex statistical modelling—in this case, linear regressions that predict Labour and Conservative vote share change between 1979 and 2019. The benefit of this approach is that we can understand the effect a characteristic—say, change in home ownership—has on the changing votes of the two parties, after accounting for all of the effects associated with other changing characteristics. Does increasing home ownership still have a negative effect on Labour vote share change after accounting for the effects of changing age profiles, changing levels of manufacturing, and so on?

In Figure 5.13 we present the effects of different variables predicting Labour's vote share change in rank order (the full models are reported in the chapter appendix, Table A5.1). If the line is grey and the line does not cross the dotted vertical line on the x-axis, the variable has a negative association with

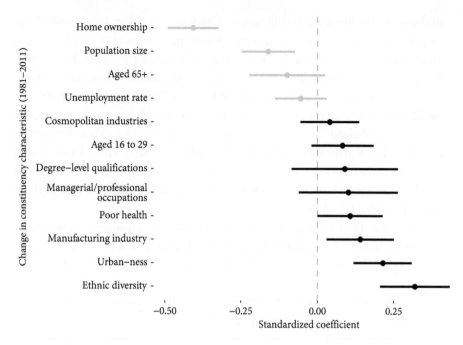

Figure 5.13 Predictors of change in Labour vote share (1979–2019)[a]

[a] The variables in this and the Conservative party model differ slightly from those outlined in Table 5.3 (the measures of left behind) due to multicollinearity and considerations relating to model fit.

Labour vote share change between 1979 and 2019. If the line is black and does not cross the dotted vertical line, there is a positive effect on Labour's vote share change. If the line crosses the dotted line, we cannot be certain enough to say that there is a significant positive or negative effect. The variables are ordered from 'most negative' to 'most positive'.

To answer the question above, change in home ownership is *the most important* constituency-level characteristic predicting Labour's vote share change. Even after accounting for all the other area-level changes, constituencies that have seen the biggest increases in home ownership have seen significant relative falls in Labour's vote. In contrast, areas that have experienced the biggest increases in ethnic diversity between 1981 and 2011 have seen the largest relative rises in Labour's vote.

For the Conservatives (see Figure 5.14), the most negative association and *the most important* predictor of their vote share change is the change in degree-level qualifications. Even after accounting for other demographic and economic changes, the bigger the increase in university graduates, the more negative the change in the Conservative vote share between 1979 and 2019.

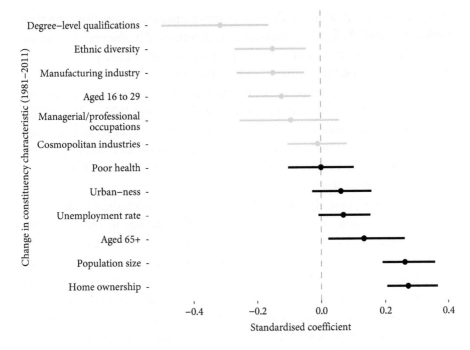

Figure 5.14 Predictors of change in Conservative vote share (1979–2019)

Perhaps unsurprisingly, ethnic diversity is also a significant negative predictor of change in Conservative vote share. In contrast to Labour, home ownership change is positively associated with Conservative vote share change. This fits with previous findings: in areas where home ownership has increased most substantially, the Conservatives have been out-performing Labour. In contrast, Labour's position, relative to the Conservatives, has improved in areas with increasing numbers of graduates, young people, and ethnic diversity.

Increasingly left behind, increasingly Conservative?

Over three decades between 1979 and 2019, the population of England and Wales has changed markedly: most areas of the country have experienced an increase in ethnic diversity, home ownership, levels of education, managerial and professional occupations, and proportions of older people of retirement age. However, there are huge variations from one constituency to the next, such that we can categorize some areas as *becoming* more left behind on different dimensions. These processes, alongside the political changes that they are associated with, are also not always consistent across this long time period. Some of the findings, therefore, are determined by the year that we use as the starting point for our analysis. Had we considered the periods 1974–2019 or 1983–2019, the findings may be rather different. With this in mind, in this discussion, we also refer to additional analysis[7] conducted in the shorter time periods between 1979 and 1992, 1992 and 2005, and 2005 and 2019. This allows us to illuminate not only the way in which the process of becoming increasingly left behind is associated with and can predict changing success for Labour and the Conservatives between 1979 and 2019, but also how this varies within these shorter time periods.

Before considering changes in left-behindedness according to the three definitions outlined, it is worth considering the findings in relation to the broader measure of socio-economic decline used in this chapter. For the Conservatives, in areas of significant socio-economic improvement, their vote share has decreased most substantially. In contrast, in areas that have seen the most significant relative economic decline, they have made considerable progress. In contrast, Labour's vote share has only increased in the constituencies that have seen the most economic improvement. Labour have been, relative to other areas, losing significant support in areas that have most significantly fallen behind, in socio-economic terms—areas in which the Conservatives have also made significant gains. Much of this change in areas of relative decline has actually occurred between 2005 and 2019. In 2019, Labour's vote collapsed in areas experiencing relative decline (mostly smaller towns), as opposed to areas that were already the poorest (mostly big cities). In contrast, the swing from the Conservatives to Labour in the most rapidly improving areas has been more consistent and has held up between 2017 and 2019.

Economically left behind

Using a more defined measure of economic left-behindedness based on change in social housing, unemployment, and poor health, the longer term trend is much less clear. While generally there have been swings to the Conservatives in areas where unemployment has fallen the least and poor health (a proxy for poverty) has increased the most, there were swings to Labour in largely urban areas where the social housing stock has been less depleted. This is matched by the statistical models predicting Labour and Conservative

[7] Due to space constraints, we do not present this analysis from shorter timeframes here but refer to some of the key findings.

vote share changes between 1979 and 2019, which show that changes in poor health and unemployment were statistically insignificant explanatory variables.

However, we have conducted additional analysis that has revealed that the period between 2005 and 2019 was markedly different to the wider time-frame. In fact, between 2005 and 2019, not only has Labour's relative support declined in areas that have seen increases in relative poverty (poor health), also changes in poor health and unemployment are both negative predictors of the change in Labour's vote share and positive predictors of the change in the Conservative vote share.

Whilst the long-term picture is unclear, there is clear evidence that, more recently, Labour's relative support is falling and the Conservatives' relative support is increasing in areas where relative economic deprivation is increasing. As previous analysis has shown, this does not imply that Labour's relative support is weakening in the most deprived areas of the country. Rather, it is decreasing in areas that are declining more rapidly or growing more slowly than others. In this case, measuring left-behindedness as a process illuminates changes that are hidden from analyses using only a static conceptualization of left behindedness.

Demographically left behind

In a time period in which the British economy has become increasingly driven by service-sector employment in larger, ethnically diverse cities with many younger graduates, areas that are moving towards this sociodemographic composition most slowly are understood in this analysis to be becoming left behind according to a demographic definition. It is certainly contestable to describe these places as increasingly left behind, particularly given the rather more serious forms of relative economic decline discussed previously. Nonetheless, as many areas that have experienced the most significant relative growth in routine and semi-routine occupations are far removed from large cities, an interesting geographical story emerges. That is, relative to their largely increasing support in many inner-city areas where there have been sharp declines in traditional forms of working-class employment, the change in Labour vote share has been below average in constituencies where these forms of employment have been increasing. Areas that, occupationally, are becoming more working class, relative to the rest of the country, are simultaneously becoming more favourable to the Conservatives.

Similarly, Labour has, on average, lost support in deindustrializing areas that have seen very limited growth in more middle-class forms of employment. In fact, in these areas that we might consider to have endured a more *prolonged decline* following deindustrialization, the fall in Labour support has been enormous. These were once Labour's heartlands—the small-town coalfields and manufacturing areas of the Midlands, Northern England, and South Wales. The Conservative Party has clearly benefited in these areas, adding weight to the hypothesis that their support has increased alongside the occupationally working-class nature of the workforce. This may also reflect the changing nature of work in these areas: from manufacturing workers represented by Labour-affiliated unions to a de-unionized and more atomized labour market of low-skilled workers.

At the same time, in areas where the population is ageing most rapidly and becoming more educationally qualified most slowly, the Conservatives have increased their relative support, whilst it has declined in areas with increasing proportions of younger people and degree-holders. The opposite is the case for Labour. This is, however, a more recent phenomenon: of the shorter time periods analysed (1979–92, 1992–2005, 2005–19), this effect of changing age composition has only occurred between 2005 and 2019. During the wider time period, areas where the increase in ethnic diversity has been slowest have also seen increased relative support for the Conservatives and a decrease in relative support for Labour. There is clear evidence that generally the Conservatives have witnessed more positive relative vote share changes in areas that are becoming demographically left behind—ageing, diversifying slowly with lower-than-average increases in gross migration and degree-holders and above average changes in typically 'working-class' occupations. This is most significantly the case in areas that have also rapidly deindustrialized, where Labour have lost ground.

Precariously left behind

If one understands areas to be becoming left behind by increasingly precarious housing and employment conditions, there is little to suggest any relative gains have been made by the Conservatives. Labour have not only made substantial gains in many areas marked by increasing housing unaffordability, declining home ownership, and a growing private rented sector, but they have also shown relative improvement in many constituencies where typically insecure forms of labour are increasingly the norm. These tend to be in urban areas, not necessarily where the proportions of young adults are increasing, but where the proportion of older, retired residents is in considerable decline. Whether one considers an area with increasing proportions of private renters and unaffordable housing to be left behind is, of course, up for debate. On the one hand, these tend to be seats in larger cities that have seen relative economic growth and an increasing number of cosmopolitan jobs held by a fast-growing graduate workforce. On the other hand, many low-income residents in these often highly unequal areas have very limited prospects of home ownership: for many, private renting in a country with restricted tenants' rights reflects a more precarious form of housing than owning their own property or accessing cheaper social housing.

Conclusion

This chapter has provided evidence of relatively clear overall trends: areas with growing numbers of older, middle- and working-class homeowners, typically removed from larger cities, have swung towards the Conservatives. Perhaps more concerning for Labour has been their precipitous decline in constituencies that have deindustrialized significantly and remained particularly working-class in character. If these, as well as broadly economically declining areas of the country, are considered to be *becoming* left behind, they present Labour with more problems than the Conservatives if the trend towards the latter continues over time. However, one may suspect that 2019 marked a low point for Labour in these areas that are becoming increasingly left behind. While their vote may never recover to the levels seen pre-Thatcher in post-industrial, working-class towns, it simply may not need to. Labour do not need to return huge majorities in these areas to win an election—they need to win most of them back whilst continuing their advance in areas that are rapidly improving.

Indeed, for the Conservatives, areas where larger proportions of people are priced out of home ownership and pushed into both the precarious rental and labour market present serious concerns. A key driver of Conservative success over this time period has been their growth in support in areas with increasing home ownership. As house price growth has, for some time, exceeded wage growth, home ownership has started to fall. Most concerning for the Conservatives is that this is not a phenomenon limited to new Labour strongholds in cities. Rather, many (though not all) constituencies across the South East of England are seeing rapidly falling home ownership, above average increasing ethnic diversity and above average increasing proportions of graduates. The Conservatives dominance in these areas is certainly under threat if they cannot widen their appeal.

Appendix

Table A5.1 Predictors of change in Labour and Conservative vote share, 1979–2019

	Change in Labour vote share (1979–2019)	Change in Conservative vote share (1979–2019)
Degree-level qualifications	0.205	−0.757***
	(0.203)	(0.196)
Managerial/professional occupations	0.281	−0.274
	(0.229)	(0.221)
Manufacturing industry	0.254**	−0.284***
	(0.102)	(0.098)
Population change (rate)	−0.130***	0.221***
	(0.035)	(0.034)
Poor health	1.102**	0.006
	(0.559)	(0.539)
Aged 16–29	0.259	−0.407**
	(0.164)	(0.158)
Aged 65+	−0.286	0.406**
	(0.181)	(0.174)
Ethnic diversity	0.299***	−0.146***
	(0.055)	(0.053)
Unemployment rate	−0.276	0.367*
	(0.216)	(0.208)
Homeowners	−0.632***	0.442***
	(0.066)	(0.063)
Cosmopolitan industries	0.124	−0.033
	(0.151)	(0.146)
Urban-ness	1.176***	0.358
	(0.268)	(0.258)
Intercept	−11.064***	5.182
	(3.715)	(3.580)
N	572	572
Adjusted R^2	0.392	0.488

Note: * $p < 0.1$, ** $p < 0.05$, *** $p < 0.01$ (standard errors in parentheses)

6

In search of Red and Blue heartlands

One of the puzzles of the electoral geography of England and Wales is the places where voters do not faithfully follow the script set by their social and economic profile. Where are the places that defy our expectations? What can these paradoxical cases tell us about British politics? This chapter examines the extent to which there are constituencies and regions of England and Wales that are seeming outliers—places where, given their sociodemographic composition, we would expect different election results than those that have occurred. The premise is that, while the demographic composition of a constituency is critical to understanding and predicting Labour and Conservative support, there remains a spatial structure to voting patterns in which specific constituencies and regions systematically under- or over-perform expectations for either party. The geographical clustering of such places suggests that there are local or regional historical, political, and cultural determinants of voting behaviour that move beyond demographic composition.

Our analysis here explores whether the constituencies and regions in which Labour and the Conservatives have 'over-performed' and 'under-performed' have changed between 1979 and 2019. Evidence is presented showing that Labour's 'heartlands' have shifted over time—where once the party over-performed significantly in former coalfield seats, in more recent elections this has shifted to Merseyside. Gradually, coalfield areas have become more electorally marginal and in line with expectations given their demographic composition. This suggests that the cultural drivers of Labour's support in former coal-mining areas have weakened at the same time as those in Merseyside have strengthened. Our findings also challenge simplistic narratives regarding the 'Red Wall'[1]—Merseyside and the coalfields of the North East, Midlands, and Yorkshire each belong to the Red Wall yet are on completely different political trajectories. For the Conservatives, this chapter reveals two

---

[1] James Kanagasooriam's original formulation of the 'Red Wall' was premised upon the same logic as our analysis here: identifying Labour-held seats where the Conservatives under-performed the prediction of constituency demographics. As Kanagasooriam and Simon (2021) point out, this important concept has been widely misunderstood and misused at times.

The Changing Electoral Map of England and Wales. Jamie Furlong and Will Jennings, Oxford University Press.
© Jamie Furlong and Will Jennings (2024). DOI: 10.1093/9780191943331.003.0006

areas of clear over-performance: Lincolnshire and the West Midlands outside of Birmingham. The party's over-performance in these two regions has generally strengthened between 1979 and 2019 while their under-performance has shifted from the former coalfields to Merseyside.

The structure of this chapter is as follows. First, vote shares of Labour and the Conservatives are mapped across England and Wales to provide evidence of consistencies and changes in the geographical patterns of support. Following this, residual values from statistical models produced at each general election between 1979 and 2019 are mapped onto constituencies in England and Wales. From this, the changes in geographical clustering of electoral over-performance and under-performance for Labour and the Conservatives are identified and discussed. Spatial analytical techniques reveal that the clustering of over- and under-performance in Merseyside and Lincolnshire are statistically significant. Analysis of individual constituencies reveals stark trends: Sefton Central—an ageing, predominantly white, suburban, wealthy constituency in Merseyside—has become, against the odds, solidly Labour; Boston and Skegness—an economically struggling Lincolnshire constituency with high levels of insecure employment—should at least be electorally competitive, but is now solidly Conservative. Not only are these regions in which the two parties out-perform predictions given their demographic composition, but they are also areas with huge and increasing majorities for the two parties. They can therefore be identified as the heartlands of Labour and Conservative support.

The geography of Labour electoral support

Figures 6.1 and 6.2 map the vote shares for the Labour Party for all constituencies across England and Wales at the 1979 and 2019 general elections. The darker the red, the higher Labour's vote share. The first point to make is that, despite changes over time that will be discussed, there is still a remarkable consistency to the geographical clustering of Labour support. In rural and small-town Southern England, especially south of the 'M4 corridor' running from London to Bristol, Labour do consistently poorly, often behind both the Conservatives and the Liberal Democrats in constituency vote shares. In contrast, Labour consistently achieve higher vote shares in urban parts of Northern England, South Wales, the far North East, Birmingham, and London.

These broader, consistent regional patterns to Labour's support—while illuminating—can lead one to overlook perhaps more subtle changes

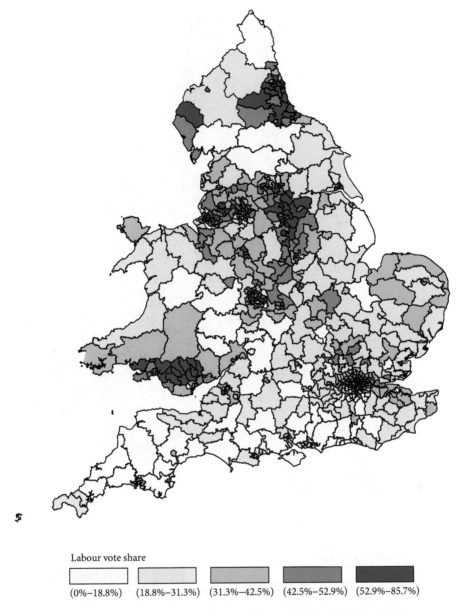

Figure 6.1 Labour constituency vote shares at the 1979 general election (1983 boundaries)

occurring within these same regions. The heavily populated belt of Northern England running roughly from Merseyside in the west to Hull on the east coast is often referred to as Labour's 'Red Wall' due to the party's long-standing and seemingly unstoppable dominance. At the 2019 election, it was widely reported that the Red Wall had collapsed, as the Conservatives

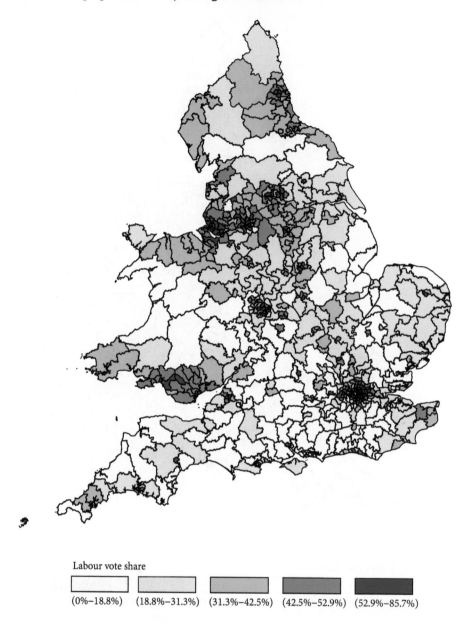

Labour vote share

(0%–18.8%) (18.8%–31.3%) (31.3%–42.5%) (42.5%–52.9%) (52.9%–85.7%)

Figure 6.2 Labour constituency vote shares at the 2019 general election

reached into former Labour heartlands. The story told by the 1979 and 2019 maps is more nuanced. In 1979, across much of this area, Labour's support was often higher in the small towns and villages centred around former coalfields than it was in the larger cities nearby. In Yorkshire and Humber, for example, contrast the constituencies in the heart of the former coalfields in Barnsley with those in Leeds (as summarized in Tables 6.1 and 6.2). In

Table 6.1 Labour and Conservative vote shares in 1979 (at 1983 boundaries):[a] a comparison between constituencies in and around Barnsley with Leeds

Area	Seat	Labour vote share	Conservative vote share	Labour area mean	Conservative area mean
Barnsley	Barnsley Central	60.6	28.2	63.8	25.5
	Barnsley East	68.9	20.3		
	Barnsley West and Penistone	60.2	30.2		
	Wentworth	65.7	23.3		
Leeds	Leeds Central	59.7	23.5	47.4	35.9
	Leeds East	55.2	30.2		
	Leeds North East	31.0	54.1		
	Leeds North West	27.5	50.3		
	Leeds West	52.2	27.1		
	Morley and Leeds South	58.5	30.5		

[a]Where boundaries have changed, the vote shares for 1979 are predicted based on a statistical model outlined in Chapter 5. This mix of observed and predicted vote shares for the 1979 general election are used throughout this chapter.

Barnsley, Labour's average vote share of 63.8% in 1979 was considerably higher than the 47.4% achieved across seats in Leeds. By 2019, the average vote in Barnsley had dropped to just 37.8%, some 26 points below the value in 1979. Yet in Leeds, the 2019 vote of 54.5% was 7.1 percentage points higher than in 1979.

This is consistent with what we see on the two maps—rather than the Red Wall collapsing, there has been a recentring of Labour's core vote from these smaller coalmining towns and villages to the larger cities of Leeds, Sheffield, Manchester, Newcastle-upon-Tyne, and Liverpool. One can see on the maps that in 1979 Labour were dominant not only on this west-east trajectory but also, just east of the Pennines, on a north-south trajectory heading from Leeds in the north down through Sheffield and to the coalfields of Derbyshire and Nottinghamshire in the Midlands. By 2019, this north-south axis has weakened considerably as Labour's core vote has receded into Leeds and Sheffield specifically. A similar pattern in the changes in Labour support occurred across other parts of Northern England and

Table 6.2 Labour and Conservative vote shares in 2019: a comparison between constituencies in and around Barnsley with Leeds

Area	Seat	Labour vote share	Conservative vote share	Labour area mean	Conservative area mean
Barnsley	Barnsley Central	40.1	21.4	37.8	32.9
	Barnsley East	37.6	27.3		
	Penistone and Stocksbridge	33.3	47.8		
	Wentworth and Dearne	40.3	35.1		
Leeds	Leeds Central	61.7	22.6	54.5	27.5
	Leeds East	49.8	35.7		
	Leeds North East	57.5	23.6		
	Leeds North West	48.6	26.8		
	Leeds West	55.1	28.9		

the Midlands, where Labour's vote share held up more strongly in bigger cities—Birmingham, Newcastle-upon-Tyne, Manchester—than it did in the smaller post-industrial towns that surround them.

The geography of Conservative electoral support

For the Conservatives, there is some consistency to the geography of their support between 1979 and 2019. The constituencies where the party's vote shares are consistently high—marked on the maps by darker shades of blue—tend to be larger seats in areas with lower population densities and less distinctly urban characteristics. In fact, this trend has become more pronounced over time: the correlation between constituency area size and Conservative vote share was 0.19 in 1979. By 2019, this figure was 0.37. For every 1 km^2 increase in constituency area size, the Conservative vote share increased on average by 0.37 percentage points at the 2019 general election. This reflects not that the Conservatives have, relative to elsewhere, become particularly strong in larger, rural constituencies, but that they have become relatively weaker in more densely populated cities.

Indeed, the pattern for the Conservatives, perhaps unsurprisingly, is the reverse of that for Labour. In 1979, the Conservative vote shares were relatively low in cities across the so-called Red Wall, but were even lower in smaller towns around the coalfields of South Yorkshire, the North East, and South Wales (Figure 6.3). By 2019, they had chipped away at Labour's

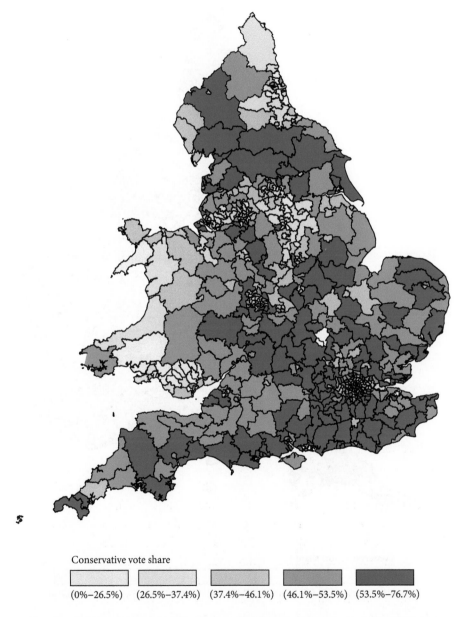

Conservative vote share

(0%–26.5%)   (26.5%–37.4%)   (37.4%–46.1%)   (46.1%–53.5%)   (53.5%–76.7%)

Figure 6.3 Conservative constituency vote shares at the 1979 general election (1983 boundaries)

dominance in these areas—again most notably one can see darker blue colours encroaching on that north-south axis of former coalfields running from West Yorkshire down to the East Midlands (Figure 6.4). In Barnsley and Leeds (referring again to Tables 6.1 and 6.2), the trend is the opposite to Labour: in 1979, the Conservatives achieved a mean vote share of 35.9%

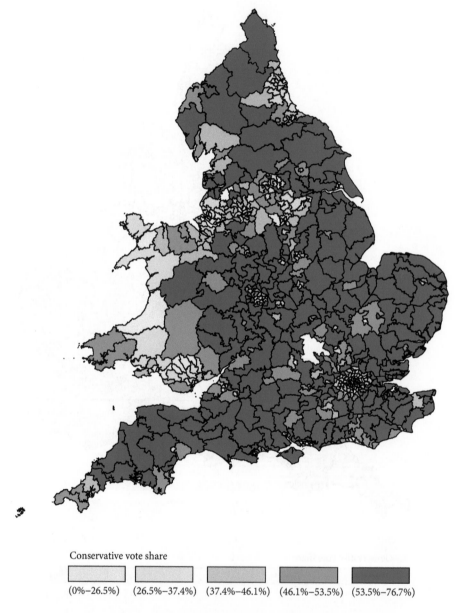

Conservative vote share

(0%–26.5%)   (26.5%–37.4%)   (37.4%–46.1%)   (46.1%–53.5%)   (53.5%–76.7%)

Figure 6.4 Conservative constituency vote shares at the 2019 general election

in Leeds compared to just 25.5% in Barnsley. By 2019, their vote share had increased across Barnsley to 32.9% but fallen in Leeds to 27.5%. These changes are perhaps a little less dramatic than those for Labour but are consistent with the idea that, within the so-called Red Wall, there are diverging patterns for both parties between larger cities and smaller towns and villages.

The spatial distribution of Labour and Conservative under- and over-performance

The maps so far have shown where Labour and Conservative electoral performances were weakest and strongest in both 1979 and 2019. But a key question remains: where did Labour and the Conservatives do better or worse than would be expected, given the sociodemographic makeup and geographical characteristics of the constituencies? How has the geography of under- and over-performance changed for each party across this time period? Indeed, we might consider an electoral stronghold or heartland for a party to be not just an area where it achieves consistently high vote shares, but one where it consistently over-achieves—areas where there are likely local, cultural factors (beyond demographics) boosting support.

To measure under- and over-performance we have first executed statistical models at each election that predict, based on sociodemographic and geographical constituency characteristics, constituency vote shares for both parties in 1979 and 2019.[2] For each constituency, at each election, we then calculate the *raw residual*—the actual vote share minus the predicted vote share from the statistical model. This value is then standardized by dividing it by an estimate of the standard deviation of the model residuals. The standardized residual for each constituency gives a measure of the distance between the expected vote share and the actual vote share. A positive value indicates that the actual vote share is higher than the predicted vote share; a negative value indicates that the actual vote share is lower than predicted. For example, in the Bradford South constituency in 2019, our model predicted Labour and Conservative vote shares of 46.5% and 41.3% compared to the actual results of 46.3% and 40.4% respectively. The residual value is therefore equal to −0.03 for Labour and −0.13 for the Conservatives—the proximity to zero capturing that the model accurately predicted the vote shares for both parties. In contrast, in Bradford West, Labour's vote share was 76.2%

---

[2] We have executed linear regression models using demographic and geographical characteristics to predict Labour and Conservative vote shares at every general election between 1979 and 2019. These linear regression models are outlined in Chapter 4 in more detail. Here we only map the standardized residual values from the 1979 and 2019 models due to space constraints.

compared to a prediction of 62.2%. The residual value of 2.14 indicates that in this constituency Labour out-performed the model considerably. For this analysis, we consider constituencies with a residual value of greater than +2 or less than −2 to be outliers—that is, constituencies where the party has significantly out- or under-performed the expectations of the model, given the area characteristics.

Figures 6.5 and 6.6 map the geographical distribution of these residuals from the statistical models predicting Labour's vote shares at the 1979 and

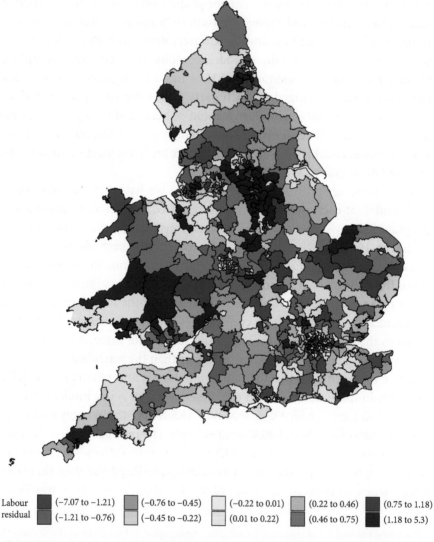

Labour residual

(−7.07 to −1.21)	(−0.76 to −0.45)
(−1.21 to −0.76)	(−0.45 to −0.22)

(−0.22 to 0.01)	(0.22 to 0.46)
(0.01 to 0.22)	(0.46 to 0.75)

(0.75 to 1.18)
(1.18 to 5.3)

Figure 6.5 Labour over- and under-performance mapped by standardized residuals at the 1979 general election (1983 boundaries)

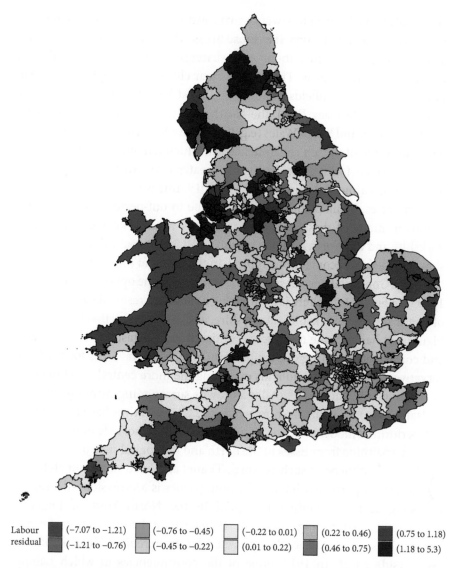

Labour residual				
■ (−7.07 to −1.21)	■ (−0.76 to −0.45)	□ (−0.22 to 0.01)	▨ (0.22 to 0.46)	■ (0.75 to 1.18)
■ (−1.21 to −0.76)	▨ (−0.45 to −0.22)	□ (0.01 to 0.22)	▨ (0.46 to 0.75)	■ (1.18 to 5.3)

Figure 6.6 Labour over- and under-performance mapped by standardized residuals at the 2019 general election

2019 general elections. In each map, constituencies coloured in *purple* are those in which the respective party *out-performed* expectations (or where the model under-predicted their vote share), whilst *orange* constituencies indicate the strongest *under-performance* (or where the model over-predicted their vote share).

Between 1979 and 2019, there has been a clear geographical shift in the areas in which Labour have over-performed, given their sociodemographic composition. In 1979, of the twenty-two constituencies in which the residual value was greater than two (i.e. those areas where the model most significantly under-predicted Labour vote shares), sixteen were in existing or former coal-mining areas. There was a clear clustering of high residual values in the former coalfields of South and West Yorkshire (e.g. Hemsworth, Rother Valley, Barnsley East), the North East (e.g. North Durham, North West Durham), and South Wales (e.g. Islwyn). By 1997 (in analysis not shown here), only one of the ten constituencies in which Labour most substantially over-performed (with a residual value greater than two) was located in a former or existing coal-mining area. By 2019, this was zero out of fourteen constituencies. Whilst Labour does continue to out-perform model expectations in many of these regions, particularly in areas of West and South Yorkshire and the North East, the overall trend is that coal-mining areas have slowly shifted to become more 'typical' in the way that they vote.

For the Conservatives, these areas have moved in the opposite direction: in 1979 (see Figure 6.7), there is a clustering of negative residual values in areas of South and West Yorkshire, Derbyshire, and South Wales that by 2019 (see Figure 6.8) had become much less prominent. In contrast, there is a notable and consistent clustering of over-performance in several areas for the Conservatives: (i) the West Midlands excluding the more central constituencies of Birmingham, and most notably in towns surrounding Birmingham (e.g. Walsall North); (ii) Lincolnshire, where the Conservatives have consistently out-performed model predictions since 1987; (iii) either side of the Thames Estuary, spanning from Essex in the north and the coastal strip of Kent in the south, in constituencies such as North Thanet and Folkestone and Hythe.

One area of particular interest for both parties is Merseyside—the region including and surrounding Liverpool in the North West of England. The strong 'coal-mining effect' of 1979—where Labour out-performed expectations and the Tories the opposite—has been replaced by a significant 'Merseyside effect'. In 1979, none of the constituencies in which Labour significantly over-performed (residual value greater than two) were in Merseyside, yet by 2019 this had increased to nine out of sixteen. The average vote share in 2019 in Merseyside is on average 16.4 percentage points higher than the vote share predicted by the model. In Sefton Central and Wirral South—two more middle-class areas some distance north and south of Liverpool, the Conservatives are predicted, given their demographics, to win both seats quite comfortably in 2019. Yet in Sefton Central, Labour secured 57.5% of the vote compared to just 27.8% for the Conservatives, and in Wirral South Labour are predicted to be almost 20 points behind the Conservatives yet finished 14 points ahead. This story played out across the whole of Merseyside,

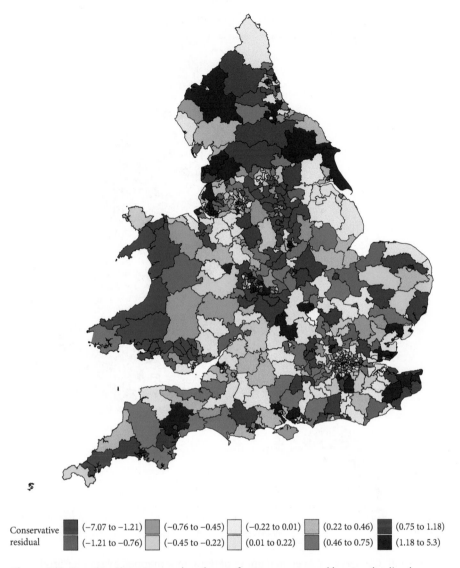

| Conservative residual | (−7.07 to −1.21) | (−0.76 to −0.45) | (−0.22 to 0.01) | (0.22 to 0.46) | (0.75 to 1.18) |
| | (−1.21 to −0.76) | (−0.45 to −0.22) | (0.01 to 0.22) | (0.46 to 0.75) | (1.18 to 5.3) |

Figure 6.7 Conservative over- and under-performance mapped by standardized residuals at the 1979 general election (1983 boundaries)

as shown in Figure 6.6 by the clustering of dark purple constituencies either side of the River Mersey in 2019. What is striking is the change from 1979, where, as Figure 6.5 shows, Labour actually under-performed and the Conservatives over-performed in some Merseyside constituencies.

One might think that the shifting of Labour's heartlands from mining towns to Merseyside fits with the narrative of their declining strength in white, working-class towns and increasing popularity in ethnically diverse,

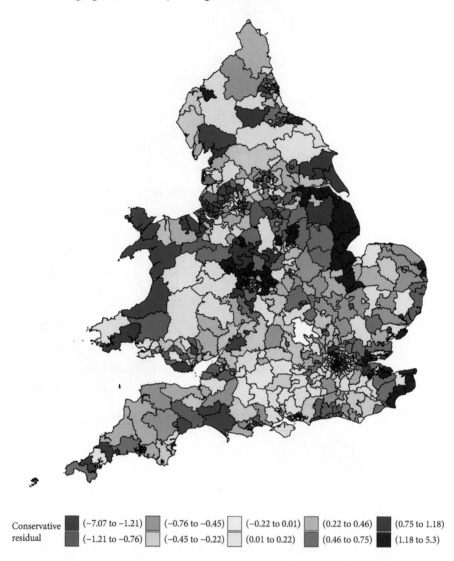

| Conservative residual | ■ (−7.07 to −1.21) | ■ (−0.76 to −0.45) | □ (−0.22 to 0.01) | ■ (0.22 to 0.46) | ■ (0.75 to 1.18) |
| | ■ (−1.21 to −0.76) | □ (−0.45 to −0.22) | □ (0.01 to 0.22) | ■ (0.46 to 0.75) | ■ (1.18 to 5.3) |

Figure 6.8 Conservative over- and under-performance mapped by standardized residuals at the 2019 general election

urban areas. However, outside of the inner-city core of Liverpool, much of suburban Merseyside is heavily white British and remains largely (with some notable exceptions) working-class. In this sense, by moving towards Labour so significantly, much of Merseyside has bucked the wider trend seen elsewhere in England and Wales—of the 'revolt on the right' among white British, working-class voters (Ford and Goodwin 2014).

At the same time, Merseyside has undoubtedly become a very poorly performing area for the Conservative Party. This is confirmed in Figure 6.9: whereas the mean Merseyside standardized residual for Labour has

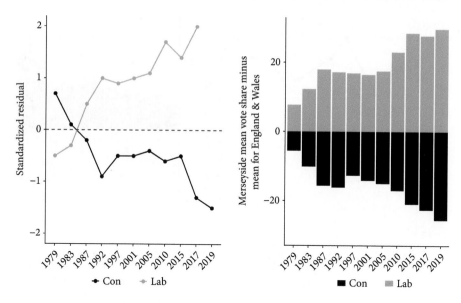

Figure 6.9 Standardized residuals and Labour/Conservative vote shares in Merseyside, 1979–2019

remarkably increased in every model year except 1997 and 2015, for the Conservatives it has decreased from 0.7 in 1979 to −1.5 by 2019—most significantly decreasing in the 2017 and 1992 models. This is not simply a case of over-performance for Labour and under-performance for the Conservatives, but also that Labour have come to achieve remarkably high vote shares and the Conservatives the opposite. Indeed, as Figure 6.9 shows, in 1979, the mean Labour vote share of 45.7% was only 7.7 percentage points above the mean Labour vote share in England and Wales of 38%. By 1987, this gap was 18 percentage points and by 2019 it was at a peak of 29.7 percentage points. In contrast, for the Conservatives, their mean Merseyside vote share was only 5.5 percentage points below their England and Wales mean in 1979. By 2019, their mean vote share in the region was some 25.5 percentage points below the England and Wales mean.

Lincolnshire perhaps best represents the opposite case to Merseyside, as an area where the Conservatives have both out-performed model predictions and have been broadly dominant in elections. In fact, at the 2017 general election, South Holland and The Deepings—a predominantly rural constituency in South Lincolnshire—produced the highest Conservative vote share in England and Wales of 69.9%. At the 2019 general election, Boston and Skegness polled second highest (76.7%) and South Holland and The Deepings third highest (75.9%). As the graph in Figure 6.10 shows, the relative Conservative performance in Lincolnshire (excluding North

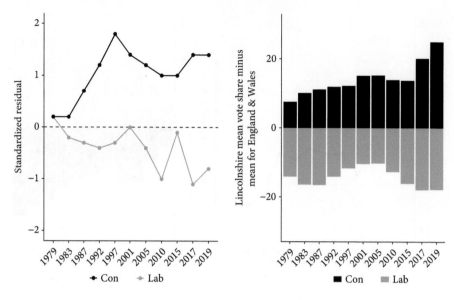

Figure 6.10 Standardized residuals and Labour/Conservative vote shares in Lincolnshire, 1979–2019

Lincolnshire/North East Lincolnshire and Lincoln),[3] compared to England and Wales as a whole, has generally increased over time. In 1979, the mean Conservative vote share in the county was only 7.5 points above the mean for England and Wales. This had increased to 15.1 points in 2001 and 24.1 points in 2019. In fact, at the 2019 general election, the mean Conservative vote share was some 70.8%. In contrast, Labour have consistently achieved vote shares considerably below their mean England and Wales performance between 1979 and 2019.

In Figure 6.10, the mean standardized residuals in Lincolnshire are plotted at each election to show the extent to which each party under- and over-performed model predictions. The positive residuals for the Conservatives indicate that they out-performed the model's predicted vote shares at every election between 1979 and 2019, most notably since 1987. In 2019, Conservative vote shares in constituencies across Lincolnshire (excluding Lincoln and North East Lincolnshire) were on average 10.9 points higher than model predictions based on sociodemographic composition. There is some within-region variation, with the residual values in the constituencies of Boston

---

[3] In the statistical analysis that follows, the constituencies that constitute the area of Lincolnshire are Boston and Skegness, Gainsborough, Grantham and Stamford, Louth and Horncastle, Sleaford and North Hykeham and South Holland and The Deepings. These reflect the constituencies considered part of Lincolnshire (as opposed to North Lincolnshire or North East Lincolnshire) by the Boundary Commission for England, minus Lincoln, which is far less politically unusual.

and Skegness, South Holland and The Deepings, and Louth and Horncastle generally higher, indicating that in these constituencies the Conservatives achieved substantially higher vote shares than one might expect given the area-level characteristics.

Understanding changing electoral geography via spatial clustering

So far, we have identified *where* Labour and Conservative absolute vote shares and relative under- and over-performance have become geographically clustered over time. Using a spatial analytical approach known as Local Indicators of Spatial Association (LISA), this can be extended to understand where these clusters are statistically significant. A local cluster map has been plotted for party vote shares and residuals at the 1979 and 2019 general elections, in order to show the changing locations where there are significant ($p<0.05$) clusters of constituencies by the type of association: constituencies with 'High-High' values are those that have a high value of the attribute and whose neighbours also have a high value; constituencies with 'Low-Low' values are those that share low values with their neighbours. For example, on the Conservative vote share maps, if a constituency has a High-High value (coloured red), both it and its neighbours have high Conservative vote shares. There are also two types of spatial outliers: constituencies coloured in a faint red (High-Low) or faint blue (Low-High). The former are constituencies with high values of the variable surrounded by neighbouring constituencies with low values; the latter is the opposite way around. In the analysis that follows, we first present maps of clustering of vote shares for the parties followed by maps of clustering of relative under- or over-performance.

Geographical clustering of Labour vote shares

The maps in Figures 6.11 and 6.12 show the statistically significant clustering of Labour's vote shares at the 1979 and 2019 general elections respectively. The regions of Low-Low clusters, where Labour generally perform poorly, are remarkably consistent across these two elections forty years apart. There are two clearly defined areas: (i) a huge expanse spanning Eastern Wales, parts of the West Midlands, the South West and the South East of England; and (ii) the East of England, most notably south from Lincolnshire to Essex. The regional clustering of High-High constituencies were in 1979 largely concentrated in coal-mining areas of West and South Yorkshire, Lancashire, South Wales, and the North East. As Figure 6.12 shows, by 2019, the statistically significant clusters of Labour support had receded in coal-mining areas—particularly in South Yorkshire where the cluster no longer exists—and had grown significantly in Merseyside and London.

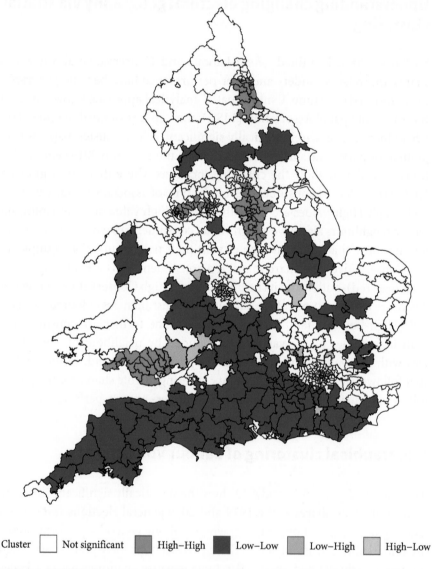

| Cluster | Not significant | High–High | Low–Low | Low–High | High–Low |

Figure 6.11 LISA cluster map showing statistically significant clustering of Labour vote shares at the 1979 general election (1983 boundaries)

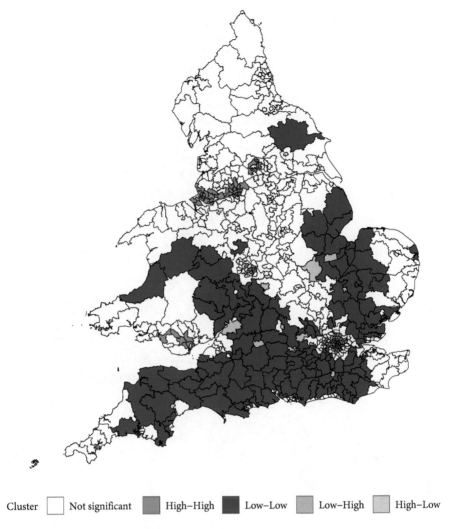

Cluster [ ] Not significant ▨ High–High ■ Low–Low ▨ Low–High ▨ High–Low

Figure 6.12 LISA cluster map showing statistically significant clustering of Labour vote shares at the 2019 general election

Geographical clustering of Labour's under/over-performance

Figure 6.13 and Figure 6.14 are local cluster maps of the *residuals* from the statistical models predicting Labour vote shares in 1979 and 2019. These maps show areas where there was statistically significant spatial clustering of Labour out-performing and under-performing model predictions. The

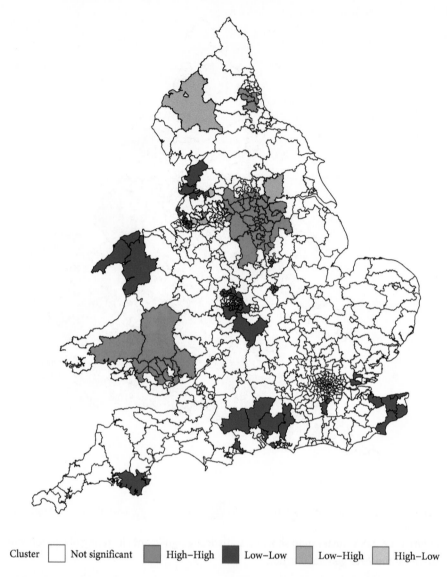

Cluster [ ] Not significant   ▨ High–High   ■ Low–Low   ▨ Low–High   ▨ High–Low

Figure 6.13 LISA cluster map showing statistically significant clustering of standardized residuals (under- and over-performance) from the 1979 model predicting Labour vote shares (1983 boundaries)

1979 map (Figure 6.13) strikingly confirms the presence of three statistically significant clusters of Labour over-performance in the coalfield regions of South and West Yorkshire, the North East close to Newcastle, and in South Wales. In contrast, there are clusters of constituencies with large, negative residuals in the West Midlands, Hampshire, and Kent, as well as parts of Merseyside and the North West. Remarkably, in 1979, Labour's vote share was lower in parts of Merseyside than one might expect given local demographic and geographicalcharacteristics. By 2019, Figure 6.14 confirms that

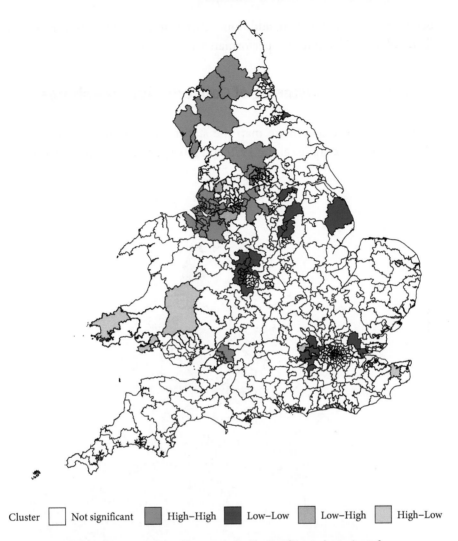

Figure 6.14 LISA cluster map showing statistically significant clustering of standardized residuals (under- and over-performance) from the 2019 model predicting Labour vote shares

the clustering of High-High residual values around the South Wales and South Yorkshire former coalfields has disappeared. In fact, parts of South Yorkshire, Nottinghamshire, and Derbyshire are now marked by Labour under-performance (Low-Low on Figure 6.14). Labour's cluster of over-performance has shifted westward across Northern England to include large parts of Merseyside, Greater Manchester, and parts of Yorkshire in and around the South Pennines. In fact, by 2019, 38 of the 63 constituencies that were within a cluster of Labour over-performance were in the North West of England (consistent with the regional trend that we observed in Figure 3.2). Low-Low clusters in Hampshire and the West Midlands have been supplemented with an additional cluster in Lincolnshire—further evidence of a significant under-performance in the region.

Geographical clustering of Conservative vote shares

In Figures 6.15 and 6.16 we map the statistically significant clustering of Conservative vote shares at the 1979 and 2019 general elections. Figure 6.15

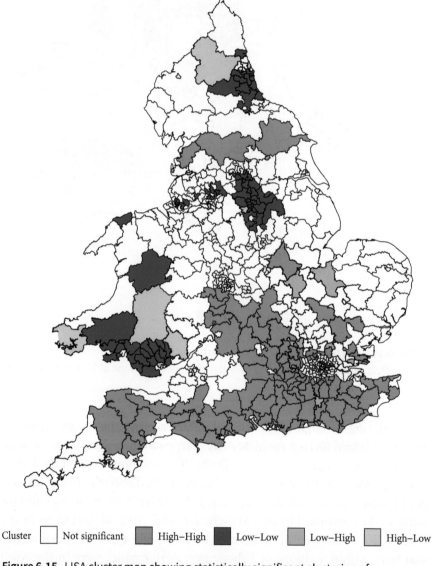

Cluster [ ] Not significant   ▓ High–High   ■ Low–Low   ▒ Low–High   ░ High–Low

Figure 6.15 LISA cluster map showing statistically significant clustering of Conservative vote shares at the 1979 general election (1983 boundaries)

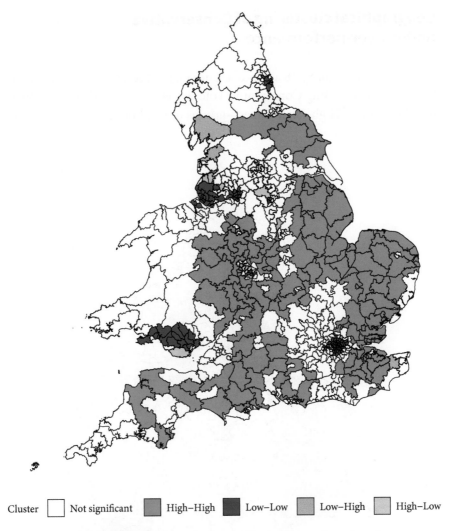

Figure 6.16 LISA cluster map showing statistically significant clustering of Conservative vote shares at the 2019 general election

shows that in 1979 high Conservative vote shares were largely clustered across a huge expanse of Southern England, while Figure 6.16 reveals that by 2019 the party was performing well in large parts of the East Midlands and West Midlands (including Lincolnshire and the areas surrounding Birmingham) as well as Eastern England. In much the opposite way to Labour, the clustering of low vote shares for the Conservatives has disappeared in the (former) coal-mining areas of South Yorkshire and the North East (though not in South Wales), and has developed across Merseyside, Greater Manchester, and London.

Geographical clustering of Conservative under/over-performance

Figure 6.17 and Figure 6.18 are local cluster maps of residuals from the statistical models predicting Conservative vote shares in 1979 and 2019. In 1979, the clustering of High-High values—groups of neighbouring constituencies

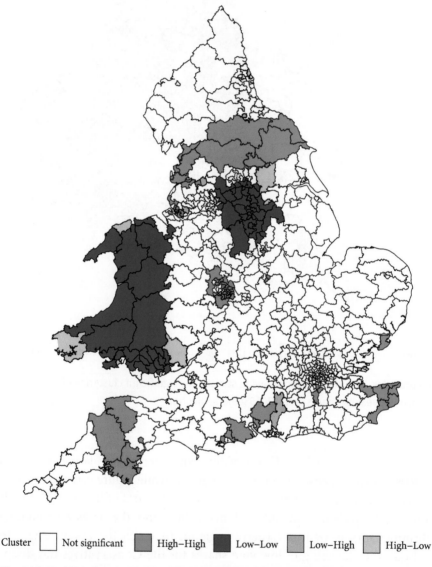

| Cluster | Not significant | High–High | Low–Low | Low–High | High–Low |

Figure 6.17 LISA cluster map showing statistically significant clustering of standardized residuals (under- and over-performance) from the 1979 model predicting Conservative vote shares (1983 boundaries)

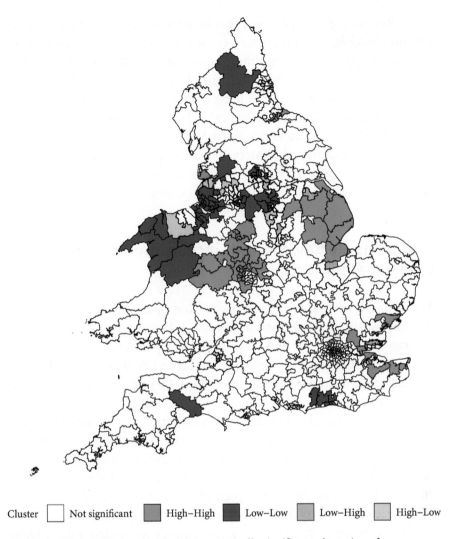

Figure 6.18 LISA cluster map showing statistically significant clustering of standardized residuals (under- and over-performance) from the 2019 model predicting Conservative vote shares

where the Conservatives out-performed model predictions—can be seen across several disparate regions: in and around Birmingham, rural North Yorkshire and Lancashire, and parts of Merseyside, Devon, Kent, and Hampshire. By 2019, rather than out-performing model expectations in urban areas of Birmingham, this over-performance had moved elsewhere in the West Midlands to the north of Birmingham, around towns and cities such as Walsall, Wolverhampton, and Stoke-on-Trent. At the same time, there is a significant increase in clustering of High-High values across Lincolnshire.

In contrast, Figure 6.17 shows that in 1979 there was a statistically significant clustering of Conservative (Low-Low) under-performance in two clear areas: (i) an area stretching across most of West and South Yorkshire and parts of Derbyshire; and (ii) almost all of Wales. By 2019, the under-performance in former mining areas of South Yorkshire and South Wales had receded, being replaced by a cluster of Low-Low values across Merseyside, Greater Manchester, North Wales, and parts of Leeds, Bradford, and Sheffield. A cluster of Conservative under-performance is also notable in the constituencies surrounding Brighton, including Hove, East Worthing and Shoreham, and Arundel and the South Downs.

Explaining Merseyside and Lincolnshire: composition or regional context?

The spatial clustering of the vote shares and model residuals have shown that the statistical models used in Chapter 4 do not adequately account for the trends in Merseyside and Lincolnshire. Despite many constituencies in Merseyside fitting a demographically left behind definition—largely white, working-class, with lower levels of education—they have become strongholds for Labour, countering the trend towards the Conservatives in similar areas elsewhere. For example, at the 2019 general election where Labour lost heavily, they secured 84.7% of the vote in Liverpool Walton 80.8% in Knowsley, and 79.4% in Bootle. In contrast, in constituencies in Lincolnshire, such as Boston and Skegness and Clacton, the Conservatives dominated, receiving 76.7% and 72.3% of the vote respectively. Yet, these parts of Lincolnshire are characterized by high levels of poor health, deprivation, and precarious forms of employment —variables typically associated with a higher Labour vote. While they have other characteristics more representative of demographically left behind areas that should make them broadly favourable to the Conservatives, given these socio-economic conditions, this level of Conservative electoral dominance is not predicted.

Of course, the first question that one asks is 'why are they so different?' Perhaps there is some missing compositional characteristics in our statistical models that might better explain the trends in these areas?[4] To test this, we

---

[4] The presence of spatial clustering (or autocorrelation) in the models invalidates key assumptions associated with OLS models: that error terms are not correlated and that observations are independent of each other. The first step to dealing with this is to identify other variables that could be included in the model that could eradicate (or at least reduce) this spatial clustering and therein better account for the trends seen in Merseyside, Lincolnshire, and other anomalous areas.

have executed the same regression models used in Chapter 4 for the 2017 and 2019 general elections but including some key additional variables:[5]

1) **Union membership (regional-level)**: A regional-level measure of union membership in 2015 has been included as constituency-level information is not available (Office for National Statistics 2016). Union membership has long been associated with support for left-wing parties (Leigh 2005; Gray and Caul 2000) and membership in Merseyside is particularly high: in 2015, the proportion of unionized employees in the region was 32.5%, compared to 24.7% for the United Kingdom and 23.0% for England (Office for National Statistics 2016). In fact, Merseyside, of all regions, had the highest proportion of employees (37.0%) whose pay was affected by collective agreement in 2015. In contrast, in the East Midlands and West Midlands—two areas where Labour have more recently under-performed—only 23.1% and 25.6% of employees had union membership.

2) **Public sector workforce**: A significant body of literature has emphasized the importance of a production sector cleavage that divides voters along two axes—public sector and private sector employees (Dunleavy 1980a, 1980b; Jensen et al. 2009)—the former being more supportive of left-wing parties and the latter right-wing parties. The statistic used here is the proportion of employees employed in the public sector (Office for National Statistics 2017a). In 2019 across the Merseyside, 23.0% of employees were employed in the public sector, compared to 16.6% of employees in England and Wales as a whole and only 13.1% in Lincolnshire (excluding Lincoln and North East Lincolnshire).

3) **Catholic population (proxy)**: In the North West, the broader region in which Merseyside sits, Catholics were estimated to make up 15.3% of the total population in 2016—the highest regional percentage in England and Wales (Bullivant 2016, p. 7). Perhaps unsurprisingly, given a quarter of Ireland's population—2 million people—came either to or through Liverpool in the 1840s during the potato famine (Sykes et al. 2013, p. 5), the proportion of Roman Catholics in the city today has been described as 'exceptional' (Davie 1993).

Since the Second World War, there has been significant evidence of a long-term party-denominational linkage between Catholics and Labour, albeit

---

[5] Two additional variables are not outlined here for brevity. They are Rural/Urban Classification (Dept for Environment, Food, and Rural Affairs 2009), rather than previous models which used the proportion not employed in agriculture and university entry rates from UCAS (2016).

one that is possibly declining (Clements 2017). As the census does not cover denominations of Christianity, a proxy measure is used in each constituency of the proportion of all schools—nursery, primary, and secondary—that are affiliated to the Catholic Church by merging separate data sources for England and Wales (Department for Education 2017; Welsh Government 2018).

Tables 6.3 and 6.4 show the proportion of schools that are Catholic in each constituency across Merseyside and Lincolnshire respectively, with pronounced differences. In Merseyside constituencies, the mean proportion of schools that are Catholic is 27.8% versus a mean of 8.8% for England and Wales and just 1.5% in Lincolnshire (excluding Lincoln). Table 6.5 lists the

Table 6.3 Proportion of schools affiliated to the Catholic Church by constituency in Merseyside

Constituency	Catholic schools (%)
Birkenhead	25
Bootle	34.9
Garston and Halewood	35.9
Knowsley	37.8
Liverpool Riverside	30.8
Liverpool Walton	28.6
Liverpool Wavertree	26.2
Liverpool West Derby	44.7
Sefton Central	27.5
Southport	17.2
St Helens North	28.6
St Helens South and Whiston	33.3
Wallasey	18.8
Wirral South	14.3
Wirral West	13.9

Table 6.4 Proportion of schools affiliated to the Catholic Church by constituency in Lincolnshire (excluding Lincoln and North East Lincolnshire)

Constituency	Catholic schools (%)
Boston and Skegness	2.1
Gainsborough	0
Grantham and Stamford	3.4
Louth and Horncastle	0
Sleaford and North Hykeham	1.6
South Holland and The Deepings	2

Table 6.5 The twenty constituencies in England and Wales with the highest proportion of schools that are affiliated to the Catholic Church

Constituency	Catholic schools (%)
Liverpool West Derby*	44.7
Knowsley*	37.8
Garston and Halewood*	35.9
Bootle*	34.9
St Helens South and Whiston*	33.3
Liverpool Riverside*	30.8
Liverpool Walton*	28.6
St Helens North*	28.6
Sefton Central*	27.5
Ribble Valley*	27.4
Wigan	26.3
Liverpool Wavertree*	26.2
Birkenhead*	25.0
Halton	25.0
Jarrow	25.0
Makerfield	24.4
Newcastle upon Tyne Central	23.8
Blaydon	23.7
Stockton North	23.7
Wythenshawe and Sale East	23.7

Note: * denotes Merseyside constituencies

twenty constituencies in the country with the highest proportion of Catholic schools. Twelve of the top twenty and nine of the top ten are located in Merseyside.

Compared to the original statistical models executed in Chapter 4, there is a slight improvement in the extent to which the variance in the dependent variables—Labour and Conservative vote shares—is 'explained' by the models incorporating these new variables. The proportion of Catholic schools, union membership, and public sector employment are all positive predictors of Labour vote share at the constituency level. Catholic schools and union membership are also negatively associated with the Conservative vote share.

But to what extent have the models become more accurate at predicting Labour and Conservative vote shares in Merseyside and Lincolnshire? Table 6.6 and Table 6.7 summarize the mean standardized residual values across Merseyside and Lincolnshire (excluding Lincoln) constituencies for the original Labour and Conservative models (from Chapter 4) and the new models (with additional variables) in 2017 and 2019.[6] Remember that

[6] The two most recent elections are chosen here for analysis in part because historical, constituency-level data is not publicly available for these additional variables used in the models.

Table 6.6 Mean standardized residual values across Merseyside and Lincolnshire for old and new models predicting Labour vote share

Year	Region	Old model	New model
2019	Merseyside	2.3	1.8
	Lincolnshire	−0.8	−0.5
2017	Merseyside	2	1.4
	Lincolnshire	−1.1	−0.8

Table 6.7 Mean standardized residual values across Merseyside and Lincolnshire for old and new models predicting Conservative vote share

Year	Region	Old model	New model
2019	Merseyside	−1.5	−1.3
	Lincolnshire	1.4	1
2017	Merseyside	−1.3	−1.2
	Lincolnshire	1.4	1

a positive mean standardized value means the party's vote over-performs the model prediction and a negative value means it under-performs it. The 'change: proximity to zero' column shows whether, by including additional variables, the new mean residual value was closer to zero, and by how much so. In all cases (i.e. in both regions, at both elections and for both parties), the new models had mean residual values that were closer to zero. It is therefore clear that, by including variables such as the proportion of Catholic schools and trade union membership, the models became a little more accurate at predicting the under- and over-performances of both parties across these two regions. However, the improvements are small. In particular, the models still significantly under-predict Labour vote shares and over-predict Conservative support in Merseyside, and they still significantly under-predict Conservative vote shares across Lincolnshire.

Space (and place) matters

The most clear-cut finding from this analysis is that, when seeking to understand the relationships between sociodemographic characteristics and electoral outcomes, space matters. The presence of clustering in the 1979 and 2019 models confirms Tobler's (1970) first law of geography: places that are near each other, both in terms of vote shares or the under- or over-performance of either party, are more similar than places that are far away. While the composition of constituencies, including any measure of how 'left behind' they might be, can accurately predict vote shares across England and Wales generally, there remains a spatial structure to the data in which specific regions under- or out- perform model predictions. At the regional level, the combination of clustering in both vote shares and model under- and over-predicting of vote shares is most noticeable in Merseyside and Lincolnshire. This chapter has identified these two areas as Labour and Conservative strongholds, or 'heartlands'. For Labour, this is a significant shift—their dominance has moved over the last few decades from the coal-fields of the North, Midlands, and Wales to big cities, and more specifically in terms of out-performing demographic predictions, Merseyside. This offers a clear challenge to any idea of a cohesive Red Wall, since Merseyside, Leeds, and Manchester are on entirely different political trajectories to the former coalfields of Yorkshire and the Midlands.

While we have identified new strongholds for Labour and the Conservatives, the mechanism behind this spatial clustering of support remains unclear. What are the unaccounted-for characteristics—shared across constituency boundaries—that are impacting upon aggregated voting behaviour? Indeed, even accounting for the Catholic population—often used as an explanation for Labour's recent stronghold on Merseyside—composition cannot account for Labour's dominance. A better understanding of this mechanism is gained, we believe, through the qualitative analysis presented in our next chapter (see Chapter 7), where we consider the shared cultural, historical, and political characteristics across these two divergent regions of Merseyside and Lincolnshire. In short, just as this chapter shows that *space* matters, understanding why involves an in-depth exploration of the unique characteristics of each *place*.

Appendix

Table A6.1 Regression summaries of the new OLS models predicting Labour vote shares at the 2019 and 2017 general elections

Dependent variables:	Labour 2019 vote share	Labour 2017 vote share
Constant	15.800***	26.400***
	(5.970)	(5.620)
Unemployment rate	0.515	0.192
	(0.336)	(0.316)

Continued

Table A6.1 *Continued*

Dependent variables:	Labour 2019 vote share	Labour 2017 vote share
Manufacturing	−0.423***	−0.316***
	(0.118)	(0.112)
Social renters	−0.035	0.026
	(0.068)	(0.064)
Degree-level qualifications	0.398***	0.058
	(0.090)	(0.082)
Secure employment (residual)	−1.330***	−2.480***
	(0.446)	(0.417)
Aged 16–29	0.240**	0.257***
	(0.103)	(0.096)
Aged 65+	−0.777***	−1.060***
	(0.150)	(0.142)
Ethnic diversity	0.235***	0.163***
	(0.036)	(0.033)
Poor health	2.130***	3.340***
	(0.409)	(0.383)
Distance to nearest cosmopolitan local authority	1.430	0.532
	(0.995)	(0.936)
Distance to nearest university	−10.300***	−11.900***
	(2.650)	(2.500)
Small urban area (reference: major urban)	0.562	0.789
	(1.030)	(0.969)
Semi-rural/rural (reference: major urban)	−0.547	−0.738
	(0.899)	(0.847)
University entry rate	−0.224***	−0.048
	(0.077)	(0.069)
Public sector	0.109**	0.088**
	(0.045)	(0.042)
Catholic schools	0.439***	0.389***
	(0.057)	(0.053)
Trade union membership	0.461***	0.417***
	(0.098)	(0.092)
Third party vote share	−0.639***	−0.621***
	(0.038)	(0.036)
N	572	572
Adjusted R^2	0.852	0.873

Note: * $p<0.1$, ** $p<0.05$, *** $p<0.01$

Table A6.2 Regression summaries of the new OLS models predicting Conservative vote shares at the 2019 and 2017 general elections

Dependent variables	Conservative 2019 vote share	Conservative 2017 vote share
Constant	86.200***	74.900***
	(6.680)	(5.380)
Unemployment rate	−0.611	−0.471
	(0.375)	(0.302)
Manufacturing employment	0.859***	0.709***
	(0.132)	(0.107)
Social renters	0.017	0.019
	(0.076)	(0.061)
Degree-level qualifications	−0.471***	−0.119
	(0.100)	(0.079)
Secure employment (residual)	1.840***	2.140***
	(0.499)	(0.399)
Aged 16–29	−0.290**	−0.332***
	(0.115)	(0.092)
Aged 65+	1.160***	1.160***
	(0.167)	(0.136)
Ethnic diversity	−0.122***	−0.133***
	(0.040)	(0.032)
Poor health	−3.640***	−3.960***
	(0.458)	(0.367)
Distance to nearest cosmopolitan local authority	−1.990*	−1.610*
	(1.110)	(0.896)
Distance to nearest university	11.900***	7.150***
	(2.960)	(2.400)
Small urban area (reference: major urban)	−2.800**	−1.560*
	(1.150)	(0.927)
Semi-rural/rural (reference: major urban)	−0.339	0.504
	(1.010)	(0.811)
University entry rate	0.107	0.098
	(0.086)	(0.066)
Public sector	−0.081	−0.064
	(0.051)	(0.040)
Catholic schools	−0.269***	−0.175***
	(0.063)	(0.051)
Trade union membership	−0.870***	−0.757***
	(0.110)	(0.088)
Third party vote share	−0.129***	−0.254***
	(0.043)	(0.035)
N	572	572
Adjusted R^2	0.781	0.838

Note: * p<0.1, ** p<0.05, p<0.01

7

Why place matters

Insights from Merseyside and Lincolnshire

As we showed in the previous chapter, two areas—Merseyside and Lincolnshire—stand out as places where election results do not fit with expectations given their compositional characteristics. Many areas of Merseyside have significant ageing, largely white, working-class populations and an under-representation of graduates. Elsewhere, these demographically left behind characteristics have been associated with a decline in Labour support and a rise in Conservative support. Yet Labour leads over the Conservatives have actually grown across Merseyside, such that the party out-performed modelled predictions based on constituency composition by an average of over 16 percentage points at the 2019 general election. Similarly, while the Conservatives should expect to do well in predominantly rural Lincolnshire given its demographic profile overall, towns such as Boston and Skegness have significant levels of urban poverty and precarious employment that, unlike in other areas, seem to do little to reduce their vote or increase Labour's support. In fact, in 2019, the Conservative vote share in Lincolnshire[1] was almost 11 points higher than predicted by our statistical models.

In this chapter, we present qualitative case studies of those two areas, drawing on interviews with local political actors and experts who consider the place-based factors that might explain the electoral over-performance of Labour on Merseyside and the dominance of the Conservatives in Lincolnshire. Several key questions are considered. If Labour's over-performance in Merseyside and the Conservative over-performance in Lincolnshire are caused by hitherto unaccounted for regional characteristics, what are these? How much of a role can be attributed to something unique in the ascendant cultures of these areas? Or might further explanations be found in the organization and activities of the main political parties? These questions cannot be answered in a quantitative manner alone. Instead, in this

---

[1] As elsewhere in the book, 'Lincolnshire' is used to refer to constituencies in the county of Lincolnshire, except Lincoln and those falling in North East Lincolnshire (constituencies around Scunthorpe and Grimsby).

The Changing Electoral Map of England and Wales. Jamie Furlong and Will Jennings, Oxford University Press. © Jamie Furlong and Will Jennings (2024). DOI: 10.1093/9780191943331.003.0007

chapter, answers are sought through qualitative data from elite interviews, the iterative exploration and observation of constituencies within the regions by the authors, and supplementary information from secondary sources. A 'place-based' approach is adopted to better understand the local contextual factors that shape the unusual political geography of these regions. By identifying these areas through spatial analysis and then attempting to explain their atypical political trajectories through in-depth qualitative methods, this research moves far beyond most studies in British electoral geography. We show that to understand Britain's electoral geography, it is necessary to appreciate the importance of local/regional identities, culture, and histories, as well as dominant narratives that shape the way electors understand their local areas. To put it more simply, there is something more than just demographics to the evolution of electoral geography.[2]

The view from the ground

Interviews with people who are actively engaged in local politics in these two regions may help illuminate why these areas are so markedly different in their politics from each other and from the rest of England and Wales. Exploring how local activists, elected representatives, journalists, and experts make sense of their local politics allows us to start to account for what is distinctive, from the perspective of those at the hard edge of politics, about these regions and their people. We conducted semi-structured interviews entirely on location in Merseyside in July 2018 and in Lincolnshire in November 2018. This was in the aftermath of the 2017 general election in a period in which there were growing internal divisions in Theresa May's Conservative government as they struggled to get sufficient support to push a Brexit deal through parliament. It was, however, prior to either the low point for the government of May 2019 or its resurgence in the polls after Boris Johnson took over as leader and led the Conservatives to victory in the December 2019 general election. Labour, on the other hand, despite surprisingly denying the Conservatives a majority at the 2017 general election, was led by the increasingly unpopular Jeremy Corbyn. Although both parties had unpopular leaders and were struggling with internal divisions, it predates the collapse in their support in spring 2019. In both interview time periods, the two parties were neck-and-neck, polling around or just below 40% of the electorate.

---

[2] Of course, our models based on sociodemographic composition explain a substantial (indeed, an impressive) amount of variation in electoral support across England and Wales, but they nevertheless do not capture the degree to which the parties over- and under-perform their expected vote in Merseyside and Lincolnshire.

Table 7.1 provides an overview of the interviews conducted, including information about the link to politics of each interviewee. Interviewees were sought from across the political spectrum in each area, as in both areas we were keen to understand not just why one party was over-achieving, but also why the other was under-achieving. All interviewees are referred to in the text by their first names only.

Table 7.1 Summary of the interviewees and their connection to politics in Merseyside/Lincolnshire[a]

Region	Name of interviewee	Role and/or connection to local politics
Merseyside	Dr Stuart Wilks-Heeg	Academic in the Department of Politics at the University of Liverpool. He has written a recent article on Labour's electoral success in Merseyside's suburbs, with a focus on Sefton Central.
	Councillor Tony Brough	Conservative councillor for the Ainsdale ward on Sefton council (since May 2018). He was previously a councillor between 2000 and 2007.
	Claire Hamilton	Political reporter for BBC Radio Merseyside since October 2012.
	Dr David Jeffery	Researcher in the Department of Politics at the University of Liverpool since 2017. He has written a Ph.D. thesis examining the causes of Conservative decline in Liverpool and is also active in the local party. In 2022 he became Chair of City of Liverpool Conservatives.
	Sheila Murphy	Labour activist organizing political and community campaigns in Liverpool. Previously, she was the Senior Regional Director of the Labour Party in the North (1997–2009).
Lincolnshire	Councillor Robert (Rob) Parker	Labour councillor for the Carholme ward. He has twice been leader of the Labour group on Lincolnshire County Council (1991–93, 1997–2013) and was leader of the Labour-Liberal Democrat Lincolnshire council (1993–7).
	Councillor Angela Mary Newton	Independent councillor for Spalding West ward since 2013. Previously a councillor for the same ward between 1981 and 1993. Opposition leader on South Holland District Council.
	Councillor Philip (Phil) Dilks	Labour councillor representing the Deeping St James ward on South Kesteven District Council since 2011. Previously a councillor on Lincolnshire County Council. Former journalist and Labour Party press officer.

Continued

Table 7.1 *Continued*

Region	Name of interviewee	Role and/or connection to local politics
	Councillor Tom Ashton	East Lindsey District Conservative Councillor for Sibsey and Stickney ward since 2015. Also elected to the Lincolnshire County Council ward of Tattershall Castle in 2017.
	Paul Kenny[b]	Previous councillor on Boston borough councillor (2011–15) and former Mayor of Boston 13–2014. Labour Party candidate for Boston and Skegness constituency in 2017.
	Pam Kenny[b]	Labour Party activist in Boston
	Jane Hancock[b]	Labour Party activist in Boston
	Keith Hancock[b]	Labour Party activist in Boston

[a]This study was approved by the Faculty of Social Sciences Research Ethics Committee at the University of Southampton (Ethics/ERGO Number: 42490). Interviewees gave written consent for their real names and job titles to be used.
[b]Originally, an interview was planned only with Paul Kenny, but on arriving at Paul's home, there were other Labour activists present, who wished to take part in the study. It then became a focus group with Paul Kenny, Pam Kenny, Jane Hancock, and Keith Hancock.

Merseyside: Labour's new heartlands

'Even in North Korea, you still have a second party': Labour's dominance on Merseyside

Whilst many of the inner-city parliamentary constituencies close to Liverpool city centre have long been Labour-dominated in general elections, some of the more suburban seats have switched over time from being Conservative under Margaret Thatcher to Labour under Tony Blair, Gordon Brown, Ed Miliband, and Jeremy Corbyn. The cause is not related to inward or outward migration (i.e. some kind of self-selection into or out of the area) since constituencies in suburban Merseyside have had some of the lowest gross migration rates in England and Wales over recent decades. This not only makes the area particularly unique but also offers some tentative counter-evidence to the 'Big Sort' thesis (Bishop and Cushing 2008)—that is, the idea that the regional political landscape is changing largely because of some kind of self-selection of individuals into the area.[3]

In the nineteenth and early twentieth century, Liverpool itself—as a busy port city—was home to widespread Conservative support from an

[3] Gallego et al. (2016) find that while there is some evidence of self-selection of individuals into parliamentary constituencies with like-minded people, this is due to non-political factors.

amalgamation of working-class Protestants concerned about Irish migration and middle-class monarchists (Belchem 2006). Indeed, Stuart describes how in the 1950s, unlike other large British cities, Liverpool maintained 'a very strong tradition of working-class conservativism' with 'the constituency Labour parties in the north end of Liverpool . . . the smallest in the country in the 1940s, 1950s in terms of membership'. The struggles that the Labour Party faced in the area are well documented by Davies (1996) and by Jeffery (2023a), who notes that, between 1945 and 1972, the Conservatives maintained their working-class base through political socialization—in short, the children of Protestants were likely to be socialized into supporting the Conservatives, even if the link between party and religion was already in decline post-Second World War.

In Liverpool itself, it was not until the 1970s and 1980s that Labour became dominant in national elections, whilst in local elections in the fifty years after Labour first took control of Liverpool city council in 1956, the party only held overall control for twenty-three (Wilks-Heeg 2019). Beyond the core city, the Conservatives were broadly dominant until the 1997 general election, when Labour took control of suburban constituencies such as Sefton Central and Wirral West—which in 2017 and 2019 were some of the unlikeliest safe Labour seats in the country.

Labour's dominance across the whole of the city today is nonetheless staggering—a point David emphatically makes: 'Even in North Korea, you still have a second party'. In inner-city areas of Liverpool, there is essentially no credible opposition in general elections whilst Labour's support is so deeply engrained: 'My uncle . . . a woodbine-smoking bricklayer from Bootle would vote for Corbyn every day of the week . . . He also voted for Tony Blair . . . He wouldn't vote any other way' (Tony). What is even more remarkable than Labour's consistent support amongst an older, white working class who have deserted them in other areas is their success in largely middle-class, white, suburban parts of Merseyside, such as the Sefton Central and Wirral West constituencies. Tony sums this up rather well: 'in Freshfield . . . per capita of the population there are more millionaires there than anywhere in the country. For them to vote Labour is bonkers but they are'. The suburban wealth of Sefton Central is clear from the wide, tree-lined streets flanked by large, red-brick Victorian houses, vast golf courses, newer gated homes, lawn tennis clubs, private schools, and a large private park (see Figures 7.1–7.4). It simply does not 'feel Labour'—this is not the young, educated, middle-class demographic that has swung towards the party in recent elections; it is older, white, and wealthy.

Figure 7.1 A row of independent shops in Crosby

Photograph © Jamie Furlong

Figure 7.2 A not atypical suburban street of large, detached homes and big gardens

Photograph © Jamie Furlong

Figure 7.3 One of many gated houses in the area

Photograph © Jamie Furlong

Figure 7.4 The grand entrance to Sacred Heart Catholic College—a Catholic comprehensive school in Crosby

Photograph © Jamie Furlong

Until 1997, these wealthier constituencies of Wirral South, Wirral West, and Crosby (which became part of Sefton Central in 2010) were generally strong areas for the Conservatives. In fact, when Labour won them in 1997, 'Tony Blair was surprised, as was Cherie who was actually from here [Sefton Central]' (Stuart). What is even more surprising is that, whereas in other areas of the country, similar suburban seats with older, white, wealthy homeowners have moved back towards the Conservatives since the height of the New Labour period, in Merseyside this process has barely occurred. We next explore possible reasons for this electoral anomaly as well as that of Merseyside more generally.

The Conservative Party and Liverpool's 'managed decline' in the 1980s

In the 1980s, Liverpool suffered from a poor reputation based on years of population decline, urban decay, economic decline, deindustrialization, and political mismanagement. After the Hillsborough and Heysel disasters, dock strikes, Toxteth riots, and local political infighting, 'many commentators simply wrote Liverpool off', labelling the city 'a huge infuriating problem which would not go away' (Crosby 2014, p. 65). While some outsiders may have callously attributed blame to the people of Liverpool, the dominant narrative within the city was that Margaret Thatcher and the Conservatives were at fault. Sheila explained that 'as far as they [the people of Liverpool] are concerned, the Tories tried to destroy it [Liverpool]. They tried to break them as people and it will take a long, long time for them to be forgiven'.

The blame attributed to the Conservatives for this troubled period in the city's history has only strengthened over time, most obviously following the publication of government documents in 2011 revealing that Margaret Thatcher's Chancellor, Geoffrey Howe, had questioned whether Liverpool should be abandoned to 'managed decline' (Parker 2019). As Claire explains: 'That's the narrative that has come back again, that the Conservatives would have seen us fail, that they would have been happy if Liverpool hadn't come back again'. The local newspaper, *The Liverpool Echo*, generally regarded as left-leaning and Labour-supporting, 'made sure as many people as possible knew about that story', Stuart noted.

While Liverpool was becoming increasingly associated with the Labour Party, many residents in suburban areas engaged in an 'act of disassociation', by declaring that they were from Lancashire not Merseyside or Liverpool, because of the city's negative image (Benbough-Jackson and Davies 2011,

p. 7). This disassociation was also political—voting Conservative was a way of enacting a political identity that was, as Stuart explains, in stark opposition to the Militant-led, Labour-controlled city centre during this time period.

The rise of the Liberals as challengers and disruptors

While Thatcher's reputation on Merseyside certainly harmed the Conservatives locally, the erosion of the party's support began well before she became leader. In fact, it was in 1972 that the Conservatives lost control of Liverpool City Council to Labour, in part as a result of their voters moving to the increasingly popular Liberal Party (Jeffery 2023a). Indeed, the 1970s and 1980s were marked by increasing support for the Liberal Party and subsequently the Liberal Democrats, across Merseyside. Through their innovative use of 'pavement politics', the Liberals built up support, both amongst those unhappy with the radical Labour council and then amongst those unhappy with Heath and then Thatcher's national Conservative government (Jeffery 2017; Wilks-Heeg 2019). The Liberals became the main party of opposition across large areas of Merseyside, with the consequence of reduced Conservative vote shares.

For many voters who had previously voted for the Conservatives, support for the Liberal Party acted as a kind of 'gateway' to New Labour. Wilks-Heeg (2019, p. 8) explains that, with Labour's move to occupy the centre ground of British politics under Tony Blair, 'Voters who had supported the Alliance in the 1980s had little difficulty switching to New Labour in 1997'. In Crosby, for example, Stuart notes that the surprise SDP victory in the 1981 by-election created a 'kind of disruptive effect' in which it took 'a chunk out of the Conservative vote long-term which they never recovered'.

Liverpool's regeneration and the increasing connection with its suburbs

Alongside the Liberals facilitating a shift in support from the Conservatives to Labour, other explanations for this shift can be found in the regeneration of Liverpool and its subsequent changing image and relationships with its hinterlands. Liverpool city centre has been transformed since the early 1990s, with significant investment, regeneration projects, and rapid population growth, particularly in affluent young professionals. Such is the change that, 'no longer stigmatised, Liverpool itself is the region's "unique selling point", its cultural and "historic" core' (Belchem 2006, p. xix). Although scholars such as McAteer (2017) and Wilks-Heeg and North (2004) have questioned the extent to which the urban transformation has addressed social and economic inequalities and included existing poorer residents, it is unquestionable that perceptions of the city from the outside have changed. Most notably, the desire to disassociate from Merseyside amongst residents of wealthier, more distant suburbs appears to have subsided somewhat.

Every interviewee agreed that suburban Merseyside has become more willing to be associated with an increasingly 'cosmopolitan' Liverpool/Merseyside and less with Lancashire or Cheshire. Initially, according to Stuart, people were quite resistant to the creation of a Merseyside County Council in the more outlying areas, something that perhaps would not be the case today: 'when I first arrived here in the late 1990s . . . people were very proud on the Wirral at that time that their postcodes were switching from Liverpool to Chester because there was a sense of prestige and higher status and so on. I don't think they feel that way now'. Winning the bid for the European Capital of Culture in 2008 only enhanced the city's image amongst people in the suburbs, according to David:

When Liverpool became cool again, the Capital of Culture in 2008, people who were living in areas like Sefton, like Crosby like the Wirral were less likely to get offended if they went on holiday and they told someone they were from the Wirral. 'Oh you're a Scouser'. They're not gonna go, 'no I'm from the Wirral'. They'll be like 'yeah actually I'm from Liverpool'.

Survey research in Sefton in 2004 found that 51% of respondents felt they belonged very or fairly strongly to Merseyside compared to 35% to Lancashire (Ipsos Mori 2004a). A similar report on the Wirral—historically part of Cheshire—came to similar conclusions (Ipsos Mori 2004b). For Stuart, 'people have developed this new relationship with the city, a kind of ease with the city that wasn't there before', that has enabled a more 'cosmopolitan' or metropolitan identity to push out from the core of the city into its suburbs. He explains that this spreading of a more 'cosmopolitan' identity is likely to have political consequences:

It changes how people see their relationship with the city and probably changes how they see themselves in some cases. A lot of this is about identity and what they feel comfortable with and with Labour being much more the party of the metropolis, I think that this is feeding into people's political identities.

Labour's increasing cosmopolitanism appears to have coincided with an increasing desire amongst residents across outer Merseyside to associate with precisely that—a 'cosmopolitan' city. Claire also explains that the establishment of a city region and associated mayor has reflected and contributed to this increasing connectedness between the core city and places such as Southport, with a greater sense of political unity: the 'city region identity has maybe shaped some of the suburbs' such that now 'there is this kind of unified, coherent zone now that is represented by a Labour person'.

Football, Hillsborough, and The Sun

There are further interrelated factors unique to Merseyside that have shaped its political trajectory: the Hillsborough disaster, the boycott of *The Sun* newspaper, and the relationship between football and politics. On 15 April 1989, 96 Liverpool football fans died in a crush at Hillsborough football stadium. In spite of the Taylor Report highlighting several critical failings by South Yorkshire police, there was significant collusion amongst politicians, the media, and the police to ensure that most of the blame was attributed to the behaviour of Liverpool fans, despite no evidence to support this (Taylor 1990). The 1985 Heysel disaster for which Liverpool fans were held broadly responsible may have clouded the judgement of politicians and the media. Conservative Prime Minister Margaret Thatcher and her government were condemned on Merseyside for allowing the fabrication of police witness statements and for failing to act on the Taylor Report. Indeed, Thatcher has since received significant criticism from politicians, the national media, and academics for the antipathy she showed towards football and football supporters (Williams 2012) and for her support of a supposedly partisan police force (Dunt 2012). One consequence, for Stuart, was widespread anti-Conservativism across the whole region:

> Almost everybody who has lived here for a long time knows somebody who was there and went through the trauma or somebody who died. So as the truth emerged in the 1990s onwards, that did I think feed quite strongly into this anti-Conservative mentality. And that wasn't just at the core of the city of Liverpool, that was really right out into the suburbs. There is a Hillsborough memorial in Crosby, there is one in the Wirral.

The Hillsborough disaster 'stitch-up' is also associated with *The Sun* newspaper, which had a headline on the following day falsely accusing fans of pick-pocketing victims and urinating on and attacking police. There has since been an orchestrated boycott of the right-wing tabloid newspaper across Merseyside and the banning of its journalists from Liverpool FC's stadium and its training ground. The strength of feeling should not be underestimated, as Stuart explains, 'I've lived here since 1998 and I've only seen someone reading *The Sun* newspaper twice . . . and in the last five years there has been a boycott of places that were even selling it so places would refuse to sell it'. According to David, '*The Sun* boycott seems to be getting stronger . . newsagents on this road has been selling it . . . let's go round and give them a piece of our mind" . . . You can see that spreading out to the Wirral, to Knowsley to Sefton'.

For David, the political effect of the boycott is likely to be most pronounced on Conservative support amongst Merseyside's working class: 'you've basically taken away the key working-class, right-wing voice in the media'. Another recent study found evidence that the drop in readership of *The Sun* led to a significant increase in pro-EU attitudes in Merseyside during the 1990s (Foos and Bischof 2022). It seems likely to have also had at least some impact on support for a broadly Eurosceptic Conservative Party in the region, particularly as the Conservatives have generally been associated with the denigrated newspaper and Labour with the Justice for the 96 campaign to hold accountable those responsible for Hillsborough. Stuart emphasizes this link: 'it was really only when Labour were in power that the issue was then looked at again with any degree of seriousness'. This undoubtedly helped forge a distinction between Labour and Conservative stances on the issue, at least in the minds of supporters.

The association between Liverpool football club and anti-establishment politics may have been amplified by Hillsborough, but the broadly left-leaning culture of the club has been long-standing. These political values arguably became closely intertwined during the 1960s and 1970s with the club's identity under manager Bill Shankly. Shankly was a staunch socialist, originally from a small mining community in Scotland. He became adored by Liverpool fans both for guiding the club to become the most successful in England, but also for his socialist principles, which fans believed he acted out when he gave tickets away for free and paid for supporters' train tickets. Half a century later, Liverpool fans continue to act out their own political identities by booing the national anthem and the King's coronation and, in the run-up to the 2017 general election, displaying banners adorned with Jeremy Corbyn's face in their famous Kop (Figure 7.6).

The presence of foodbanks at both Anfield (Liverpool's stadium) and Goodison Park (Everton's stadium) also acts as a link between the football clubs and the local Labour Party, at the same time as solidifying the image of the clubs and city as socialistic: 'you've got football supporters foodbank organizing which is done at Liverpool and Everton and that is

Figure 7.5 A banner declaring 'we're not English we are Scouse' at Anfield, Liverpool Football Club

© Andrew Teebay/Liverpool Echo

Figure 7.6 Liverpool fans unveil a banner supporting Jeremy Corbyn during the Premier League match at Anfield, Liverpool Football Club, Sunday 7 May 2017

© PA Images/Alamy

all, I think it's Walton CLP (Constituency Labour Party) members that have started or they're certainly heavily involved' (Claire). Indeed, the Fans Supporting Foodbanks initiative was part-founded by Ian Byrne, who subsequently became Labour MP for the Liverpool West Derby constituency at the 2019 general election. For some supporters, Liverpool FC is simply not an apolitical football club, as a recent fan's blog post confirms:

> Liverpool FC, befitting the city they're based in, have always been a club you can't fully separate from politics. The city's history as a bastion of the working class, of unions, and of anti-Tory sentiment that peaked during the Thatcher years and has remained strong ever since informs the club's local fanbase. (Chomyn 2017)

Merseyside exceptionalism: performing an anti-Conservative or pro-Labour Scouse identity

> 'An oppositional culture often finds its raison d'être in that which it opposes'.
>
> **(Benbough-Jackson and Davies 2011, p. 2)**

> 'The whole literature on Liverpool is "Liverpool is exceptional, it is a place beyond England". It's bollocks! But it's part of the popular conception'.
>
> **(David)**

All of the factors that we have discussed here have contributed to a pre-existing perception of Liverpool's exceptionalism: that the city and its inhabitants are somehow different to other cities and their populations in northern England. The social, political, and cultural peculiarities of Liverpool and its past are, alongside critical examinations of any notion of exceptionalism, widely discussed in academic literature (see Croll 2003; Belchem 2006; Powell 2007; Ball 2017; Jeffery 2023a, 2023b). Whether Liverpool's difference is real or imagined, there is a strong Scouse identity that many people understand to be loosely constructed in opposition to notions of the establishment, Englishness, and conservativism. It is a widely held belief that, for many people on Merseyside, their Scouse identity is more important than their English identity (Millward and Rookwood 2011). Indeed, alongside the 'we are not English we are Scouse' banner at Anfield (Figure 7.5), there is an inscription on a pillar in the Museum of Liverpool with a quote from the late politician Margaret Simey: 'The magic of Liverpool is that it isn't England'. Stuart identifies this clear sense of difference with other English cities as people frequently repeat on Merseyside that 'Liverpool has more in common with Marseille or Naples than it does with Manchester or Sheffield or Leeds'. However, the anti-Englishness of Scouse identity is contested in recent research by Jeffery (2023b), which showed little evidence for the 'Scouse not English' trope, but rather that the two identities actually coexisted amongst many Merseyside residents.

It may even be the case that a 'cosmopolitan' Liverpool today is defined by its residents in relation to a more 'introspective and parochial Lancashire' (Benbough-Jackson and Davies 2011, p. 6). This fits with Liverpool's history as a diverse port city and a commonly held narrative that the city was and still is a place of openness where difference is accepted and celebrated (Phillips and Brown 2011). While this self-defined openness and oppositional identity may manifest in a less Eurosceptic attitude and a rejection of English nation-alism, the Conservatives may also be negatively associated with notions of both Englishness and the establishment more broadly. Tony explains this connection: 'Part of Liverpudlian psychology is to challenge the establish-ment . . . And so the Conservatives will always be seen as the establishment party as so to challenge the Conservatives would be seen to be quite sensible'. Voting Labour or at least being anti-Conservative may be, just like the accent or supporting Liverpool or Everton FC, a way of performing Scouse iden-tity. David notes how challenging this is for local Conservative activists: 'You could knock on as many doors as you wanted, and you still wouldn't be able to convince enough people on the merit of your argument because it's like a hand on your shoulder stopping you from voting [Conservative] because it goes against your identity'. This idea that Scouse identity is defined and performed in opposition to conservativism was perhaps crystallized in the period of decline during the 1980s:

> In the 80s it did seem like the rest of the country was against Liverpool . . . it was like a self-defence mechanism. If everyone is calling Liverpool a shithole, instead of trying to compete with the rest of the country on these Thatcherite terms of eco-nomic progress and efficiency, we are going to compete on solidarity and on being compassionate. (David)

Claire identified that Labour, much like Catholicism and football may be a positive signifier of Scouse identity:

> I think it goes to the heart of a sort of Scouseness in that it is passionate and it is kind of an emotional connection I think in some ways that people feel that relationship to those things that we've already mentioned—religion and football—and maybe the Labour Party is still part of that for a lot of people.

This leads one to ask: is Scouse identity more strongly connected to being pro-Labour or anti-Conservative? The only study to assess this using survey data with Merseyside residents found that a slightly higher proportion (64%) of self-identifying Scousers felt that 'real' Scousers should not vote for the Conservatives than those who felt that 'real' Scousers should vote Labour (57%) (Jeffery 2023b). Either way, identifying as Scouse was *the most important* factor (above and beyond other demographic and attitudinal characteristics) determining support (or lack of) for both parties, showing its clear structuring effect on voting behaviour in the region.

Local organization of political parties

Inevitably, coinciding with their electoral strengths and weaknesses, the organizational structures and access to resources of the two main parties have diverged. Due to Labour's popularity in Merseyside, they have many more local activists ready to go door-knocking than the Conservatives. The enormous majorities for Labour in inner-city seats mean that many young, enthusiastic activists in Liverpool can campaign in more marginal suburban constituencies: 'if you live in Bootle or Walton or Knowsley you know what your result is going to be but you're looking to Wirral West, Weaver Vale, Southport and you think, "right well we'll go and help out there"' (Claire). Stuart notes that, with a good public transport system across the metropolitan area, 'it's quite easy [for Labour] to move people out to campaign in Southport or the Wirral'.

In contrast, Sheila points out that 'the Tories just haven't got the bodies. On the Wirral the Tories actually employ a company to go out and deliver their leaflets'. This is a result of both their wider unpopularity but also a support base that is increasingly older and less mobile. Tony explained that 'we used to have what often shouldn't be referred to as the blue rinse brigade . . ., well that generation has passed through and there aren't those people coming behind'. As Stuart points out, it is also more difficult to motivate activists to campaign or to stand for election without a strong organizational structure behind them and with the inevitable prospect of losing: 'people don't want to stand for election just to get annihilated. People don't want to campaign. And that kind of spreads outwards I think so the party is by now organizationally very weak right across Merseyside'.

The collapse of the Liberal Democrats and the failure of UKIP

As discussed earlier, the success of the Liberals (via the SDP-Liberal Alliance) in the 1980s acted as a 'gateway' to many people on Merseyside voting Labour in national elections under Tony Blair. In other areas that have populations that are similar to the outskirts of Merseyside—predominantly older and white—many voters have found their way back to their initial home in the Conservatives. In suburban Merseyside, Labour have actually become electorally stronger. Two simultaneous political processes may have contributed to this anomaly. The first is that, in a time period in which the Conservative brand was largely toxic on Merseyside, the Liberal Democrats went into coalition government in 2010 with the Conservative Party led by David Cameron. Sheila notes the effect on local elections:

> With the Lib Dems going into coalition with the Tories, we just hammered them continually . . . The numbers that we [Labour] won by was just ridiculous and that was not a lot to do with the Labour Party but to do with the Lib Dems nationally, working with the Tories because the Tories as you know are just hated.

The second political process that has contributed to this anomaly is the failure of UKIP across Merseyside. At the 2015 general election, whereas elsewhere in the country Labour benefited from the collapse of the Liberal Democrats but simultaneously lost votes to UKIP, across Merseyside the latter process was far less substantial. In fact, despite the largely white, working-class composition of many areas of Merseyside, UKIP struggled to have any political impact. For Tony, this reflects the broad support for multiculturalism across Merseyside: 'People's colour and creed, that's not an issue in my view in Liverpool. We don't have that sort of racial issue . . . You can go up to Yorkshire and find that it's still alive and kicking. Here it isn't'. David similarly locates UKIP's lack of appeal in the self-perception of Liverpool as an open, port city: 'I think it's this identity . . . Liverpool sees itself as this open, welcoming city, we were built on immigration'. Yet, he notes how this self-identification as a multicultural city does not fit with reality of a city with relatively limited ethnic diversity: 'this myth of Liverpool being a melting pot probably contributes to this idea that UKIP aren't doing too well'. Performing the Scouse identity for many people would certainly not consist of voting for a party perceived by some to be parochial, English, and racist.

UKIP's failures across Merseyside in 2015 appears to have had a knock-on effect on election outcomes in 2017. In large parts of England, the Conservatives saw large increases in their vote shares in areas where UKIP were strong in 2015 but subsequently collapsed in 2017 (Heath and Goodwin 2017). For many ex-Labour voters or previous non-voters, UKIP acted as a 'gateway' to subsequently voting for the Conservatives—a party who were endorsing and broadly supportive of Brexit (Mellon et al. 2018). As so few voters moved to UKIP in the first place across Merseyside, this 'gateway' simply did not exist.

Reflections on Merseyside

To summarize, there are many place-based factors that have contributed to the electoral under-performance of the Conservatives and the over-performance of Labour across Merseyside. The widespread anti-conservativism that has become part of Scouse identity seems to have strengthened in the 1980s and 1990s, first when the city suffered from serious economic decline and later as police, media, and government responses to the Hillsborough disaster caused significant anger towards PM Margaret Thatcher and the Conservatives. These feelings appear to have strengthened over time. It is not simply anti-Conservativism but also a pro-Labour orientation, as people suggest the Labour Party is often integral to Scouse identity: 'Somebody told me in Kirkby once . . . that it's like a religion Labour to people. They're Catholic, they vote Labour, they support Everton or Liverpool. Those are things that people identify with' (Claire). Political factors have since reinforced the situation, with the gateway that the Liberals/Liberal Democrats offered as a transition from Conservative to Labour for many voters not subsequently being matched by a UKIP 'gateway' acting in reverse. The challenge for the Conservatives is made greater as Labour's dominance has allowed them to become strongly organized across Merseyside, with many young, enthusiastic activists ready to campaign.

Lincolnshire: agricultural trade unionism to Conservative Party stronghold

'Being a member of Labour in South Holland is like being a member of a Rare Breed Society'

Just as Merseyside has not always been the cradle of the Labour Party that it is today, the history of rural Lincolnshire is not without challenges to economic orthodoxy. In fact, in the 1870s, Lincolnshire was an important area in the agricultural labourers' movement often referred to as the 'revolt of the field' (Dunbabin 1963). Phil identifies that 'historically, this was the home of trade unionism, certainly in the agricultural sector'. That seems quite difficult to believe today, given the dominance of the Conservative Party and the relative insignificance of the Labour Party in general elections across south Lincolnshire. The interviewees representing the Labour Party all emphasized quite how challenging the region is for them, sometimes with humour: 'being a member of Labour in South Holland is like being a member of a Rare Breed Society' (Paul).

The strength of anti-Labour sentiment is so strong that, to appeal to voters, Phil removes any mention of the Labour Party from the boards that people put up in support of him in the local elections: 'I stand as "Fair Deal Phil" to kind of soften the Labour bit. I can't claim that it said "vote Labour"'. In Figure 7.7—a campaign leaflet that Phil used in 2013—the attempt at disassociation from the Labour Party is clear.

The composition of south Lincolnshire is highly unusual in the English context. There is perhaps no other area of England that has such a significant older, white, rural population yet at the same time is predominantly working-class and has a high number of Eastern European migrants (Figure 7.8). Taking Boston and Skegness, for example, in 2011, the constituency was the third furthest away from a university and had the fifth highest proportion of the population employed in precarious forms of employment, the sixth lowest proportion employed in 'cosmopolitan' industries (South Holland and the Deepings had the second lowest), the seventeenth highest proportion employed in agriculture, the second highest proportion employed in routine and semi-routine occupations, and an above average proportion of migrants. Of 572[4] constituencies in England and Wales, according to the measure that we calculated in Chapter 6, Boston and Skegness ranked 24th highest in terms of socio-economic decline between 1979 and 2019. On the same measure, South Holland and the Deepings ranked 147th. Keith summarizes the frustration felt by local Labour Party activists who feel that elsewhere in the country, the poor economic conditions, working-class history, and austerity measures might create more favourable conditions for campaigning:

> The place is falling around people's ears with the hospital, the doctor's, the schools, things like that. Yes, it's caused by central government initially...People can see it's happening but when it comes to voting...you still can't get them to vote Labour!... No matter what happens it's going to be an X for the local Conservative.

---

[4] This is one less than the 573 constituencies of England and Wales as the Speaker's seat has been removed from the analysis.

DSJ Election - Thursday 7am-10pm

DEEPINGS ADVERTISER SAYS:

"Conservatives let us down..."

'Vote Fair Deal Phil Dilks...'

A local businessman has accused the Conservatives of attempting to mislead DSJ voters over the recent Deeping traffic lights debacle.

In this week's Deepings Advertiser, Managing Director Andy Pelling urges DSJ residents to vote Fair Deal Phil Dilks in Thursday's election for a new county councillor.

Mr Pelling played a key role in the campaign to scrap the £1 million traffic light scheme.

Local Conservatives fought to save the scheme which was approved by the Conservative-run council.

But in election leaflets, local Conservatives attempted to claim credit for scrapping the scheme.

Mr Pelling says he would probably vote 'right of centre' in national elections but was upset about claims made by local Conservatives.
He adds: "I feel local people have been let down."

> "In local elections, it's all about the candidate, not the party...
>
> "If you want local people to represent you, vote for Fair Deal Phil Dilks."
>
> Andy Pelling
> Managing Director
> Deepings Advertiser

Figure 7.7   A leaflet used by Phil Dilks in the run up to the 2013 Local Elections in Deeping St James
© Jamie Furlong

Figure 7.8 North Street, Bourne, does not give the impression of an economically thriving area
Photograph © Jamie Furlong

A culture of deference to landowners and farmers

In the nineteenth century, a dominant narrative about rural politics was that rural electors existed in 'deferential communities' and voted in accord with the wishes of their landlords or the primary landowners in the local area who they regarded as economically and socially superior (Moore 1976). This was highly likely prior to the Ballot Act of 1872, which ensured that elections were held by secret ballot, limiting the sway that landowners could have on employees (Newby 1979). In a study of nineteenth-century Lincolnshire's politics, Olney (1973, p. 249) to some extent contested this idea but still concluded that 'the broad but intangible truth is that the "heavy" agriculturalists of Lincolnshire, and particularly the arable farmers, suffered from Conservativism almost as an occupational disease. They seemed to inhale it from the very furrows that they ploughed'. There is certainly something very distinctive about the physical geography of the area (Figure 7.9).

Interviewees associated with the Labour Party were keen to emphasize the persistence of a deference to the 'landed gentry' even today. Phil describes the

Figure 7.9 The unusual geography of the Fens of south Lincolnshire, close to Spalding
Photograph © Jamie Furlong

moment that, as an employee for the *Louth Standard* newspaper, he covered Jeffery Archer's political rally in 1974:

> It was absolutely packed with people wanting to meet Mr Archer and he pulled up, all the other candidates sat on the podium, and we had to wait for Mr Archer, and he came like a bride at a wedding . . . The doors at the back of the hall opened up and this Rolls Royce arrived. Fucking Rolls Royce! . . . And Mr Archer gets out and he comes down the aisle. And as he comes down the aisle people doffed their caps at him.

The extent to which this is typically deference or also protecting one's own economic interests is questionable, as exemplified by numerous stories of farm workers voting Conservative to protect the interests of their landowner but also their own employment:

> It's almost like a feudal system here. Because basically there is no industry other than to do with land work . . . and the ones that are actually working are in fear

of their jobs if they don't vote for their governor. In other words, 'we work on the land, when it comes to voting they're paying my wages, I'm going to vote for them' (Keith).

I've known people who have told me working on the land that the day before the election the foreman or the boss, the farmer, would call all the workers together in the yard and tell them to make sure they got out to vote tomorrow for the Conservatives because if you vote Labour on Thursday you will not have a job on Friday... It's the age of deference . . . and it hasn't entirely gone. (Phil)

Only further local research would determine how dominant the culture of deference described here has been in Lincolnshire and whether it has, beyond anecdote, ever shaped the unusual politics of the area. Nonetheless, socialization plays a key role in the way in which people acquire political values, such that even if deference were never explicitly expressed, growing up and working in an area dominated by agriculture and landowners could lead people to implicitly acquire and express similar values. What is more, the economic incentive to vote the same way as the local landowner/employer may hold more weight in a poorly connected area where there are few other industrial jobs for farm labourers and communities are tightly bonded.

Negative experiences of national and local Labour governance

Just as there was a dominant narrative that the Conservatives failed to support Merseyside in the 1980s, interviewees referred to some voters in Lincolnshire who felt that Tony Blair's Labour government overlooked or were openly antagonistic to the concerns of people in rural areas. Tom explains: 'I don't think the experience of the countryside during the Blair years was one which it is likely to forget in a hurry'. Labour have received significant blame for the ban on fox hunting and the rise in immigration from Eastern Europe in the Boston area: 'I remember the countryside marches, I remember the BSE crisis, and . . . the immigration that we saw at the time, which has had a demonstrable effect on how people vote'. Tom's experience suggested that many voters in Lincolnshire developed a negative, long-lasting impression of the Labour Party that has not disappeared since. A significant portion of this discontent relates to the enlargement of the European Union in 2004 and 2007 and the subsequent increase in the number of Eastern European immigrants in south Lincolnshire:

Lots of people blamed Labour and Tony Blair and Gordon Brown for in 2004 when Germany and other places in Europe put like an 18 month holding situation before they allowed people to come, Gordon and Tony they listened to the Farmers Union and they listened to the CBI who then said to them 'don't put restrictions on people coming' . . . I told them it would be the Achilles heel of the Labour Party and Tony Blair would be known as 'the man who let all the foreigners in'. (Paul)

Paul points out that it is not just the rise in immigration that some residents negatively associated with the Labour Party, but also the introduction of a minimum wage in 1999. The influx of workers from more deprived areas of the country could no longer be relied upon by farmers, as conditions in their own areas improved at the same time as local workers required more substantial pay packets: 'When [the influx of workers] stopped because of better living standards and they got jobs in those [other] areas, they stopped coming. You've got the minimum wage issue and at that stage they were realizing that the only way you could get local labour, you'd have to get labour to come and live in Boston'.

Immigration: a critical issue

Concerns around immigration in south Lincolnshire have been featured extensively in the national media, both relating to the rise in support for UKIP between 2010 and 2015 and subsequently the vote to leave the European Union in June 2016 (e.g. Harris et al. 2015; Chakelian 2016; Jack 2019). The increase in the relative number of migrants in the region—most notably in Boston and in South Holland—was due initially to a large Portuguese population but subsequently was driven primarily by high levels of inward migration of people from Eastern Europe following the expansion of the European Union in 2004 and 2007. In south Lincolnshire, many migrants are employed in agriculture or food processing industries (Robinson and Reeve 2006; Green et al. 2007; Tuckman and Harris 2009). There is much to suggest that the changing population did not go unnoticed by local residents: 'People don't talk about much else [than immigration] in that place [Boston] actually' (Rob).

There has been a fairly widespread backlash against immigration in the area that, at its most extreme, has resulted in cases of racism and xenophobia (Barnes and Cox 2007; Lumsden et al. 2018). Keith explained: 'It's almost like Boston is still stuck a little bit in the past, whether it's someone with a different colour of skin or they come from another part of the world; it's not good news'. This nostalgia for the past ties closely with the way in which newcomers from elsewhere in Britain were considered a threat to the sense of community, 'rural way of life', and perceived identity of south Lincolnshire in the 1980s (Broun 2020).

The extent to which these feelings are more prevalent in Lincolnshire than elsewhere, or how often they manifest in racism or xenophobia is not entirely clear. Nonetheless, Phil noted two recent instances of racism, the first referring to a Polish man who was the Labour Party 2017 candidate and constituency chairman for South Holland and the Deepings: 'A friend of his wife challenged her in the street and said, "I don't understand why you're still here" . . . She replied, "what do you mean? It's my home" . . . "No, your home is in Poland. You should go back to Poland" . . . And she was so upset that she has gone home'. He also told a similar story reflecting strong local opposition to immigration regarding local residents' responses to the possibility of a Traveller site in the area during the 1990s:

> The district went fucking mad. All these little communities saying, 'we don't want bloody gyppos here.' And we had a public meeting in the leisure centre here . . . Somebody got up in that meeting and said 'we had some travellers and they moved in three or four doors down from us and unfortunately they had to move away because somebody put a brick through the windows.' And the mood of the audience was 'yeah fucking right, get rid of them'.

Much like in Merseyside where the *Liverpool Echo* is accused of, and at times quite clearly displays, a left-wing bias, newspapers in south Lincolnshire were criticized for legitimizing such racist and xenophobic beliefs after the initial arrival of migrants from Portugal: 'The local press started to get very racist. It allowed unreasonable behaviour or attitudes to be aired so people would say comments and normally where the press would say no we are not going to record that, they did and they allowed lots of letters . . . awful letters' (Phil). While we cannot find historical news articles in Lincolnshire to support Phil's claim, there is widespread evidence of the overwhelmingly negative way in which, much more recently, Gypsies, Travellers, and Roma people are portrayed by the British press (James 2020; Okely 2014; Richardson and O'Neill 2012).

While the relative level of racism or xenophobia in the area cannot be determined from these anecdotes, there has been a strong rejection of pro-immigration ideas across Lincolnshire, particularly in the south of the county, where UKIP performed particularly well in the 2015 general election. One cause of this is the perception that south Lincolnshire is largely declining or becoming left behind—a common theme throughout the interviews that mirrors our own findings. People are susceptible to blaming these economic conditions on high levels of immigration, according to Rob: 'if you're out of work or you can't get a house, then you look for reasons and you can be directed by political parties towards a scapegoat'. This is compounded by the fact that the out-migration of younger, educated residents leaves many remaining residents with fewer marketable qualifications in direct competition with foreign workers for jobs in shops, packing in factories, and working on the land: 'All the talented people leave Boston and the kids that are left behind to be honest about it aren't able to do much more than use their hands in terms of manual jobs ... And that's easily done by someone coming in from elsewhere who is willing to work for less' (Rob). Anti-immigrant sentiment is likely to be harsher as much of the incoming labour is low-skilled work, with significant research showing that public responses to this type of immigration tend to be more negative (Hainmueller and Hiscox 2010). Kaufmann (2017) has shown that this is even more likely the case when the speed of ethnic change is rapid.

Immigration: Labour's pain, UKIP's gain

The rapid population change in south Lincolnshire first occurred under the most recent Labour government following the enlargement of the EU in 2004 and 2007. According to Paul, many of those with negative feelings about the rise in the number of immigrants have attached some of the blame for this on Labour: 'people will say they're from a Labour background but over the last few years on immigration they've got used to not voting Labour'. He explains how the increasingly urban, 'cosmopolitan', and socially liberal nature of the Labour Party has perhaps not helped this situation: 'I think some people feel the Labour Party have left them behind'. An increasingly frustrated section of the white British population coincided with a recently arrived immigrant population from the EU, many of whom were not eligible to vote. Indeed, a high proportion of recent arrivals to the UK combined with low naturalization rates meant that in 2015, only an estimated 5% of Polish residents had voting rights (Ford and Grove-White 2015, p. 7). Given that most (but not all) migrant groups register relatively high vote shares for Labour, political disenfranchisement or disengagement of Eastern Europeans in south Lincolnshire may well have benefited the Conservatives at Labour's expense. However, UKIP have also gained from these population changes: 'I think after 2011, UKIP was the principal beneficiary of all or most of that discontent [about immigration]' (Tom). Such was the discontent, Paul explains how in the 2015 local elections, UKIP 'just put one candidate up but they could have put any-body up, and they won. They didn't need to canvass. They didn't need to make a message'.

At the Lincolnshire County elections in 2013, UKIP took sixteen seats from the Conservatives, most of which were in the south and south-east of the county. Two years later, they tied with the Conservatives for control of Boston council but failed to win the Boston and Skegness constituency in the gen-eral election (placing second), despite receiving 33.8% of the vote. UKIP's true popularity in 2015 may have been even higher, only obscured by tactical voting: 'if they were a solid Conservative voter, looking at the choice of either a Labour Miliband government or a Cameron government, in Lincolnshire they would have held back in the general election. I don't think they held back in the locals' (Tom).

UKIP as a 'gateway' to the Conservatives or UKIP and then back home again?

In Merseyside, the lack of support that UKIP won in 2015 appears to have benefited Labour as it limited the potential for UKIP to act as a 'gateway' for some voters between voting Labour pre-2015 to voting Conservative in 2017 and 2019. In Lincolnshire, UKIP's strength at the general election in 2015 may have aided this process, as Rob explains: 'Soft Labour vot-ers . . . found themselves easily able to get to the Conservatives by going through UKIP. They would never have countenanced the idea of going from Labour to the Conservatives but found a route through UKIP'. One rea-son why some of these former UKIP voters—particularly those that had come from the Conservatives—may have switched to the Conservatives in 2017 was the pro-Brexit stance taken up by Theresa May and most of her party.

The extent to which voters that moved from UKIP to the Conservatives had previously voted Labour in Lincolnshire is not particularly clear, as Angela's opinion exemplifies: 'they [former UKIP voters] went back to the Conserva-tives mainly. It was pretty obvious to me that that's where they'd come from'. It may well have been the case, as has been found elsewhere (Sobolewska and Ford 2020), that in 2015 UKIP gained many disaffected voters who had voted Conservative in 2010 but previously for Labour under Tony Blair: 'these are people who could well have voted Labour in 1997 and 2001. To use Boston and Skegness constituency as an example, in 1997 Labour got within 600 odd votes, in 2001, 500 odd votes before it started going the other way' (Tom).

Insecure labour and the lack of unionization

While immigration has aroused a negative response from some residents in south Lincolnshire, it has also resulted in a significant population of the working class—that is, recent EU migrants—being disenfranchised. Labour's left-of-centre economic policies may have had less traction in an area where many of the potential beneficiaries of such policies are not able to vote. Even those migrants with voting rights are unlikely to be members of trade unions that might be affiliated to the Labour Party and afford a sense of class solidarity or group interest that might impact voting behaviour. Low unionization may reflect a legacy of a trade union movement that 'has not always been a good friend to migrant workers, often mistakenly viewing them as willing help-mates to employers seeking to cut wage rates and other terms and conditions' (UNISON 2013). It may also be the result of characteristically low rates of union membership of Eastern European migrants specifically (Hardy and Clark 2005). Paul describes how 'the union movement have never really grasped Eastern Europeans', such that they are more easily accepting of exploitative conditions:

> You'll hear the farmers say this and the people who own the factories, 'what we like about the Eastern Europeans is that they'll come in for their shift, and if we say to them 'work another 5 hours' they say 'yeah, ok, no problem.' When they say things like 'there's no work today, come back tomorrow' . . .some of the locals would say 'fuck off.' We have scenarios here when you go into the town centre . . .and about twenty buses turn up . . .They'll take you to the factory at about 5 or 6 o clock . . .and if they don't need you they'll say to them on the bus 'we don't need you tonight.' You either wait for the bus or you make your own way home.

In contrast to the public sector or large private sector companies that might offer, or at least not oppose, the unionization of employees, much of the agricultural workforce is organized by more resistant employers: 'If they're controlled by gangmasters . . . if you're a trouble maker which is what union members will be classed as . . . "don't bother coming to me for work if you're a trouble maker. I've got 50 men to replace you"' (Jane). In contrast to the dominance of the insecure, agriculture workforce around south Lincolnshire, other towns across the Midlands and even in the far north of the county (e.g. Grimsby and Scunthorpe) retain some heavier industry and have industrial legacies with most likely larger unionized workforces.

Geographical and cultural disconnectedness: support for independents

The occupational structure of the working class is certainly not the only char-acteristic that makes this region unique. All of the interviewees identified a strong sense of independence across Lincolnshire that in part comes from the geographical and cultural isolation of the area. Many linked this sense of independence to the idea of self-sufficiency—that ultimately keeping the government and London at a distance is perceived as being much better for the local area: 'We are in the East Midlands but Nottingham is a long way from Boston. The self-confident want to be left on their own and are not too bothered about the people who do need the state. And the self-confident are the decision-makers' (Rob).

This culturally ingrained desire for self-determination perhaps also offers some explanation for the success of independent candidates in local elec-tions. Rob makes the link with the politics of rural parts of the United States: '"I'm not going to be told by Washington [DC] what's going to go on. Leave me to my own devices at a distance" . . . therefore they stand as individ-ual people with the respect of not being told what to do'. As a result, he argues, 'the party structure is not very solid . . . here it's Labour, Liberal Democrat, Conservative, Independent, or Independent and another Inde-pendent'. There are currently two highly competitive independent groups active on Lincolnshire County Council, holding four seats between them. It would perhaps be speculative to suggest these independent councillors limit support for other parties competing against Conservative dominance of the region. Nonetheless, in 2007 for example, one independent group— the Boston Bypass Party—clearly acquired votes from former Labour voters, as Paul explains: 'in 2007 we all got knocked out by the Boston Bypass Party. We lost all of our seats in one clean swoop'. Even if independents only directly affect Labour support in local elections, it can reinforce the idea that Labour have little chance of winning across much of Lincolnshire and weaken the organizational structure of the local party going into a general election.

Party organization: 'how are Labour functioning in the more far-flung parts of the county? They're not!'

In a mirror image of Merseyside, the aforementioned factors have resulted in a dominant and organizationally strong Conservative Party and a weak

Labour Party. More resources in the form of contracted staff and access to buildings from which to run campaigns means that standing for the Conservatives was perceived as much easier than representing any other party. Angela suggested, 'if I was to stand as a Conservative, I wouldn't have to work hard like I do'. She continues to explain her reasoning: 'the MPs here except Lincoln are Conservative and they've all got agents and those agents have got offices in your town . . . All of the volunteers flock to there because they've got paid people who can collate a lot of the information that councillors want'. This is in sharp contrast to the Labour Party organization that is perhaps most bleakly summarized by Rob: 'how are Labour functioning in the more far-flung parts of the county? They're not!' Part of this weakness is top-down, in that the Labour Party cannot afford to allocate resources to constituencies in south Lincolnshire that are not considered remotely winnable, as Jane explains: 'To get assistance from the main party, we've got to be a marginal. And as far as Labour is concerned, we are so far, we are just miles away from any conceivable victory'. Instead, as Phil points out, in the run up to a general election, activists are encouraged to campaign in more marginal seats in the region, such as Lincoln and Peterborough, weakening Labour's position locally even further:

> Because we are not a target area with key seats, you don't get the same backup that the party at a regional basis is able to provide to Lincoln for example which is a marginal seat. Or Peterborough even. And you also then get the culture says quite rightly that we in a general election should go to Peterborough so it makes it even worse here.

In Merseyside, the seats in the urban core of Liverpool are perceived as so 'safe' that Labour will send activists to the suburbs to campaign. Lincoln— the only seat Labour held in 2017 outside of the far north of the county—is extremely marginal, meaning few activists would ever leave to campaign in the more rural areas. Tom explains that 'we [the Conservatives] can cover the area in a way that I think Labour would struggle to . . . I suppose Labour could bus its people out of Louth and Lincoln but if it's going to contest seats it is going to concentrate on Louth and Lincoln where it can make a difference'. The shortage of activists in the rural areas also leads to a shortage of Labour candidates, with local elections in some wards frequently fought without anyone standing from the Labour Party. For Rob, the shortage of Labour candidates is exacerbated by low levels of education: 'the more urban it is, the more likely it is you are going to have relatively educated people to provide leadership'.

Conclusion: place matters

At the most recent general election in 2019, every single parliamentary constituency in Merseyside had a higher Labour vote share and (bar Southport) a lower Conservative vote share than predicted by our Chapter 4 statistical models based on sociodemographic characteristics. This is not just a reflection of a local culture that is pro-Labour. In fact, in Merseyside there has been a clear story that explains how, since the 1970s, a Scouse identity has been constructed in opposition to Thatcher, *The Sun*, and more broadly the Conservative Party. The links between the cultures, identities, and politics of the region have been explained by mainstream commentators and academics alike. Although there has been some media attention related to Brexit specifically, much less has been written about Lincolnshire and why it has been such a stronghold for the Conservative Party. Perhaps it is because, on the surface at least, the causes of Lincolnshire's unusual politics are more diffuse.

Some of the explanation for Conservative dominance in Lincolnshire appears to lie in the fact that the statistical models cannot account for the precise and especially unusual composition of the area—particularly in Boston and Skegness and South Holland and the Deepings. For example, there are large numbers of recently arrived migrants from Eastern Europe, who are largely employed in routine occupations with seemingly low levels of union membership and significant disenfranchisement. These factors—combined with the ageing, white, working-class British population with low levels of education living in a relatively declining area where the rapid increase in immigration has been blamed on the previous Labour government—create a challenging situation for the Labour Party, as Jane reiterates: 'I honestly wouldn't even do a jumble sale in Boston in aid of the Labour Party. You'd have to disguise it somehow'.

In contrast, the Conservatives have benefited from the collapse of UKIP's widespread local support and their pro-Brexit stance in an area of the country that registered the highest vote to leave the European Union. In addition to these factors, many of the interviewees identified the broader cultural phenomenon of a long-standing deference to farming and landowners in part because of their status and wealth and in part because they are the key employers in the local area. While the short-term story in the media has often been one of UKIP gains and the Brexit vote in Lincolnshire, the long-term narrative should be the strength of the Conservative support here, in an area that in many respects might be considered demographically left behind.

8
Conclusion

There are rare moments in time when the political order is rapidly over-turned, and the geography of electoral competition is realigned decisively. At other times, the incremental march of social and economic forces slowly but surely leads to a structural shift in electoral geography. Cox (1986) traces the development of a party-oriented electorate in Britain to the period imme-diately after the second Reform Act in 1867, with voters before then often splitting their votes in double-member districts. At that time, Britain's elec-toral politics was heavily aligned on the urban–rural cleavage. Accordingly, Schonhardt-Bailey (2003) shows that the split in the Conservative Party over free trade in 1846 aligned with the agricultural interests of electorates, with the free trade Peelite faction eventually merging with the Whigs and the Radi-cals to establish the Liberal Party in 1859. As such, Britain's historical electoral geography reflected a split between rural-agricultural (protectionist) inter-ests and urban (free trade) interests. The urban–rural cleavage of 1846 casts a long shadow over the spatial distribution of party support in modern British politics, with the modern Conservative Party still dominant in rural areas of England today.

In an ecological study based on electoral and census data much like this book, Wald (1983) alternatively argues that between 1885 and 1918 there was a decline in alignment of patterns of voting in Britain with religion rather than urban-rural interests. The emergence of social class as the dominant cleavage of British politics during the early twentieth century led the Labour Party to displace the Liberals as the main opposition to the Conservative Party (Stephens 1982). In the new electoral alignment, Labour's vote was heavily concentrated in urban, industrial areas that tended to have larger working-class populations. This matches the geography of support for left parties in other industrial democracies (Rodden 2019). The general election of 2019 is notable for representing perhaps the most significant rupture of that electoral geography for nearly a hundred years. Labour's vote is still concentrated in major urban areas, large towns, and major cities, but the party's support has receded in its industrial heartlands. The Conservatives, on the other hand, have made clear inroads into those demographically left

The Changing Electoral Map of England and Wales. Jamie Furlong and Will Jennings, Oxford University Press.
© Jamie Furlong and Will Jennings (2024). DOI: 10.1093/9780191943331.003.0008

behind areas. At the 2019 general election, this may have translated for the first time into significant seat gains for the Conservatives, but, as our analysis has shown, this shift has been a long time in the making.

It is not surprising that these longer term trends are overlooked, given the disorienting nature and uncertain direction of British politics in recent years. Following the Great Recession of 2008–9 and demise of New Labour, we have witnessed the collapse of the Liberal Democrats as an electoral force, the rise and fall of UKIP, the rise of the SNP in Scotland and the unsuccessful Scottish independence referendum in 2014, election of Jeremy Corbyn as leader of the Labour Party and its leftward shift under him, the vote to leave the EU, three general elections in five years (2015, 2017, and 2019), widely unexpected general election results (2015 and 2017), a UK government (under Theresa May) in disarray over its Brexit deal and receiving just 9% of the vote in the May 2019 European parliament elections, a Prime Minister removed by their party over persistent scandal (Boris Johnson), and the shortest-serving PM in British history (Liz Truss). In this context, voting behaviour is more volatile than ever and relationships between voters and political parties increasingly strained (Green and Prosser 2016; Sanders 2017; Fieldhouse et al. 2020). Despite the captivating nature of this volatility and the electoral horse race, it is important to not lose sight of the long-term changes that have occurred in the electoral geography of England and Wales.

Drawing attention to long-term trends is not an exercise in ignoring short-term volatility. Governments with sizeable parliamentary majorities today appear less secure than in the not-too-distant past, and substantial swings between parties seem far more possible from one election to the next. This volatility is likely, of course, to also be expressed geographically. Just as, at the 2019 general election, commentators referred to the collapse of the 'Red Wall'—a realignment in British politics as former Labour strongholds in post-industrial towns of Northern England and the Midlands turned to the Conservatives—it is not difficult to imagine future references to Labour 'rebuilding the Red Wall' as the political pendulum swings back and some constituencies are regained. However, even if Labour won back many of these seats and the Red Wall, on the surface, looked the same as before, the geographical distribution of votes across this area is likely to be rather different to even 1997, let alone 1979. In future elections, the strongholds of Labour's support will not be the former mining towns and villages of South Yorkshire or County Durham, but the major urban centres of Liverpool, Manchester, Leeds, Sheffield, and Birmingham, alongside cities and university towns elsewhere in the country. In this sense, our analysis serves as a call for a more nuanced understanding of the electoral geography of England and Wales than is offered by popular uses of concepts like the Red and Blue Wall (not least because the Red Wall now has some blue bricks, and the Blue Wall is not a contiguous set of constituencies and many may soon be yellow!).

The drivers of changing electoral geography

As we have argued, these changes in electoral geography are driven by long-term trends in the social and economic structure of Britain and their geographical expression. Those trends relate to the decline of traditional industry and shrinking of the working class, expansion of higher education, the clustering of economic activity in major cities and high-tech towns (often coexisting with higher numbers of service workers in insecure employment), high levels of inward migration especially into major urban centres, and an ageing population that increasingly resides outside major cities. Those trends are bound up with the development of the contemporary capitalist model in post-industrial societies (Ford and Jennings 2020), which is why similar trends are observed across many other countries, of growing support for right parties and candidates in rural and peripheral areas. A growing number of studies explore the role of resentment towards urban elites as a driver of populist forces (Cramer 2016; McKay et al. 2023). In the modern global economy, countries seek to drive economic growth and dynamism through agglomeration of firms and high skilled workers—relying on inflows of younger graduates, professionals, migrants, and those in relatively low-paid service work (supporting the economic activities and lifestyles of knowledge economy workers). Areas that we refer to as demographically left behind, on the other hand, are increasingly characterized by ageing populations, with lower levels of education, the decline of industry, and relatively low levels of ethnic diversity.

These trends give rise to (divergent) compositional effects on voting patterns, due to the propensity of certain groups to favour one party over another, as more or less of these groups are found in particular places over time. For example, the weakening individual-level link between social class and voting for Labour has eroded the party's support in its industrial heartlands among those populations, even as those populations have declined. At the same time, the increasing tendency of younger voters and university graduates to vote for Labour (Sobolewska and Ford 2020; Sturgis and Jennings 2020; Ford et al. 2021) has led to it securing very high levels of support in major cities and university towns. Together, these changes in social structure have therefore produced distinct spatial distributions of electoral preferences.

We have also shown how the regional fortunes of the parties have changed considerably over the period from 1945 to 2019. The Labour Party has consistently over-performed its national vote share in Wales, Yorkshire and the Humber, and the North East, and under-performed it in the East, South East, and South West (with support in the East and West Midlands hovering just slightly above the national average). It has seen rising levels of support over this period in the North West, where it now dominates—aided by the party's dominance of the cities of Liverpool and Manchester. For most of the post-war period, Labour's support in London tended to track the national average. Over the last decade, however, it has rapidly increased its dominance in the nation's capital, making it the party's strongest region. Scotland, in contrast has seen a realignment from Labour to the SNP, and a collapse in support relative to its national average.

In our analysis we have shown that region has become an increasingly strong predictor of constituency vote share for both parties, and especially for the Conservatives over the post-war period, though the trend has fluctuated since the 1980s. In a more granular analysis of place types, we charted the long-term decline of Conservative support in the inner suburbs of core cities, and the party's growing support in industrial town constituencies between 2015 and 2019. Rural constituencies have seen a long-term decline in support for Labour, but since 1997 the Conservative Party has grown its vote in these places considerably—thanks to feelings of rural resentment towards the New Labour government in the earlier period and greater propensity of rural seats to vote for Brexit (Jennings and Stoker 2019). More broadly what these dynamics capture is a growing link between population density and Labour's vote. In 2019, the strength of that relationship was greater than at any point since 1945. Relatedly, analysis of the party's electoral efficiency shows how the clustering of Labour support in urban centres contributes to significant numbers of wasted votes in safe constituencies.

How places vote

Research has shown that the Labour Party has become increasingly popular amongst younger people (Curtice 2017; Bell and Gardiner 2019; Sturgis and Jennings 2020), university graduates (Surridge 2016; Hobolt 2018), and ethnic minorities (Andrews 2017; Katwala and Ballinger 2017), typically at the expense of the Conservatives. At the same time, the Conservatives appear to hold greater appeal amongst older people (Bell and Gardiner 2019) and those without educational qualifications (Skinner and Mortimore 2017). The former are often crudely lumped together as 'cosmopolitan'; the latter as 'left behind'.

This division has geographical manifestations with Labour losing ground to the Conservatives in what we have termed demographically left behind areas, where the population is older, whiter, and in possession of fewer educational qualifications than cosmopolitan inner-city areas. We have offered conclusive evidence of this geographical realignment in which support for the Conservatives has become stronger in areas with significant manufacturing industries rather than cosmopolitan service-sector jobs, a high ratio of old to young people and generally less transient, less ethnically diverse populations. For Labour, the opposite is the case: the association with demographically left behind compositional characteristics has been decreasing over time. While this geographical realignment accelerated at the 1997 general election and the post-Brexit elections of 2017 and 2019, this represents a long-term trend. Indeed, the relationships between Labour and Conservative vote shares and constituency age, occupational, and education profiles have generally moved in the same direction across elections from 1979 to 2019. As such, our analysis offers clear evidence that, while the 2017 and 2019 general elections saw Brexit significantly contribute to these changing relationships (Fieldhouse and Bailey 2023), the reshaping of the *electoral geography* of England and Wales is a product of long-term social, economic, and political forces. The trends shaping the electoral geography of demographically left behind places have been present across many decades. In 2019, the acceleration of this process, combined with a large fall in Labour's vote overall, led to significant seat losses to the Conservatives in the party's traditional strongholds, leading many commentators to overlook the long-term nature of these dynamics.

While there is evidence that the Labour Party holds increasing appeal in cosmopolitan urban areas characterized by a large proportion of ethnic minorities, younger people, and graduates, it would be premature to refer to them as the party of middle-class areas. In fact, in areas characterized by high levels of home ownership and managerial/professional workers, there has been remarkable stability, with the Conservatives continuing to be electorally ascendant. Similarly, in the poorest areas of Britain (those areas we call economically left behind)—often the same urban areas that are home to younger graduates and a more ethnically diverse population—the Labour Party is more dominant than ever. Extending the findings of Jennings and Stoker (2017), our analysis shows that poverty remains *the* key predictor of

Labour success at every election from 1979 to 2019. It is possible to conclude, therefore, that left behind areas remain strongly oriented towards Labour, providing we are willing to recognize the deprivation of ethnically diverse urban areas as a form of left-behindedness, rather than only base the concept on the demographics behind the rise in support for the populist right (e.g. Ford and Goodwin 2014).

While two areas might have a similar sociodemographic composition at the point in time of a particular election, one may be on an upward economic trajectory, the other a downward trajectory—one becoming more left behind, another moving ahead. Just as perceived decline and feelings of resentment are associated with shifts towards the extreme right amongst individuals (Gest et al. 2017; Gidron and Hall 2017, 2020), these divergent trends of relatively improving and declining places are also critical to understanding changes in electoral geography. In areas that have become more demographically left behind, relative support for the Conservatives has increased quite dramatically at Labour's expense. This phenomenon— particularly strong between 2005 and 2019 and in areas that have rapidly deindustrialized and experienced more prolonged decline—lends support to the idea that the class-based model is continuing to decrease in salience, at least as far as electoral geography is concerned. In fact, were the positive association between declining areas and Conservative vote share change to continue to strengthen, the 'two-class, two-party model' identified by Butler and Stokes (1969) could one day operate in reverse.

While we have presented evidence of Conservative Party support increasing in areas that are, relative to others, becoming more working class, and at least more recently, failing to keep up economically, the same trend is not seen in areas that have seen the biggest increases in precarious forms of employment and housing. Areas where homeowners are being replaced by less secure private renters—particularly in London and the North West— have seen remarkable relative increases in Labour support and decreases in Conservative support. Similar findings across a shorter, more recent time frame (2015–17) are revealed by Denver (2018). The same pattern holds true for areas where both housing unaffordability and employment insecurity have risen most substantially.

Given the changing relationships between the social class, educational, and age compositions of areas and party support, it should come as no surprise that some of the places we might call 'strongholds' of Labour and Conservative support have changed as well. For Labour, this has been extremely pronounced: where once the party achieved its highest vote shares in the coal-mining towns of South Yorkshire and the North East, it now achieves huge majorities in Merseyside. For the Conservatives, there has been more consistency, though they have become particularly dominant in rural Lincolnshire and parts of the East and West Midlands that were once more competitive. These strongholds are not just places where party vote shares are high, but where, given their sociodemographic compositions, the parties outperform expectations. Indeed, many parts of Merseyside are largely white, working class with few graduates—precisely the kind of political makeup that should have seen increasing support for the Conservatives. Similarly, while south Lincolnshire shares some of those characteristics, it also has high levels of economic deprivation and precarious forms of work—characteristics that should make Labour at least competitive. Yet, even after accounting for the unusual religious makeups and divergent levels of trade union membership and public sector occupations of Merseyside and Lincolnshire, statistical models still cannot fully explain the remarkable dominance of Labour in the former and the Conservatives in the latter.

We have explored these notable case studies of Merseyside and Lincolnshire in more depth, drawing on interviews with local political actors and experts who consider the place-based cultural, historical, and political factors that help explain this diffusion of voting behaviour across constituencies within these regions. In this way, our approach moves beyond existing electoral geographical research in the UK that has used rigorous quantitative methodologies to identify the presence of contextual effects (MacAllister et al. 2001; Johnston et al. 2005) but have rarely examined how or why these effects operate to produce unusual political cases. In Merseyside, we have revealed the way in which the emergence of the Liberals in the 1970s acted as a gateway for Conservative voters to eventually vote for the Labour Party. A culmination of events, from Thatcher's government suggesting Liverpool be left to 'managed decline' to support for the police force stitch-up of the Hillsborough disaster and the subsequent boycotting of *The Sun* newspaper, have led to a Scouse identity being constructed in opposition to the Conservatives and more broadly the 'establishment'. The interlinked nature of the city's football clubs, foodbanks, Catholicism, the left-leaning *Liverpool Echo*, the Labour Council, and the city's cosmopolitan regeneration, serve to reaffirm this identity and create a unique regional-level political culture that has resulted in Labour dominance and Conservative failure—even in places where demographics should favour the latter.

While much has been written of Merseyside's unusual politics, Lincolnshire received very little political attention until UKIP achieved success in the south of the county in 2015, pre-empting the particularly high estimated Leave vote share in the EU referendum in constituencies such as

Boston and Skegness. This is perhaps because the contextual causes of the unexplained Conservative dominance are a little more diffuse than those behind Labour's success in Merseyside. Nonetheless, our analysis reveals possible explanations in a regional cultural deference to landowners and the unusual combination of geographical/cultural disconnectedness, high levels of insecure, low-skilled labour, and responses to a recent influx of workers from Eastern Europe. As such, the findings emphasize the ever-present need—as identified more than thirty years ago by Agnew (1990) and Reynolds (1990)—for contextual approaches that understand not just the importance of spatial location but the way in which political attitudes and actions are moderated through place (Massey and Thrift 2003).

What might the future look like?

Wise observers of politics will know that demography is not destiny, but the trends that we have charted here point to possible future paths that might be taken by Britain's electoral geography that merit some reflection. First, the drift of younger people and university graduates in a socially liberal direction (Sobolewska and Ford 2020) and their spatial clustering in major cities and university towns suggest that the geographical polarization that we observe might, everything else being equal, become even more extreme in future. Such an outcome would see Labour building vast majorities in parts of London, Manchester, Liverpool, Sheffield, Leeds, and Bristol, for example, while recruiting far fewer voters in marginal towns in 'Middle England'. Continued electoral inefficiency of this sort would require the party to consistently win the national vote by large margins to have a hope of securing a parliamentary majority.

Of course, Labour's 'cosmopolitan' vote could yet come under threat in those densely populated urban centres from the Green Party, appealing to younger, more liberal voters concerned about postmaterial issues such as climate change. It is also possible that migration of those younger, diverse, graduates out of cities to suburbs and home counties outside London across the South—as a natural part of the life course—could tip the balance of many constituencies currently held by the Conservatives and lead to a rebalancing of that electoral inefficiency. Many of those seats are already under threat from the Liberal Democrats, due at least in part to a backlash against Brexit in Remain-voting areas. If the Conservative Party's Southern heartlands increasingly start to turn yellow or red, while it retains an electoral foothold in former industrial parts of Northern England, it will be hard not to argue that the electoral geography of England and Wales has been turned upside down.

An alternative view might be that, with the growth of higher education, as larger cohorts of graduates move through the population, polarization might decrease as older generations in places will be more likely to have gone to university and share some of the same experiences and values of younger generations. Historically, as individuals have aged, they have become more likely to vote Conservative (Tilley and Evans 2014). However, amongst Millennials, this process has so far halted—a likely cohort effect in which experiences such as the global financial crisis of the late 2000s, the expansion of university education, growing up amongst greater ethnic diversity, the EU referendum, the proliferation of insecure labour, and the lack of housing affordability has resulted in a more distinct and hardened set of values (Burn-Murdoch 2022). This may reflect more broadly socially liberal values amongst younger voters than specifically economically left-wing values (Cadywould 2017), especially as there is some evidence that younger generations have adopted Thatcherite economic individualist values (Grasso et al. 2019). Either way, as the Millennial cohort of voters (and Gen Z if they follow the same pattern) replace older voters over time, there is a significant problem for the Conservatives if they hold on to their more socially liberal values. This process, referred to as generational replacement (Abramson and Inglehart 1992), represents a potential existential threat to the Conservative Party. Of course, the death of Tory England has been foretold before, just as the Labour Party was widely considered to be in a death spiral as recently as May 2021 following the local elections and Hartlepool by-election defeat.

The ageing of the population is not without future electoral challenges for the Labour Party. That Labour's average vote share only increased between 1979 and 2019 in the 20% of constituencies that have become younger illuminates the challenge they face to reverse this trend in areas with ageing populations—in particular, largely white, suburban, or small-town constituencies. The 2021 census revealed that the proportion of the UK population aged over 65 has increased from 16.4% in 2011 to 18.6% in 2021 (Office for National Statistics 2023a), and projections suggest this age group will make up almost a quarter of the population by 2043 (House of Commons Library 2021). While the historical trend of becoming more conservative with age appears to have weakened, as the older population grows, Labour's relative unpopularity with this group could still be an obstacle to achieving power. Many seats with especially old populations are found in former Labour heartlands—demographically left behind constituencies, including many that Labour lost to the Conservatives in 2019, such as Workington, Vale of Clwyd, Bishop Auckland, Rother Valley, and Don Valley. Although they certainly do not need these areas to become their 'heartlands' once again, there are very few routes to power for the party that do not involve regaining many of these kinds of seats.

From a purely strategic point of view with an aim of maximizing vote efficiency, Labour may decide that it is willing to regain support in its former heartlands where voters tend towards socially conservative values at the expense of cosmopolitan cities where voters are generally more socially liberal. However, adopting more socially conservative positions to appeal to voters in these more demographically left behind areas may have limited benefit other than alienating its support amongst its younger, more cosmopolitan base (Abou-Chadi & Wagner 2020). To some extent, the 2019 local elections (Labour's vote share—28%) and subsequent European parliament elections (Labour's vote share—14%) should serve as a warning for Labour that the socially liberal, largely urban, and more likely university-educated side of its support does not have the same historical ties to the party as its former working-class core. This chimes with Dalton's (2007) idea that voters with higher levels of education and political knowledge are less likely to rely on party loyalty when making their vote choice.

While compared to demographically left behind constituencies, the threat to Labour might be lower in the most cosmopolitan constituencies where they have substantial majorities, and these voters are greater in number. However, younger graduates are likely to make up increasing numbers of more marginal constituencies outside of larger cities (Warren 2018). Even small losses to the Greens and Liberal Democrats could see Labour lose a substantial number of seats if they are simultaneously not retaining or regaining support in more demographically left behind areas. This same process of younger, university-educated middle classes moving out of London is likely to pose a more substantial threat in traditional Conservative heartlands. As they struggle to afford the space to bring up a family in the capital, large numbers are moving out to commutable locations across the South East and elsewhere, taking with them their socially liberal values that make them more Labour-inclined (Burn-Murdoch 2023; Warren 2018). Future research will no doubt show the extent to which these graduates retain their values and voting preferences, but it seems clear that the combination of increasing proportions of university graduates and growing ethnic diversity is likely— unless trends change—to cause the Conservative Party significant problems in some of its own strongholds, particularly in Southern England.

For the Conservatives, it is not only the spreading out of younger graduates across Britain's geography that poses an electoral risk, but an increasing ethnic diversity in more electorally marginal smaller towns and suburbs. Population projections suggest that ethnic minority groups will grow most rapidly outside of the largest cities over the next forty years (Rees et al. 2017). As ethnic diversity becomes more embedded into everyday life in these areas, they may become more favourable to the Labour Party, though the future voting habits of specific ethnic minority groups will be especially important.

Given the anaemic state of Britain's economy, and stagnation of real wages over more than a decade combined with an increasingly insecure labour market, the unaffordability and shortage of housing across large parts of England and Wales represents an increasing problem with the potential to have significant electoral consequences. The growing number of younger people unable to buy homes, and shortages of available housing, are contributing to the establishment of renters as a voting bloc. Indeed, there has been a significant increase in the proportion of households that are privately renting from 34.3% in 2011 to 37.3% in 2021 (Office for National Statistics 2023b), with renting particularly common in cities and larger towns. In our analysis, social and private renting is strongly linked to support for Labour. The demise of the Thatcherite dream of home ownership for younger generations may therefore lead to falling support for the Conservatives in constituencies where affordability becomes a key issue. After the 2015 general election, private renting was described as 'the Conservatives' electoral Achilles' heel, especially in London' (Lund 2015, p. 503). The possible election-defining impact of the growing number of private renters has become well documented and should be of concern to the Conservatives given current trends in their support (Craw 2014; Akehurst 2017; Singh 2018). While the party has strong ties to homeowners and arguably has prioritized their concerns above private and social renters, housing unaffordability is not just an issue in Labour's city constituencies, but large parts of the South East in particular, where the Conservatives could face an increased challenge in retaining their traditional support.

The comparative implications

Our analysis has been focused on the case of Britain, and England and Wales specifically for the most part. However, our theoretical arguments and empirical findings offer important advances to wider debates over growing polarization between urban and peripheral-rural areas in advanced democracies across the world (e.g. Rickardsson 2021; Taylor et al. 2023). This book complements such studies and importantly builds on the arguments put for-ward in Jonathan Rodden's (2019) *Why Cities Lose*. Our analysis tells the same story of how the position of parties on social issues, combined with key trends in socio-economic geography, have led to the sorting of voters into parties and a shift in the geographical distribution of support—with left parties (Labour) increasingly concentrated in urban areas and right par-ties (the Conservatives) concentrated in smaller towns and rural areas. The British case offers its own distinctive features, most notably the role of Brexit in accelerating the Labour Party's loss of support in its traditional, industrial heartlands between the 2015 and 2019 general elections. What we have added to those important existing accounts of geographical divides is a focus on the specific demographic characteristics driving these aggregate-level trends—showing how the strengthening association of age, education, and ethnic diversity, for example, with party support have contributed to the growing significance of population density in shaping electoral competition between left and right parties. Similar trends, of left parties losing support in left behind former heartlands, are observed in a range of political systems and countries, including Canada (Armstrong et al. 2022), the USA (Scala et al. 2015; Taylor et al. 2023), the Netherlands (van Gent et al. 2014; Harteveld et al. 2022), and Italy (Faggian et al. 2021).

As we noted early in the book, these trends in social structure are intrinsi-cally entangled with the contemporary capitalist model in advanced indus-trial countries. The dominant policy model of those countries has fuelled the growth of the graduate class, decline and marginalization of the work-ing class, high migration and rapidly rising ethnic diversity, and the growing geographical segregation of populations between core and peripheral areas. Across different sorts of political system, these trends have impacted on the spatial distribution of political preferences. Accordingly, Maxwell (2019) finds that (demographic) compositional effects lead to more socially lib-eral, pro-immigration attitudes found in large cities. Luca et al. (2023) also find that in more economically developed countries cities tend to cultivate and nurture more socially liberal values. The economic and cultural gravi-tational pull of major cities for younger, educated, professional, and more diverse populations that are left- and liberal-leaning means that the result-ing geographical divides in voting may be sustained for some time. Though of course, the extent to which this city–town (or even urban–rural) cleavage continues to structure British electoral geography could be limited by ethnic minorities and younger graduates migrating from dense, city seats to sub-urban and smaller town constituencies while simultaneously retaining their left- or liberal-leaning values.

Methodological challenges and opportunities

The key question that guides research in electoral geography is 'why do particular parties draw more electoral support from some places than from others?' (Pattie and Johnston 2009). In short, electoral geographers typically seek to understand the way in which space, place, and electoral processes interact to produce geographical patterns in political attitudes, voting behaviour, and party support. We believe this book makes a number of important methodological contributions to achieve this aim, and ultimately, advance the study of electoral geography in the British context. It extends key research in the field by applying new methods to estimate constituency characteristics across a forty-year window, new data spanning this time frame and new approaches, such as combining quantitative and qualitative analysis, to understand where parties under- and over-perform and why these geographical exceptions exist. In doing so, like Johnston and Pattie (2006) and Johnston et al. (1988) before that, this research seeks to be one of the defining accounts of electoral geography in Britain and wider context for years to come.

Most constituency-level analysis of a similar kind in Britain has been restricted to shorter time periods due to boundary changes between elections. By using areal interpolation to accurately project census data onto constituency characteristics for which it is otherwise unavailable (e.g. 2011 census data on the 2005 constituencies boundaries), and by carefully harmonizing data across four censuses, we have been able to produce robust analysis of the characteristics associated with levels of Labour and Conservative support across eleven general elections, from 1979 to 2019. The same approach has been used to project data from the 1981 census onto constituency boundaries used in 2019, allowing us to identify the socio-economic and demographic factors associated with *changes* in electoral support over a forty year period (1979–2019). We hope that this approach will be adopted by other political scientists to produce more detailed, longer term ecological analyses of party support in Britain and elsewhere.

The spatial analytical methods used in Chapter 6 also serve to answer calls for research in electoral geography to move beyond the arbitrary boundaries of parliamentary constituencies and assess processes that operate at wider spatial scales (Jensen et al. 2013). Our research is a rare example[1] in British electoral geography of analysing the statistically significant spatial

---

[1] One notable exception is Cutts and Webber (2010) who examined the presence of global and local spatial autocorrelation at the 2005 general election alongside the predictive capabilities of spatial regression models.

clustering of vote shares and model residuals, the latter to understand where both Labour and Conservative parties under- and over-perform over time. This allows for the identification of areas in England and Wales—Merseyside and Lincolnshire—where constituency composition cannot fully account for the levels of support both parties receive. These areas are marked by the unusually strong influence of regional, local, cultural, and historical factors on party support. In other words, we can identify places that are politically *exceptional*.

For these regional effects to have any plausibility (i.e. that we are not just missing key compositional characteristics in our analysis), research must link it to a place-based history of political development. That is precisely the strength of our analysis: semi-structured interviews with political actors have revealed the historical, geographical, and cultural factors that have contributed to dominant political cultures and election results in Merseyside and Lincolnshire that cannot be easily accounted for sociodemographic composition. In short, they help us explain the otherwise unexplainable. This approach is also a response to still pertinent calls for research in electoral geography to shift in focus from the attributes of political spaces to political places as 'historically constituted entities' (Pringle 2003). In reality, we combine both approaches, using spatial analytical methods to identify precisely *where* these political exceptions are, and qualitative methods to understand *why* they persist. In Merseyside, it provides an empirical extension to the work of Wilks-Heeg (2019); in Lincolnshire it is the first study of its kind to focus on Conservative support and not favourability towards UKIP and leaving the EU. In terms of research in electoral geography, it serves as a call for more mixed methods approaches. For example, localized survey and ethnographic methods might be combined to better understand local political cultures and identities, where these are not sufficiently captured by national surveys or ecological predictors.

While this research provides a much-needed combination of understanding electoral geography in terms of *space* as well as *place*, there are of course still limitations. Conducting analysis with parliamentary constituencies as the unit of study is important, particularly in a first-past-the-post system where the distribution of voters across parliamentary constituencies determines who takes power. However, this aggregate-level approach restricts any conclusions to the constituency-level, for it would be an ecological fallacy to make inferences about the behaviour of individuals in any particular area. For example, knowing that areas with more people living in poor health are more likely to vote for Labour, or that the proportion of people in poor health is consistently the most important predictor of Labour support, does not reveal whether individuals in poor health are more or less likely to vote for Labour. At no point can the reader make conclusions from this analysis about the relationship between the characteristics of individuals and their voting preferences. Future research could combine individual and compositional, constituency-level statistical analysis through multi-level modelling, to understand how individual and constituency characteristics interact to influence voting behaviour.

Afterword

Places, of course, do not vote, but they play a fundamental role in electoral politics through the aggregation of preferences within a given geographical area and translation of those preferences into representation. They form the local context in which people work, shop, socialize, and go about their daily lives. Places are where they encounter schools, police, hospitals, and other frontline public services, and often seek employment. They also can be the source of identities and cultures that shape political worldviews, be it in rural farming communities or industrial towns with long trade union heritages. Place-based resentments have been linked to the effective appeal of populism in the US (Cramer 2016) and elsewhere. The roots of the demographic composition of most places tend to run deep. These are usually the product of centuries of social and economic development, sometimes influenced directly by the interventions of government, which can intersect with the sorts of political cleavages famously identified by Lipset and Rokkan (1967)—urban–rural, core–periphery, and labour–capital. As we have shown, the electoral geography of England and Wales continues to be shaped by elements of each of these socio-structural cleavages: with Labour's vote increasingly located in major urban centres (including the national capital) with high proportions of younger generations, university graduates, and those in low-paid precarious employment, and the Conservatives' vote increasingly concentrated in less densely populated areas, with older populations, where industrial employment is in decline and there are lower rates of inward migration.

The reason that place-based differences can be so powerful in countries like the UK and the US, with their first-past-the-post single member districts and electoral college for presidential elections, is that votes are translated into who wins in a way that can be highly disproportionate, depending on the distribution of preferences. The importance of electoral geography to the success of any political party should not be understated. Of course, there are occasional elections, such as the 1979, 1997, and 2019 general elections, where political forces might sweep a party to a landslide win almost irrespective of the geography of their support. But in a first-past-the-post electoral system, the changing distribution of voters across Britain, combined with the changing relationships between parties and voters, will have a defining impact on the outcome of most elections. It is therefore crucial that both Labour and the Conservatives understand the unique political challenges that they face because of the changing makeup of British society, and how this varies from place to place. Our expectation is, then, that the electoral geography revealed at the 2019 general election will continue to be important in future elections, but will be subject to considerable fluctuations of the political weather, not least as voters are increasingly volatile and prone to switching to other parties. We hope that in this book we have set out how electoral geography is shaped by long–term forces and can alter significantly the chances of parties taking office.

References

Abou-Chadi, T., and Wagner, M. (2020). Electoral fortunes of social democratic parties: do second dimension positions matter? *Journal of European Public Policy*, 27(2): 246–72. https://doi.org/10.1080/13501763.2019.1701532

Abramson, P. R., and Inglehart, R. (1992). Generational replacement and value change in eight West European societies. *British Journal of Political Science*, 22(2): 183–228. https://doi.org/10.1017/s0007123400006335

Agnew, J. (1990). From political methodology to geographical social theory? A critical review of electoral geography, 1960–87. In Johnston, R. J., Shelley, F. M., and Taylor, P. J. (eds) *Developments in Electoral Geography*. London: Routledge, 15–21.

Agrawal, S., and Phillips, D. (2020). *Catching up or Falling Behind? Geographical Inequalities in the UK and How they have Changed in Recent Years*. London: Institute for Fiscal Studies. http://library2.nics.gov.uk/pdf/dso/2020/0607.pdf (Accessed 19 December 2023)

Ainsley, C. (2018). *The New Working Class: How to Win Hearts, Minds and Votes*. Bristol: Policy Press.

Akehurst, S. (2017). The power of Generation Rent was felt for the first time: Did renters cost Theresa May her majority? *City Metric*, June 20. https://www.citymetric.com/politics/power-generation-rent-was-felt-first-time-did-renters-cost-theresa-may-her-majority-3124 (Accessed 15 August 2019)

Andrews, K. (2017). The votes of ethnic minorities made a big difference to the general election: Labour should take note. *The Independent*, 15 June. http://www.independent.co.uk/voices/ethnic-minority-vote-general-election-labour-jeremy-corbyn-racial-faultlines-anti-immigration-a7791101.html (Accessed 20 October 2017)

Ansell, B., and Adler, D. (2019). Brexit and the politics of housing in Britain. *Political Quarterly*, 90(S2): 105–16. https://doi.org/10.1111/1467-923X.12621

Armstrong, D. A., Lucas, J., and Taylor, Z. (2022). The urban-rural divide in Canadian federal elections, 1896–2019. *Canadian Journal of Political Science*, 55(1): 84–106. https://doi.org/10.1017/S0008423921000792

Autor, D., Dorn, D., Hanson, G., and Majlesi, K. (2020). Importing political polarization? The electoral consequences of rising trade exposure. *American Economic Review*, 110(10): 3139–83.

Ball, J. (2017). 'Militant Liverpool' as Liverpool exceptionalism: The rise, fall and character of the City Council, 1983–1987. *Transactions of the Historic Society of Lancashire and Cheshire*, 166: 145–186. https://doi.org/10.3828/transactions.166.10

Bank of England. (2016). *A Millennium of Macroeconomic Data*. London: Bank of England.

Barclay, A. (2020). When religious voting becomes volatile: The case of Jewish voters in Britain. *Politics and Religion*, 13(3): 544–74. https://doi.org/10.1017/S1755048320000188

Barnes, I., and Cox, V. (2007). EU migrants as entrepreneurs in Lincolnshire exploiting the enterprise culture. The *International Journal of Entrepreneurship and Innovation*, 8(3): 209–18. https://doi.org/10.5367/000000007781698545

Bartolini, S., and Mair P. (1990). *Identity, Competition, and Electoral Availability: The Stabilization of European Electorates 1885–1985*. Cambridge: Cambridge University Press.

Beatty, C., and Fothergill, S. (2020). The long shadow of job loss: Britain's older industrial towns in the 21st century. *Frontiers in Sociology*, 5. https://doi.org/10.3389/fsoc.2020.00054

Belchem, J. (2006). *Merseypride: Essays in Liverpool Exceptionalism.* 2nd edn. Liverpool: Liverpool University Press.

Bell, T., and Gardiner, L. (2019). My generation, baby: The politics of age in Brexit Britain. *Political Quarterly*, 90(S2): 128–41. https://doi.org/10.1111/1467-923X.12623

Benbough-Jackson, M., and Davies, S. (2011). Introduction: Merseyside and culture. In *Merseyside: Culture and Place.* Newcastle: Cambridge Scholars, 1–21.

Benzeval, M., Bond, L., Campbell, M., Egan, M., Lorenc, T., Petticrew, M., and Popham, F. (2014). *How does Money Influence Health?* York: Joseph Rowntree Foundation. https://www.jrf.org.uk/sites/default/files/jrf/migrated/files/income-health-poverty-full.pdf (Accessed 14 October 2019)

Bishop, B., and Cushing, R. G. (2008). *The Big Sort: Why the Clustering of Like-Minded America is Tearing us Apart.* Boston: Houghton Mifflin.

Bowyer, B. (2008). Local context and extreme right support in England: The British National Party in the 2002 and 2003 local elections. *Electoral Studies*, 27(4): 611–20. https://doi.org/10.1016/j.electstud.2008.05.001

Broun, J. L. (2020). Place, identity and social conflict in post-industrial England: Cases from South Lincolnshire in the 1980s. *Contemporary British History*, 34(3): 331–57. https://doi.org/10.1080/13619462.2020.1716732

Brown, J. R., and Enos, R. D. (2021). The measurement of partisan sorting for 180 million voters. *Nature Human Behaviour*, 5: 998–1008. https://doi.org/10.1038/s41562-021-01066-z

Bullivant, S. (2016). *Contemporary Catholicism in England and Wales: A Statistical Report Based on Recent British Social Attitudes Survey Data.* London: St Mary's University, Benedict XVI Centre for Religion and Society. https://www.stmarys.ac.uk/research/centres/benedict-xvi/docs/2018-feb-contemporary-catholicism-report-may16.pdf (Accessed 17 January 2019)

Burn-Murdoch, J. (2022). Millennials are shattering the oldest rule in politics. *Financial Times*, 30 December. https://www.ft.com/content/c361e372-769e-45cd-a063-f5c0a7767cf4 (Accessed 5 October 2023)

Burn-Murdoch, J. (2023). London's parasitical housing market is driving away young families. *Financial Times*, 21 April. https://www.ft.com/content/d6bc22ed-d6d8-464b-b706-b4d478c6baf1 (Accessed 5 October 2023)

Butler, D., and Stokes, D. E. (1969). *Political Change in Britain: Forces Shaping Electoral Choice.* New York: St. Martin's Press.

Cadywould, C. (2017). Three challenges Labour must grapple with before it can deliver a progressive majority. LSE British and Irish Politics and Policy. https://blogs.lse.ac.uk/politicsandpolicy/labour-long-term-challenges (Accessed 5 October 2023)

Campbell, R., and Shorrocks, R. (2021). Finally rising with the tide? Gender and the vote in the 2019 British Elections. *Journal of Elections, Public Opinion and Parties*, 31(4): 488–507. https://doi.org/10.1080/17457289.2021.1968412

Catney, G. (2015). Exploring a decade of small area ethnic (de-)segregation in England and Wales. *Urban Studies*, 53: 1691–1709.

Catney, G. (2016). The changing geographies of ethnic diversity in England and Wales, 1991–2011. *Population, Space and Place*, 22: 750–65.

Catney, G., Wright, R., and Ellis, M. (2021). The evolution and stability of multi-ethnic residential neighborhoods in England. *Transactions of the Institute of British Geographers*, 46: 330–46. https://doi.org/10.1111/tran.12416

Centre for Cities. (2016). *The Great British Brain Drain*. London: Centre for Cities. https://www.centreforcities.org/wp-content/uploads/2016/11/16-11-18-The-Great-British-Brain-Drain.pdf (Accessed 19 December 2023)

Chakelian, A. (2016). A view from Brexitland: Boston, the town that voted strongest to leave the EU. *New Statesman*, 1 July. https://www.newstatesman.com/politics/uk/2016/07/view-brexitland-boston-town-voted-strongest-leave-eu (Accessed 7 March 2019)

Chomyn, N. (2017). Klopp talk: 'I will never vote for the right'. The Liverpool Offside, 23 November. https://liverpooloffside.sbnation.com/liverpool-fc-news-coverage/2017/11/23/16694130/jurgen-klopp-politics-left-wing-shankly-socialism-never-vote-for-right (Accessed 4 August 2019)

Chrisp, J., and Pearce, N. (2019). Grey power: Towards a political economy of older voters in the UK. *Political Quarterly*, 90: 743–56. https://doi.org/10.1111/1467-923X.12737

Clements, B. (2017). Catholic voters in Britain: What are their political preferences? *British Politics and Policy*, 16 May. http://blogs.lse.ac.uk/politicsandpolicy/catholic-voters-in-britain-what-are-their-political-preferences/ (Accessed 8 June 2018)

Corlett, A., and Judge, L. (2017). *Home Affront: Housing across the Generations*. Resolution Foundation. https://www.resolutionfoundation.org/app/uploads/2017/09/Home-Affront.pdf (Accessed 11 August 2019)

Cramer, K. J. (2016). *The Politics of Resentment: Rural Consciousness in Wisconsin and the Rise of Scott Walker*. Chicago: University of Chicago Press.

Craw, D. W. (2014). The generation rent vote could decide the 2015 election. https://www.generationrent.org/generation_rent_decide_2015_election (Accessed 14 August 2019)

Crewe, I. (1973). The politics of 'affluent' and 'traditional' workers in Britain: An aggregate data analysis. *British Journal of Political Science*, 3(1): 29–52. https://doi.org/10.1017/S0007123400007687

Crewe, I. M., and Fox, A. D. (2011). *British Parliamentary Constituencies, 1979–1983*. [Data set] UK Data Service. SN: 1915. http://doi.org/10.5255/UKDA-SN-1915-1 (Accessed 2 February 2017)

Crewe, I, S.ärlvik, B., and Alt, J. (1977). Partisan dealignment in Britain 1964–1974. *British Journal of Political Science*, 7(2): 129–90. http://doi.org/10.1017/S0007123400000922.

Croll, A. (2003). Communing with 'the laity': Exceptionalism, postmodernism and the urban biography. *Urban History*, 30(2). https://doi.org/10.1017/S0963926803001068

Crosby, A. G. (2014). Perceptions of Liverpool 1530–2010: The historical evidence of 51 contemporary observers. *The Local Historian*, 44(1): 51–68.

Cox, G. W. (1986). The development of a party-orientated electorate in England, 1832–1918. *British Journal of Political Science*, 16(2): 187–216. https://doi.org/10.1017/S0007123400003884

Curtice, J. (2017). Who voted Labour in 2017? NatCen, 24 September. http://www.natcen.ac.uk/blog/who-voted-labour-in-2017?_ga=2.1622454.682480170.1506331403-2069454732.1462541675 (Accessed 26 September 2017)

Curtice, J., and Park, A. (eds) (1999). *Critical Elections: British Parties and Voters in Long-Term Perspective*. London: SAGE Publications, 124–47.

Curtice, J., and Steed, M. (1982). Electoral choice and the production of government: The changing operation of the electoral system in the United Kingdom since 1955. *British Journal of Political Science*, 12(3): 249–98. https://doi.org/10.1017/S0007123400002970

Cutts, D., Goodwin, M., Heath, O., and Surridge, P. (2020). Brexit, the 2019 general election and the realignment of British politics. *Political Quarterly*, 91: 7–23. https://doi.org/10.1111/1467-923X.12815

Cutts, D., and Webber, D. J. (2010). Voting patterns, party spending and relative location in England and Wales. *Regional Studies*, 44(6): 735–60. https://doi.org/10.1080/00343400903107744

Daddow, O. (2013). The use of force in British foreign policy: From new labour to the coalition. *Political Quarterly*, 84: 110–18. https://doi.org/10.1111/j.1467-923X.2013.02428.x

Dalton, R. J. (2007). Partisan mobilization, cognitive mobilization and the changing American electorate. *Electoral Studies*, 26(2): 274–86. https://doi.org/10.1016/J.ELECTSTUD.2006.04.009

Damore, D. F., Lang, R. E., and Danielsen, K. A. (2020). *Blue Metros, Red States: The Shifting Urban-Rural Divide in America's Swing States*. Washington, DC: Brookings Institution.

Davie, G. (1993). Believing without Belonging: A Liverpool Case Study/Croyance sans appartenance: Le cas de Liverpool. *Archives des Sciences Sociales des Religions*, 81: 79–89. https://doi.org/10.3406/assr.1993.1636

Davies, S. (1996). *Liverpool Labour: Social and Political Influences on the Development of the Labour Party in Liverpool, 1900–1939*. Edinburgh: Edinburgh University Press.

Department for Education (2017). *Schools in England*. [Data set]. https://www.gov.uk/government/publications/schools-in-england (Accessed 17 October 2019)

Department for Environment, Food and Rural Affairs (2009). *Parliamentary Constituencies*. [Data set]. https://www.ons.gov.uk//methodology/geography/geographicalproducts/ruralurbanclassifications/2001ruralurbanclassification (Accessed 9 September 2019)

Dempsey, N., and Johnston, N. (2018). Political disengagement in the UK: Who is disengaged? (House of Commons Library briefing paper 7501). https://researchbriefings.parliament.uk/ResearchBriefing/Summary/CBP-7501 (Accessed 17 October 2019)

Denver, D. (2018). The results: How Britain voted. *Parliamentary Affairs*, 71(suppl_1), 8–28. https://doi.org/10.1093/pa/gsx059

de Dominicis, L., Dijkstra, L., and Pontarollo, N. (2022). Why are cities less opposed to European integration than rural areas? Factors affecting the Eurosceptic vote by degree of urbanization. *Cities*, 130: 103937.

Dormann, C. F., Elith, J., Bacher, S., Buchmann, C. M., Carl, G., Carré, G., and Lautenbach, S. (2013). Collinearity: A review of methods to deal with it and a simulation study evaluating their performance. *Ecography*, 36(1): 27–46. https://doi.org/10.1111/j.1600-0587.2012.07348.x

Dunbabin, J. P. D. (1963). The 'revolt of the field': The agricultural labourers' movement in the 1870s. *Past and Present*, 26(1): 68–97. https://doi.org/10.1093/past/26.1.68

Dunleavy, P. (1980a). The political implications of sectoral cleavages and the growth of state employment: Part 1, the analysis of production cleavages. *Political Studies*, 28(3): 364–83. https://doi.org/10.1111/j.1467-9248.1980.tb00475.x

Dunleavy, P. (1980b). The political implications of sectoral cleavages and the growth of state employment: Part 2, cleavage structures and political alignment. *Political Studies*, 28(4): 527–49. https://doi.org/10.1111/j.1467-9248.1980.tb01257.x

Dunt, I. (2012). Hillsborough: Was it Thatcher's fault? http://www.politics.co.uk/news/2012/09/13/hillsborough-was-it-thatcher-s-fault (Accessed 23 February 2019)

The Economist. (2021). The truth behind the Tories' northern strongholds. *The Economist*, 31 March.

Electoral Calculus. (n.d.). *1992 (Actual) Election Result*. [Data set]. https://www.electoralcalculus.co.uk/flatfile.html (Accessed 17 October 2019)

Enos, R. D. (2017). *The Space between us: Social Geography and Politics*. Cambridge: Cambridge University Press.

Evans, G., and Tilley, J. (2012). How parties shape class politics: Explaining the decline of the class basis of party support. *British Journal of Political Science*, 42(1): 137–61. https://doi.org/10.1017/S0007123411000202

Evans, G., and Tilley, J. (2017). *The New Politics of Class: The Political Exclusion of the British Working Class*. Oxford: Oxford University Press.

Faggian, A., Modica, M., Modrego, F., and Urso, G. (2021). One country, two populist parties: Voting patterns of the 2018 Italian elections and their determinants. *Regional Science Policy and Practice*, 13: 397–413.

Farrall, S., Gray, E., and Jones, P. M. (2020). The role of radical economic restructuring in truancy from school and engagement in crime. *British Journal of Criminology*, 60(1): 118–40. https://doi.org/10.1093/bjc/azz040

Fieldhouse, E. A. (1995). Thatcherism and the changing geography of political attitudes, 1964–87. *Political Geography*, 14(1): 3–30.

Fieldhouse, E., and Bailey, J. (2023). A new electoral map? Brexit, realignment and the changing geography of party support in England. *Political Geography*, 102(102862): 1–10. https://doi.org/10.1016/j.polgeo.2023.102862

Fieldhouse, E., Green, J., Evans., G., Schmitt, H., van der Eijk, C., Mellon, J., and Prosser, C. (2017). *British Election Study 2017 Constituency Results file, version 1.0*. [Data set]. https://www.britishelectionstudy.com/data-object/2017-bes-constituency-results-with-census-and-candidate-data (Accessed 9 November 2018)

Fieldhouse, E., Green, J., Evans, G., Mellon, J., Prosser, C., Schmitt, H., and van der Eijk, C. (2020). *Electoral Shocks: The Volatile Voter in a Turbulent World*. Oxford: Oxford University Press. https://doi.org/10.1093/oso/9780198800583.001.0001

Fitzgerald, J. (2020). *Close to Home: Local Ties and Voting Radical Right in Europe*. Cambridge: Cambridge University Press.

Foos, F., and Bischof, D. (2022). Tabloid media campaigns and public opinion: Quasi-experimental evidence on euroscepticism in England. *American Political Science Review*, 116(1): 19–37. https://doi.org/10.1017/S000305542100085X

Ford, R., and Goodwin, M. (2014). *Revolt on the Right: Explaining Support for the Radical Right in Britain*. London: Routledge.

Ford, R., and Grove-White, R. (2015). Migrant voters in the 2015 general election. Migrants' Rights Network and Centre on Dynamics of Ethnicity, University of Manchester. https://www.barrowcadbury.org.uk/wp-content/uploads/2015/01/Migrant_Voters_2015_paper.pdf (Accessed 7 March 2019)

Ford, R., and Jennings, W. (2020). The changing cleavage politics of Western Europe. *Annual Review of Political Science*, 23: 295–314. https://doi.org/10.1146/annurev-polisci-052217-104957

Ford, R., Jennings, W., and Somerville, W. (2015). Public opinion, responsiveness and constraint: Britain's three immigration policy regimes. *Journal of Ethnic and Migration Studies*, 41(9): 1391–411. https://doi.org/10.1080/1369183X.2015.1021585

Ford, R., Bale, T., Jennings, W., and Surridge, P. (2021). *The British General Election of 2019*. Basingstoke: Palgrave.

Furlong, J. (2018). Twitter thread on 'Accounting for demographics and geographical location, where in the country did Labour over-perform (green-dark green on map) in 2017?' Twitter, 13 November. https://twitter.com/jamiewfurlong/status/1062280372082348032 (Accessed 19 December 2023)

Furlong, J. (2019). The changing electoral geography of England and Wales: Varieties of 'left-behindedness'. *Political Geography*, 75. https://doi.org/10.1016/j.polgeo.2019.102061

Gallego, A., Buscha, F., Sturgis, P., and Oberski, D. (2016). Places and preferences: A longitudinal analysis of self-selection and contextual effects. *British Journal of Political Science*, 46(3): 529–50. https://doi.org/10.1017/S0007123414000337

van Gent, W. P. C., Jansen, E. F., Smits, J., and H, F. (2014). Right-wing radical populism in city and suburbs: An electoral geography of the Partij Voor de Vrijheid in the Netherlands. *Urban Studies*, 51(9): 1775–94. https://doi.org/10.1177/00420980 13505889

Gest, J., Reny, T., and Mayer, J. (2017). Roots of the radical right: Nostalgic deprivation in the United States and Britain. *Comparative Political Studies*, 51(13): 1694–1719. https://doi. org/10.1177/0010414017720705

Gidron, N., and Hall, P. A. (2017). The politics of social status: Economic and cultural roots of the populist right. *British Journal of Sociology*, 68: S57–S84. https://doi.org/10.1111/1468-4446.12319

Gidron, N., and Hall, P. A. (2020). Populism as a problem of social integration. *Comparative Political Studies*, 53(7): 1027–59. https://doi.org/10.1177/0010414019879947

Goodhart, D. (2017). *The Road to Somewhere: The Populist Revolt and the Future of Politics*. London: Hurst & Co.

Goodwin, M., and Heath, O. (2016). The 2016 referendum, Brexit and the left behind: An aggregate-level analysis of the result. *Political Quarterly*, 87(3): 323–32. https://doi.org/10. 1111/1467-923X.12285

Goodwin, L. D., and Leech, N. L. (2006). Understanding correlation: Factors that affect the size of r. *Journal of Experimental Education*, 74(3): 249–66. https;//doi.org/10.3200/JEXE. 74.3.249-266

Graham, M. H. (2003). Confronting multicollinearity in ecological multiple regression. *Ecology*, 84(11): 2809–15. https://doi.org/10.1890/02-3114

Grasso, M. T., Farrall, S., Gray, E., Hay, C., and Jennings, W. (2019). Thatcher's children, Blair's babies, political socialization and trickle-down value change: An age, period and cohort analysis. *British Journal of Political Science*, 49(1): 17–36. https://doi.org/10.1017/S0007123416000375

Gray, M., and Caul, M. (2000). Declining voter turnout in advanced industrial democracies, 1950 to 1997: The effects of declining group mobilization. *Comparative Political Studies*, 33(9): 1091–1122. https://doi.org/10.1177/0010414000033009001

Green, J. (2021). Why did the Conservatives win? In N. Allen and J. Bartle (eds) *Breaking the Deadlock*. Manchester: Manchester University Press, 174–97. https://doi.org/10.7765/9781526152374.00013

Green, J., and Jennings, W. (2017). *The Politics of Competence*. Cambridge: Cambridge University Press.

Green, J., and Prosser, C. (2016). Party system fragmentation and single-party government: The British general election of 2015. *West European Politics*, 39(6): 1299–310. https://doi. org/10.1080/01402382.2016.1173335

Green, A. E., Jones, P., and Owen, D. (2007). *Migrant Workers in the East Midlands Labour Market*. East Midlands Development Agency. http://irep.ntu.ac.uk/id/eprint/431/1/202835_migrantworkersintheeastmidalndslabourmarket2007.pdf (Accessed 7 March 2019)

Green, J., Jennings, W., McKay, L. and Stoker, G. (2023) Perceptions of local economic Decline: Who perceives decline, and why does it matter? Paper Prepared for the Annual Conference of the European Political Science Association, 24 June 2021.

Hainmueller, J., and Hiscox, M. J. (2010). Attitudes toward highly skilled and low-skilled immigration: Evidence from a survey experiment. *American Political Science Review*, 104(1): 61–84. https://doi.org/10.1017/S0003055409990372

Hall, P. A., Evans, G., and Kim, S. I. (2023). *Political Change and Electoral Coalitions in Western Democracies*. Cambridge: Cambridge University Press.

Hanretty, C. (2017). Areal interpolation and the UK's referendum on EU membership. *Journal of Elections, Public Opinion and Parties*, 27(4): 466–83. https://doi.org/10.1080/17457289.2017.1287081

Hardy, J., and Clark, N. (2005). EU enlargement, workers and migration: Implications for trade unions in the UK and Poland. The Global Unions Research Network International Workshop 'Trade Unions, Globalization and Development—Strengthening Rights and Capabilities of Workers'. Novo Hamborgo, Brazil. https://www.tuc.org.uk/research-analysis/reports/eu-enlargement-workers-and-migration-implications-trade-unions-uk-and (Accessed 5 March 2019)

Harris, J., Domokos, J., Stevenson, R., and Payne-Frank, N. (2015). Election 2015: Fear and loathing in Farageland. *The Guardian*, 14 April. https://www.theguardian.com/commentisfree/video/2015/apr/14/boston-lincolnshire-nigel-farage-ukip-migrants-video (Accessed 7 March 2019)

Harteveld, E., van der Brug, W., de Lange, S., and van der Meer, T. (2022). Multiple roots of the populist radical right: Support for the Dutch PVV in cities and the countryside. *European Journal of Political Research*, 61: 440–61. https://doi.org/10.1111/1475-6765.12452

Heath, A. F., Fisher, S., Sanders, D., and Sobolewska, M. (2011). Ethnic heterogeneity in the social bases of voting at the 2010 British general election. *Journal of Elections, Public Opinion and Parties*, 21(2): 255–77. https://doi.org/10.1080/17457289.2011.562611

Heath, A. F., Fisher, S. D., Rosenblatt, G., Sanders, D., and Sobolewska, M. (2013). *The Political Integration of Ethnic Minorities in Britain*. Oxford: Oxford University Press.

Heath, O. (2015). Policy representation, social representation and class voting in Britain. *British Journal of Political Science*, 45(1): 173–93. https://doi.org/10.1017/S0007123413000318

Heath, O. (2018). Policy alienation, social alienation and working-class abstention in Britain, 1964–2010. *British Journal of Political Science*, 48(4): 1053–73. https://doi.org/10.1017/S0007123416000272

Heath, O., and Goodwin, M. (2017). The 2017 general election, Brexit and the return to two-party politics: An aggregate-level analysis of the result. *Political Quarterly*, 88: 345–58. https://doi.org/10.1111/1467-923X.12405

Hirschman, A. O. (1964). The paternity of an index. *American Economic Review*, 54(5): 761.

Hobolt, S. B. (2018). Brexit and the 2017 UK general election. *Journal of Common Market Studies*, 56(S1): 39–50. https://doi.org/10.1111/jcms.12751

Hobolt, S., Leeper, T., and Tilley, J. (2021). Divided by the vote: Affective polarization in the wake of the Brexit referendum. *British Journal of Political Science*, 51(4): 1476–93. https://doi.org/10.1017/S0007123420000125

House of Commons Library. (2012). *Education: Historical Statistics SN/SG/4252*. London: UK Parliament.

House of Commons Library. (2020a). *General Election Results from 1918 to 2019*. London: UK Parliament. https://commonslibrary.parliament.uk/research-briefings/cbp-8647/

House of Commons Library. (2020b). *General Election 2019: Full Results and Analysis*. [Data set]. https://commonslibrary.parliament.uk/research-briefings/cbp-8749/ (Accessed 4 October 2023)

House of Commons Library (2021). *Housing an Ageing Population: A Reading List*. https://commonslibrary.parliament.uk/research-briefings/cbp-9239/ (Accessed 5 October 2023)

House of Commons Library (2023). *Higher Education Student Numbers*. https://researchbriefings.files.parliament.uk/documents/CBP-7857/CBP-7857.pdf (Accessed 10 December 2023)

Ipsos Mori (2004a). *Local Government Review—Views of Residents in the Sefton Metropolitan Borough Council area, Merseyside.* London: The Boundary Committee for England. https://www.ipsos.com/sites/default/files/migrations/en-uk/files/Assets/Docs/Archive/Polls/rep60sef.pdf (Accessed 13 February 2019)

Ipsos Mori (2004b). *Local Government Review—Views of Residents in Wirral Metropolitan Borough Council Area.* London: The Boundary Committee for England. https://www.ipsos.com/sites/default/files/migrations/en-uk/files/Assets/Docs/Archive/Polls/rep57wir.pdf (Accessed 13 February 2019)

Iversen, T., and Soskice, D. (2019). *Democracy and Prosperity: Reinventing Capitalism through a Turbulent Century.* Princeton: Princeton University Press.

Jack, I. (2019). The trip from London to Lincolnshire showed me the Brexit divide's depth. *The Guardian,* 16 February. https://www.theguardian.com/commentisfree/2019/feb/16/trip-london-lincolnshire-brexit-divide (Accessed 7 March 2019)

James, Z. (2020). Gypsies' and Travellers' lived experience of harm: A critical hate studies perspective. *Theoretical Criminology,* 24(3), 502–20. https://doi.org/10.1177/1362480620911914

Jeffery, D. (2017). The strange death of Tory Liverpool: Conservative electoral decline in Liverpool, 1945–1996. *British Politics,* 12(3): 386–407. https://doi.org/10.1057/s41293-016-0032-6

Jeffery, D. (2023a). *Whatever Happened to Tory Liverpool? Success, Decline and Irrelevance since 1945.* Liverpool: Liverpool University Press.

Jeffery, D. (2023b). The impact of local identities on voting behaviour: A scouse case study. *British Politics.* https://doi.org/10.1057/s41293-023-00242-1

Jefferys, P. (2013). London has certainly seen a big increase in private renters but it's not the city with the biggest proportion of private renters in England. *British Politics and Policy,* 4 February. https://blogs.lse.ac.uk/politicsandpolicy/renting-not-just-for-londoners (Accessed 11 August 2019)

Jennings, W., and Stoker, G. (2015). The bifurcation of politics: The impact of cosmopolitan versus shrinking urban dynamics. Paper presented at the European Urban Research Association conference 'Transforming cities, transformative cities', Sibiu, Romania, 17–20 September 2015. https://antipolitics.soton.ac.uk/files/2015/08/StokerJenningsShrinkingCosmopolitanUrban-1.pdf (Accessed 1 August 2023)

Jennings, W., and Stoker, G. (2016). The bifurcation of politics: Two Englands. *Political Quarterly,* 87(3): 372–82. https://doi.org/10.1111/1467-923X.12228

Jennings, W., and Stoker, G. (2017). Tilting towards the cosmopolitan axis? Political change in England and the 2017 general election. *Political Quarterly,* 88(3): 359–69. https://doi.org/10.1111/1467-923X.12403

Jennings, W., and Stoker, G. (2019). The divergent dynamics of cities and towns: Geographical polarisation and Brexit. *Political Quarterly,* 90(S2): 155–66. https://doi.org/10.1111/1467-923X.12612

Jennings, W., McKay, L., and Stoker, G. (2021). The politics of levelling up. *Political Quarterly,* 92(2): 302–11. https://doi.org/10.1111/1467-923X.13005

Jensen, C. D., Lacombe, D. J., and McIntyre, S. G. (2013). A Bayesian spatial econometric analysis of the 2010 UK general election. *Papers in Regional Science,* 92(3): 651–66. https://doi.org/10.1111/j.1435-5957.2012.00415.x

Jensen, J. L., Sum, P. E., and Flynn, D. T. (2009). Political orientations and behavior of public employees: A cross-national comparison. *Journal of Public Administration Research and Theory,* 19(4): 709–30. https://doi.org/10.1093/jopart/mun031

Johnson, B. (2020). Leicester: Up to 10,000 could be victims of modern slavery in textile factories. *Sky News Online*, 13 July. https://news.sky.com/story/leicester-up-to-10-000-could-be-victims-of-modern-slavery-in-textile-factories-12027289 (Accessed 10 November 2022)

Johnston, R. J., and Pattie, C. J. (1998). Composition and context: Region and voting in Britain revisited during Labour's 1990s revival. *Geoforum*, 29(3): 309–29. https://10.1016/S0016-7185(98)00013-X

Johnston, R., and Pattie, C. J. (2006). *Putting Voters in Their Place: Geography and Elections in Great Britain*. Oxford: Oxford University Press.

Johnston, R. J.,Pattie, C. J., and Allsopp, J. G. (1988). *A nation dividing? The Electoral Map of Great Britain 1979–1987*. London: Longman.

Johnston, R., Jones, K., Sarker, R., Propper, C., Burgess, S., and Bolster, A. (2004). Party support and the neighbourhood effect: Spatial polarisation of the British electorate 1991–2001. *Political Geography*, 23(4): 367–402. https://doi.org/10.1016/j.polgeo.2003.12.008

Johnston, R., Propper, C., Burgess, S., Sarker, R., Bolster, A., and Jones, K. (2005). Spatial scale and the neighbourhood effect: Multinomial models of voting at two recent British general elections. *British Journal of Political Science*, 35(3): 487–514. https://doi.org/10.1017/s0007123405000268

Johnston, R., Jones, K., Propper, C., and Burgess, S. (2007). Region, local context, and voting at the 1997 general election in England. *American Journal of Political Science*, 51(3): 640–54. https://doi.org/10.1111/j.1540-5907.2007.00272.x

Kanagasooriam, J. (2019). Twitter thread on where the U.K. Conservative party has historically, and is still, under-performing, and why that's interesting for any upcoming election. Twitter, 14 August. https://twitter.com/JamesKanag/status/1161639282450321409

Kanagasooriam, J., and Simon, E. (2021). Red wall: The definitive description. *Political Insight*, 12(3): 8–11. https://doi.org/10.1177/20419058211045127

Katwala, S., and Ballinger, S. (2017). *Mind the Gap: How the Ethnic Minority Vote Cost Theresa May her Majority*. London: British Future. http://www.britishfuture.org/wp-content/uploads/2017/09/Mind-the-gap-report-2017.pdf (Accessed 20 October 2017)

Kaufmann, E. (2017). Levels or changes? Ethnic context, immigration and the UK Independence Party vote. *Electoral Studies*, 48: 57–69. https://doi.org/10.1016/j.electstud.2017.05.002

Laver, M., and Budge, I. (eds) (1992). *Party Policy and Government Coalitions*. Basingstoke: Macmillan.

Law, C. M. (1967). The growth of urban population in England and Wales, 1801–1911. *Transactions of the Institute of British Geographers*, 41: 125–43. https://doi.org/10.2307/621331

Lazar, S., and Sanchez, A. (2019). Understanding labour politics in an age of precarity. *Dialectical Anthropology*, 43: 3–14. https://doi.org/10.1007/s10624-019-09544-7

Lehmann, P., Franzmann, S., Burst, T., Regel, S., Riethmüller, F., Volkens, A., Weßels, B., and Zehnter, L. (2023). *The Manifesto Data Collection*. Manifesto Project (MRG/CMP/MARPOR). Version 2023a. Berlin: Wissenschaftszentrum Berlin für Sozialforschung (WZB)/Göttingen: Institut für Demokratieforschung (IfDem). https://doi.org/10.25522/manifesto.mpds.2023a

Leigh, A. (2005). Economic voting and electoral behaviour: How do individual, local and national factors affect the partisan choice? *Economics and Politics*, 17(2): 265–96. https://doi.org/10.1111/j.1468-0343.2005.00154.x

Lipset, S. M., and Rokkan, S. (eds) (1967). *Party Systems and Voter Alignments: Cross-National Perspectives*. New York: Free Press.

Local Trust. (2019). Left behind? Understanding communities on the edge. https://localtrust.
org.uk/wp-content/uploads/2019/08/local_trust_ocsi_left_behind_research_august_2019.
pdf (Accessed 15 December 2023)

Luca, D., Terrero-Davila, J., Stein, J., and Lee, N. (2023). Progressive cities: Urban–rural polarisation of social values and economic development around the world. *Urban Studies*, 60(12):
2329–50. https://doi.org/10.1177/00420980221148388

Lumsden, K., Goode, J., and Black, A. (2018). 'I will not be thrown out of the country because
I'm an immigrant': Eastern European migrants' responses to hate crime in a semi-rural context in the wake of Brexit. *Sociological Research Online*, 24(2): 167–84. https://doi.org/10.
1177/1360780418811967

Lund, B. (2015). The electoral politics of housing. *Political Quarterly*, 86(4): 500–6. https://
doi.org/10.1111/1467-923X.12205

McAllister, I., and Rose, R. (1988). *United Kingdom Ecological Data, 1981–1987*. [Data set] UK
Data Service. SN: 2081. http://doi.org/10.5255/UKDA-SN-2081-1 (Accessed 17 October
2018)

MacAllister, I., Johnston, R., Pattie, C., Tunstall, H., Dorling, D., and Rossiter, D. (2001) Class
dealignment and the neighbourhood effect: Miller revisited. *British Journal of Political
Science*, 31(1): 41–59. https://doi.org/10.1017/S0007123401000035

MacAllister, I., Fieldhouse, E., and Russell, A. (2002). Yellow fever? The political geography of
liberal voting in Great Britain. *Political Geography*, 21(4): 421–47. https://doi.org/10.1016/
S0962-6298(01)00077-4

McAteer, B. (2017). The Social Impacts of Urban Waterfront Regeneration Projects. http://
theprotocity.com/social-impacts-urban-waterfront-regeneration-projects/ (Accessed 22
February 2019)

McCann, P., and Ortega-Argilés, R. (2021). The UK 'geography of discontent': Narratives,
Brexit and inter-regional 'levelling up'. *Cambridge Journal of Regions, Economy and Society*,
14(3): 545–64. https://doi.org/10.1093/cjres/rsab017

McKay, L., Jennings, W., and Stoker, G. (2023). Understanding the geography of discontent:
Perceptions of government's biases against left-behind places. *Journal of European Public
Policy*: 1–30. https://doi.org/10.1080/13501763.2023.2277381

McKee, K., Hoolachan, J., and Moore, T. E. (2017). The precarity of young people's housing
experiences in a rural context. *Scottish Geographical Journal*, 133(2): 115–29.

McLennan, W. (2019). General election 2019: Did students seal Labour's victory in Canterbury? *BBC News*, 14 December. https://www.bbc.co.uk/news/election-2019-50776173
(Accessed 19 December 2023)

McMahon, D., Heath, A., Harrop, M., and Curtice, J. (1992). The electoral consequences of
north–south migration. *British Journal of Political Science*, 22(4): 419–43. https://doi.org/
10.1017/S0007123400006475

Marcinkiewicz, K. (2018). The economy or an urban–rural divide? Explaining spatial patterns
of voting behaviour in Poland. *East European Politics and Societies*, 32(4): 693–719. https://
doi.org/10.1177/0888325417739955

Martin, R., Gardiner, B., Pike, A., Sunley, P., and Tyler, P. (2021). *Levelling Up Left
Behind Places: The Scale and Nature of the Economic and Policy Challenge*. London:
Routledge.

Martínez-Fernández, C., Audirac, I., Fol, S., and Cunningham-Sabot, E. (2012). Shrinking
cities: Urban challenges of globalization. *International Journal of Urban and Regional
Research*, 36(2): 213–25. https://doi.org/10.1111/j.1468-2427.2011.01092.x

Massey, D., and Thrift, N. (2003). The passion of place. In Johnston, R., and Williams, M. (eds)
A Century of British Geography. London: British Academy, 275–302

Maxwell, R. (2019). Cosmopolitan immigration attitudes in large European cities: Contextual or compositional effects? *American Political Science Review*, 113(2): 456–74. https://doi.org/10.1017/S0003055418000898

Mellon, J., Evans, G., Fieldhouse, E., Green, J., and Prosser, C. (2018). Brexit or Corbyn? Campaign and inter-election vote switching in the 2017 UK general election. *Parliamentary Affairs*, 71(4): 719–37. https://doi.org/10.1093/pa/gsy001

Millward, P., and Rookwood, J. (2011). 'We all dream of a team of Carraghers': Comparing the semiotics of 'local' and Texan Liverpool fans' talk. *Sport in Society*, 14(1): 37–52. https://doi.org/10.1080/17430437.2011.530009

Moore, D. C. (1976). *The Politics of Deference: A Study of the Mid-Nineteenth Century British Political System*. Hassocks: Harvester Press.

Moretti, E. (2012). *The New Geography of Jobs*. New York: Houghton Mifflin Harcourt

Newburn, T. (2001). Modernisation, New Labour and criminal justice policy. *Criminal Justice Matters*, 46(1): 4–5. https://doi.org/10.1080/09627250108553653

Newburn, T. (2007). 'Tough on crime': Penal policy in England and Wales. *Crime and Justice*, 36(1): 425–70. https://doi.org/10.1086/592810

Newby, H. (1979). *The Deferential Worker: A Study of Farm Workers in East Anglia*. Madison, WI: University of Wisconsin Press.

Norris, P. (2001). *The British Parliamentary Constituency Database 1992–2001*. Release 1.2. [Data set]. https://www.pippanorris.com/data/ (Accessed 9 November 2018)

Norris, P. (2005). *The British Parliamentary Constituency Database 1992–2005*. Release 1.3. [Data set]. https://www.pippanorris.com/data/ (Accessed 9 August 2017)

Norris, P. (2010). *May 6th 2010 British General Election Constituency Results*. Release 5.0. [Data set]. https://sites.google.com/site/pippanorris3/research/data#TOC-May-6th-2010-British-General-Election-Constituency-Results-Release-5.0 (Accessed 9 November 2018)

O'Connor, S. (2017). Left behind: Can anyone save the towns the UK economy forgot? *The Financial Times*, 16 November. https://www.ft.com/blackpool (Accessed 1 October 2017)

Office for National Statistics. (2002). *UK Standard Industrial Classification of Economic Activities 2003*. London: The Stationery Office https://webarchive.nationalarchives.gov.uk/ukgwa/20160105160709/http://www.ons.gov.uk/ons/guide-method/classifications/archived-standard-classifications/uk-standard-industrial-classification-1992–sic92-/uk-sic-2003.pdf (Accessed 15 April 2024)

Office for National Statistics. (2003). *2001 Census Aggregate Data*. [Data sets]. https://www.nomisweb.co.uk/census/2001/all_tables (Accessed 9 November 2018)

Office for National Statistics. (2013) *2011 Census Aggregate Data*. [Data sets]. https://www.nomisweb.co.uk/census/2011/all_tables (Accessed 9 November 2018)

Office for National Statistics. (2015). *House Price Statistics for Small Areas: 1995 to 2014*. [Data set]. https://www.gov.uk/government/statistics/house-price-statistics-for-small-areas-1995-to-2014 (Accessed 11 August 2019)

Office for National Statistics. (2016). *Trade Union Membership Statistics 2015. Labour Force Survey*. [Data set]. https://www.gov.uk/government/statistics/trade-union-statistics-2015 (Accessed 5 February 2019)

Office for National Statistics. (2017a). Business Register and Employment Survey Public/Private Sector. [Data set]. https://www.nomisweb.co.uk/datasets/newbres6pp (Accessed 6 February 2019)

Office for National Statistics. (2017b). *Households by Deprivation Dimensions*. [Data set] QS119EW. https://www.nomisweb.co.uk/census/2011/qs119ew (Accessed 15 April 2024)

Office for National Statistics. (2018a). *Earnings and Hours Worked, Place of Residence by Parliamentary Constituency*. [Data set] ASHE Table 10. https://www.ons.gov.

uk/employmentandlabourmarket/peopleinwork/earningsandworkinghours/datasets/ placeofresidencebyparliamentaryconstituencyashetable10 (Accessed 11 August 2018).

Office for National Statistics. (2018b). *People in Employment on Zero Hours Contracts*. [Data set] EMP17. https://www.ons.gov.uk/employmentandlabourmarket/peoplein work/employmentandemployeetypes/datasets/emp17peopleinemploymentonzerohours contracts (Accessed 19 March 2018)

Office for National Statistics. (2018c). *UK Business: Activity, Size and Location*. [Data set]. https://www.ons.gov.uk/businessindustryandtrade/business/activitysizeandlocation/ datasets/ukbusinessactivitysizeandlocation (Accessed 11 August 2019).

Office for National Statistics. (2020). *Population Estimates for the UK, England and Wales, Scotland and Northern Ireland: Mid-2019*. https://www.ons.gov.uk/peoplepopulation andcommunity/populationandmigration/populationestimates/bulletins/annualmidyear populationestimates/mid2019estimates (Accessed 6 October 2023)

Office for National Statistics. (2021). *Census Unearthed: Explore 50 Years of Change from 1961*. https://www.ons.gov.uk/peoplepopulationandcommunity/housing/articles/ censusunearthedexplore50yearsofchangefrom1961/2021-08-09

Office for National Statistics. (2023a). *Profile of the Older Population Living in England and Wales in 2021 and Changes since 2011*. https://www.ons.gov.uk/peoplepopulationand community/birthsdeathsandmarriages/ageing/articles/profileoftheolderpopulationliving inenglandandwalesin2021andchangessince2011/2023-04-03 (Accessed 5 October 2023)

Office for National Statistics. (2023b). *Housing, England and Wales: Census 2021*. https://www.ons.gov.uk/peoplepopulationandcommunity/housing/bulletins/ housingenglandandwales/census2021 (Accessed 5 October 2023)

Office of Population Censuses and Surveys. (1997). *1991 Census Aggregate Data*. [Data sets]. https://www.nomisweb.co.uk/query/select/getdatasetbytheme.asp?theme=77 (Accessed 9 November 2019)

Office of Population Censuses and Surveys. (2000). *1981 Census Aggregate Data*. [Data sets]. https://www.nomisweb.co.uk/query/select/getdatasetbytheme.asp?theme=78 (Accessed 9 November 2018)

Okely, J. (2014). Recycled (mis)representations: Gypsies, Travellers or Roma treated as objects, rarely subjects. *People, Place and Policy Online*, 65–85. https://doi.org/10.3351/ ppp.0008.0001.0006

Olney, R. J. (1973). *Lincolnshire Politics 1832–1885*. London: Oxford University Press.

Parker, S. (2019). The leaving of Liverpool: Managed decline and the enduring legacy of Thatcherism's urban policy. *British Politics and Policy*, 17 January. https://blogs.lse.ac.uk/ politicsandpolicy/the-leaving-of-liverpool (Accessed 22 February 2019)

Patias, N., Rowe, F., and Arribas-Bel, D. (2023). Local urban attributes defining ethnically segregated areas across English cities: A multilevel approach. *Cities*, 132: 103967.

Pattie, C., Dorling, D., and Johnston, R. (1997). The electoral geography of recession: Local economic conditions, public perceptions and the economic vote in the 1992 British general election. *Transactions of the Institute of British Geographers*, 22(2): 147–61. http://www. jstor.org/stable/622306

Pattie, C., and Johnston, R. (1999). Context, conversation and conviction: Social networks and voting at the 1992 British general election. *Political Studies*, 47(5): 877–89. https://doi. org/10.1111/1467-9248.00235

Pattie, C., and Johnston, R. (2000). 'People who talk together vote together': An exploration of contextual effects in Great Britain. *Annals of the Association of American Geographers*, 90: 41–66. https://doi.org/10.1111/0004-5608.00183

Pattie, C., and Johnston, R. (2009). Electoral Geography. In Kitchin, R., and Thrift, N. (eds) *International Encyclopedia of Human Geography*. Elsevier Science, 405–22.

Pattie, C. J., Johnston, R. J., Schipper, M., and Potts, L. (2015). Are regions important in British elections? Valence politics and local economic contexts at the 2010 general election. *Regional Studies*, 49(9): 1561–74. https://doi.org/10.1080/00343404.2013.847271

Payne, S. (2019). UK general election: Can Boris Johnson break Labour's 'red wall'? *Financial Times*, 6 November. https://www.ft.com/content/fbd00ed6-ffd1-11e9-be59-e49b2a136b8d

Pearce, N. (2016). Labour is caught in a bind between its metropolitan and working-class heartlands. *The Guardian*, 3 July. https://www.theguardian.com/commentisfree/2016/jul/02/brexit-labour-divisions-way-forward (Accessed 10 July 2017)

Phillips, J. M., and Brown, J. (2011). Matriarchal narratives of identity and community, and the re-branding of a city. In Benbough-Jackson, M., and Davies, S. (eds) *Merseyside: Culture and Place*. Newcastle: Cambridge Scholars, 214–40.

Pike, A., MacKinnon, D., Coombes, M., Champion, T., Bradley, D., Cumbers, A., Robson, L., and Wymer, C. (2016). *Uneven Growth: Tackling City Decline*. Joseph Rowntree Foundation. https://www.jrf.org.uk/sites/default/files/jrf/files-research/tackling_declining_cities_report.pdf (Accessed 7 August 2018)

Pike, A., Béal, V., Cauchi-Duval, N., Franklin, R., Kinossian, N., Lang, T., Leibert, T., MacKinnon, D., Rousseau, M., Royer, J., Servillo, L., Tomaney, J., and Velthuis, S. (2023). 'Left behind places': A geographical etymology. *Regional Studies*. https://doi.org/10.1080/00343404.2023.2167972

Powell, R. C. (2007). Jacqueline Nassy Brown 'Dropping anchor, setting sail': Geographies of race in Black Liverpool. *Antipode*, 39(2): 355–57. https://doi.org/10.1111/j.1467-8330.2007.00525.x

Pringle, D. G. (2003). Classics in human geography revisited. Commentary 2. *Progress in Human Geography*, 27(5): 607–9. https://doi.org/10.1191/0309132503ph451xx

Prosser, C., and Fieldhouse, E. (2017). A tale of two referendums: The 2017 election in Scotland. British Election Study. 2 August. https://www.britishelectionstudy.com/bes-findings/a-tale-of-two-referendums-the-2017-election-in-scotland/#.YZRTeWDP1jE

Rees, P. H., et al. (2017). Population projections by ethnicity: Challenges and solutions for the United Kingdom. In Swanson, D. A. (ed.), *The Frontiers of Applied Demography*. Cham, Switzerland: Springer, 383–408.

Reid, B., and Liu, G. J. (2019). One nation and the heartland's cleavage: An exploratory spatial data analysis. In Grant, B., Moore, T. and Lynch, T. (eds) *The Rise of Right-Populism*. Singapore: Springer, 5–22.

Reynolds, D. R. (1990). Whither electoral geography? A critique. In Johnston, R., Shelley, F. M., and Taylor, P. J. (eds) *Developments in Electoral Geography*. London: Croom Helm, 22–38.

Richardson, J., and O'Neill, R. (2012). 'Stamp on the Camps': The social construction of Gypsies and Travellers in media and political debate. In Richardson, J., and Ryder, A. (eds) *Gypsies and Travellers: Empowerment and Inclusion in British Society*. Bristol: Policy Press, 169–86.

Rickard, S. J. (2020). Economic geography, politics, and policy. *Annual Review of Political Science*, 23: 187–202. https://doi.org/10.1146/annurev-polisci-050718-033649

Rickardsson, J. (2021). The urban–rural divide in radical right populist support: The role of resident's characteristics, urbanization trends, and public service supply. *Annals of Regional Science*, 67: 211–42. https://doi.org/10.1007/s00168-021-01046-1

Riva, M., Terashima, M., Curtis, S., Shucksmith, J., and Carlebach, S. (2011). Coalfield health effects: Variation in health across former coalfield areas in England. *Health Place*, 17(2): 588–97. https://doi.org/10.1016/j.healthplace.2010.12.016

Robinson, D., and Reeve, K. (2006). *Neighbourhood Experiences of New Immigration: Reflections from the Evidence Base*. Joseph Rowntree Foundation. https://www.jrf.org.uk/report/experiences-new-immigration-neighbourhood-level (Accessed 7 March 2019)

Rodden, J. (2010). The geographic distribution of political preferences. *Annual Review of Political Science*, 13: 321–40.

Rodden, J. (2019). *Why Cities Lose: The Deep Roots of the Urban-Rural Political Divide*. New York: Basic Books.

Sanders, D. (2017). The UK's changing party system: The prospects for a party realignment at Westminster. *Journal of the British Academy*, 5: 91–124. https://doi.org/10.5871/jba/005.091

Sanders, D., Fisher, S. D., Heath, A., and Sobolewska, M. (2014a). The democratic engagement of Britain's ethnic minorities. *Ethnic and Racial Studies*, 37(1): 120–39. https://doi.org/10.1080/01419870.2013.827795

Sanders, D., Heath, A., Fisher, S., and Sobolewska, M. (2014b). The calculus of ethnic minority voting in Britain. *Political Studies*, 62(2): 230–51. https://doi.org/10.1111/1467-9248.12040

Sassen, S. (2019). *Cities in a World Economy*. 5th edn. Thousand Oaks, CA: SAGE Publications. https://doi.org/10.4135/9781071872710

Savage, M., Devine, F., Cunningham, N., Taylor, M., Li, Y., Hjellbrekke, J., Le Roux, B., Friedman, S., and Miles, A. (2013). A new model of social class? Findings from the BBC's Great British Class Survey Experiment. *Sociology*, 47(2): 219–50. https://doi.org/10.1177/0038038513481128

Scala, D. J., Johnson, K. M., and Rogers, L. T. (2015). Red rural, blue rural? Presidential voting patterns in a changing rural America. *Political Geography*, 48: 108–18. https:/doi.org/10.1016/j.polgeo.2015.02.003

Schaeffer, M. (2014). *Ethnic Diversity and Social Cohesion: Immigration, Ethnic Fractionalization and Potentials for Civic Action*. Farnham: Ashgate

Schonhardt-Bailey, C. (2003). Ideology, party and interests in the British Parliament of 1841–47. *British Journal of Political Science*, 33(4): 581–605. http://www.jstor.org/stable/4092197

Scott, R. (2022). Does university make you more liberal? Estimating the within-individual effects of higher education on political values. *Electoral Studies*, 77: 102471.

Simon, E. (2022). Explaining the educational divide in electoral behaviour: Testing direct and indirect effects from British elections and referendums 2016–2019. *Journal of Elections, Public Opinion and Parties*, 32(4): 980–1000. https://doi.org/10.1080/17457289.2021.2013247

Singh, M. (2018). The Tories face eviction from office unless they help Generation Rent. https://capx.co/the-tories-fave-eviction-from-office-unless-they-help-generation-rent (Accessed 15 August 2019)

Skinner, G., and Mortimore, R. (2017). How Britain voted in the 2017 election. https://www.ipsos.com/ipsos-mori/en-uk/how-britain-voted-2017-election (Accessed 13 June 2019)

Sobolewska, M., and Ford, R. (2020). *Brexitland*. Cambridge: Cambridge University Press.

Social Mobility Commission. (2017). *State of the Nation 2017: Social Mobility in Great Britain*. London: Social Mobility Commission.

Standing, G. (2011). *The Precariat: The New Dangerous Class*. London: Bloomsbury Academic.

Standing, G. (2015). The precariat and class struggle. *RCCS Annual Review*, 7(7): 3–16. https://doi.org/10.4000/rccsar.585

Stephens, H. W. (1982). Party realignment in Britain, 1900–1925: A preliminary analysis. *Social Science History*, 6(1): 35–66. https://doi.org/10.2307/1170846

Storper, M. (2013). *Keys to the City*. Princeton: Princeton University Press.

Sturgis, P., and Jennings, W. (2020). Was there a 'youthquake' in the 2017 general election? *Electoral Studies*, 64: 102065.

Sturgis, P., Brunton-Smith, I., Kuha, J., and Jackson, J. (2014). Ethnic diversity, segregation and the social cohesion of neighbourhoods in London. *Ethnic and Racial Studies*, 37(8): 1286–309. https://doi.org/10.1080/01419870.2013.831932

Surridge, P. (2016). Education and liberalism: Pursuing the link. *Oxford Review of Education*, 42(2): 146–64. https://doi.org/10.1080/03054985.2016.1151408

Sutton Trust. (2018). *Home and Away: Social, Ethnic and Spatial Inequalities in Student Mobility*. London: Sutton Trust.

Sykes, O., Brown, J., Cocks, M., Shaw, D., and Couch, C. (2013). A city profile of Liverpool. *Cities*, 35: 299–318. https://doi.org/10.1016/j.cities.2013.03.013

Taylor, Lord Justice. (1990). *The Hillsborough Stadium Disaster: Final Report of the Inquiry by the Rt Hon Lord Justice Taylor*. London: HMSO. https://web.archive.org/web/20140330053408/http://southyorks.police.uk/sites/default/files/hillsboroughstadiumdisasterfinalreport.pdf (Accessed 23 February 2019)

Taylor, Z., Lucas, J., Armstrong, D. A., and Bakker, R. (2023). The development of the urban-rural cleavage in Anglo-American democracies. *Comparative Political Studies*, 0(0). https://doi.org/10.1177/00104140231194060

Tilley, J., and Evans, G. (2014). Ageing and generational effects on vote choice: Combining cross-sectional and panel data to estimate APC effects. *Electoral Studies*, 33: 19–27

Tobler, W. (1970). A computer movie simulating urban growth in the Detroit region. *Economic Geography*, 46(suppl_1): 234–40. https://doi.org/10.2307/143141

Tomlinson, J. (2020). De-industrialization: Strengths and weaknesses as a key concept for understanding post-war British history. *Urban History*, 47(2): 199–219. https://doi.org/10.1017/S0963926819000221

Tomlinson, J. (2021). Deindustrialisation and 'Thatcherism': Moral economy and unintended consequences. *Contemporary British History*, 35(4): 620–42. https://doi.org/10.1080/13619462.2021.1972416

Tuckman, A., and Harris, L. (2009). *The Employment of Migrant Labour in the East Midlands*. Acas. https://www.acas.org.uk/media/2620/The-Employment-of-Migrant-Labour-in-the-East-Midlands/pdf/The-Employment-of-Migrant-Labour-in-the-East-Midlands-accessible-version.pdf (Accessed 7 March 2019)

UCAS (2016). *End of Cycle Report 2016 Data Files*. [Data set]. https://www.ucas.com/corporate/data-and-analysis/ucas-undergraduate-releases/ucas-undergraduate-analysis-reports/ucas-undergraduate-end-cycle-reports (Accessed 13 July 2017)

UNISON (2013). *Organising Migrant Workers*. UNISON. https://www.unison.org.uk/content/uploads/2013/06/On-line-Catalogue173513.pdf (Accessed 7 March 2019)

Wald, K. D. (1983). *Crosses on the Ballot: Patterns of British Voter Alignment since 1885*. Princeton: Princeton University Press.

Waldron, R. (2021). Housing, place and populism: towards a research agenda. *Environment and Planning A: Economy and Space*, 53(5): 1219–29. https://doi.org/10.1177/0308518x211022363

Walks, R. A. (2005). City-Suburban Electoral Polarization in Great Britain, 1950–2001. *Transactions of the Institute of British Geographers*, 30(4): 500–17. http://www.jstor.org/stable/3804510

Warren, I. (2018). Watch out, Tories: Your southern strongholds are turning red. *The Guardian*, 9 May. https://www.theguardian.com/commentisfree/2018/may/09/tories-southern-red-south-england-london#comments (Accessed 18 June 2019)

Warren, I. (2017). How the Conservatives lost their home counties heartland. *The Guardian*, 12 October. https://www.theguardian.com/commentisfree/2017/oct/12/conservatives-lost-home-counties-influx-young-people-london-south-east (Accessed 19 December 2023)

Watson, M. (2018). Brexit, the left behind and the let down: The political abstraction of 'the economy' and the UK's EU referendum. *British Politics*, 13(1): 17–30. https://doi.org/10.1057/s41293-017-0062-8

Welsh Government. (2018). *Address List of Schools in Wales*. [Data set]. https://gov.wales/statistics-and-research/address-list-of-schools/?lang=en (Accessed 17 January 2019)

Wilks-Heeg, S. (2019). Safe Labour suburbia? The changing politics of the Merseyside suburbs. *Political Quarterly*, 90(1): 53–63. https://doi.org/10.1111/1467-923X.12528

Wilks-Heeg, S., and North, P. (2004). Cultural policy and urban regeneration: A special edition of *Local Economy*. *Local Economy*, 19(4): 305–11. https://doi.org/10.1080/0269094042000286819

Williams, J. (2012). 'The truth' of the Hillsborough disaster is only 23 years late. *British Politics and Policy*, 12 September. http://blogs.lse.ac.uk/politicsandpolicy/archives/26897 (Accessed 23 February 2019)

Wolfinger, R., and Rosenstone, S. (1980). *Who Votes?* New Haven: Yale University Press.

Index

For the benefit of digital users, indexed terms that span two pages (e.g., 52–53) may, on occasion, appear on only one of those pages.

A

age
  generational replacement, 223
  older voters, 20, 23*f*, 45–47, 96–98, 97*f*,
    127–128, 128*f*, 223–224
  population ageing, 26, 39, 42–43, 45–47,
    148, 223–224
  places, 45–47
  values, 45–47
  voting in general elections, 20, 22*f*, 23*f*,
    96–98, 97*f*, 109*f*, 110*f*, 126–128, 127*f*,
    128*f*, 144*f*, 145*f*, 150*t*, 181*t*, 183*t*
  younger voters, 6–7, 20, 42, 46–47, 96–98,
    97*f*, 222–225
agglomeration, 42–43
Alliance, 43, 83*t*, 199–200
Anti-establishment, 195, 197–198, 221
Attlee, Clement, 63–64
authoritarianism, *see* values

B

Ballot Act of 1872, 204
Blair, Tony, 206
Blue Wall, 216–217
Brexit
  electoral geography of, 10–14, 12*f*, 13*f*,
    47–48, 214, 219
  realignment, 10–11
Brexit Party, 26–27
Brown, Gordon, 206

C

Cameron, David, 199–200, 210
cleavages
  age, 96
  class, 16–17, 18–20, 20*f*, 215–216
  geographical
    city-town, 225–226
    core-periphery, 80
    cosmopolitan-left behind, 111–114, 131,
      198, 218–219, 224
    London-rest of the UK, 40

    North-South, 17–18, 40, 62
  Parochial-cosmopolitan, 37
    labour-capital, 16 n.15
    owner-worker, 16 n.15
    production sector, 176–177
    socio-economic, 16
    urban-rural, 62–63, 72–75, 215–216
social class
  cleavage, *see* cleavage
  consciousness, 16
  dealignment, 18–20, 20*f*, 21*f*, 25–26, 39–40,
    89–90, 94–95, 95*f*
  decline of working-class occupations, 38–39
  measurement, 19–20 n.20, 35*t*, 95*f*
  middle class, 5–6, 14–15, 17–19, 19–20 n.20,
    33, 39–40, 43, 58, 69–70, 88–89, 93–96,
    94 n.5, 95*f*, 112, 142–143, 148,
    162–163, 188, 219–220, 224
  new working class, 3, 30, 43, 48, 89–90
  voting in general elections, 18–20, 20*f*, 21*f*,
    25–26, 93–96, 93*f*, 95*f*, 125, 126*f*, 131,
    149
  working class, 4, 17, 19–20 n.20, 20*f*, 21*f*, 26,
    29, 38–40, 50*t*, 51–54, 58–60, 88–90,
    93–96, 93*f*, 95*f*, 113–114, 147–149,
    163–164, 187–188, 200, 212, 215–216
Clegg, Nick, 5–6
clustering (geographical)
  of demographic groups, 37–39, 42–43,
    225–226
  of electoral under-or over-performance,
    159–167, 169–172, 174–176
  of vote shares, 151–159, 167–168, 172–173
coalfield/coal-mining towns, *see* places (types
    of)
cohort effect, 223
compositional effects, 217–218, 226
conservativism (social conservativism), 57, 57
    n.7, 58–60, 59*f*
constituencies
  Alyn and Deeside, 52*t*
  Amber Valley, 52*t*, 111–112, 128*f*

constituencies (*Continued*)
Arundel and the South Downs, 176
Barking, 52*t*
Barnsley Central, 155*t*, 156*t*
Barnsley East, 155*t*, 156*t*, 161–162
Barrow and Furness, 51–54, 52*t*, 69, 71 n.4
Bassetlaw, 11, 11 n.9, 71 n.4
Batley and Spen, 142
Battersea, 55*t*
Beaconsfield, 54, 55*t*
Bermondsey and Old Southwark, 52*t*
Berwick-upon-Tweed, 71–72 n.5
Bethnal Green and Bow, 52*t*, 55*t*
Bethnal Green and Stepney, 52*t*
Bexhill and Battle, 52*t*
Bexleyheath, 52*t*
Birkenhead, 178*t*, 179*t*
Birmingham Edgbaston, 70 n.3
Birmingham Hodge Hill, 2–3, 3*f*
Birmingham Ladywood, 2–3, 3*f*, 52*t*, 55*t*,
139–140
Birmingham Selly Oak, 70 n.3
Birmingham Small Heath, 52*t*, 55*t*
Birmingham Sparkbrook, 52*t*, 55*t*
Bishop Auckland, 1–2, 1–2 n.1, 2*f*, 11, 11
n.9, 71 n.4, 223–224
Blackpool South, 3*f*, 89–90
Blaenau Gwent, 52*t*
Blaydon, 179*t*
Blyth Valley, 1–2–2 n.1, n.3, 2*f*, 71 n.4
Bolsover, 2*f*, 8, 71 n.4
Bootle, 176, 178*t*, 179*t*, 188, 199
Boston and Skegness, 15, 52*t*, 125, 152,
165–167, 165–166 n.3, 176, 178*t*, 184,
186*t*, 202, 210, 214, 221–222
Bournemouth East, 52*t*, 131
Bow and Poplar, 52*t*
Bradford South, 159–160
Bradford West, 159–160
Brecon and Radnor, 71–72 n.5
Brecon and Radnorshire, 71–72 n.5
Brent Central, 55*t*, 131–132
Brent East, 55*t*
Brent South, 55*t*
Bristol West, 5*f*, 6, 8, 14–15, 26–27, 55*t*, 70
n.3, 112, 125, 129–131, 134–135
Calder Valley, 10–11 n.8, 142
Camberwell and Peckham, 52*t*
Cambridge, 7*f*, 7–8, 126–127
Canterbury, 6–7, 7*f*, 10, 26–27, 112
Cardiff Central, 55*t*, 70 n.3
Cardiff North, 70 n.3
Cardigan, 71–72 n.6

Carlisle, 69
Carmarthen East and Dinefwr, 71–72 n.6
Castle Point, 15, 52*t*
Ceredigion, 71–72 n.6
Ceredigion and Pembroke North, 71–72 n.6
Charnwood, 52*t*
Cheadle, 52*t*, 54, 55*t*, 139–140
Chelsea, 54
Chelsea and Fulham, 55*t*
Chesham and Amersham, 55*t*
Chester, 136
Christchurch, 51–54, 52*t*
Cities of London and Westminster, the, 55*t*
City of London and Westminster South, the,
55*t*
Clacton, 15, 52*t*, 176
Clitheroe, 16–17
Copeland, 69
Corby, 52*t*
Crosby, 52*t*, 189*f*, 190*f*, 191–192, 193–194
Croydon North, 55*t*
Croydon South, 52*t*, 55*t*
Denton and Reddish, 142
Deptford, 16–17
Derbyshire Dales, 142
Don Valley, 71 n.4, 223–224
Dudley East, 51–54, 52*t*
Dudley North, 128–129, 142–143
Dudley South, 129–131, 142–143
Dulwich, 55*t*
Dulwich and West Norwood, 55*t*
Dwyfor Meirionnydd, 71–72 n.6
Ealing Southall, 55*t*
Easington, 4*f*
Eastbourne, 52*t*
East Devon, 52*t*
East Ham, 55*t*, 129–131, 134–135
East Worthing and Shoreham, 176
Edinburgh South, 9
Epsom and Ewell, 55*t*
Esher, 54, 55*t*
Esher and Walton, 55*t*
Exeter, 7*f*, 7–8
Fareham, 52*t*
Folkestone and Hythe, 162
Fulham, 54, 55*t*
Fylde, 69
Gainsborough, 71–72 n.5, 165–166 n.3, 178*t*
Gainsborough and Horncastle, 71–72 n.5
Garston and Halewood, 178*t*, 179*t*
Glasgow East, 8–9
Glasgow North East, 8–9
Glasgow South West, 8–9

Glasgow Springburn, 8–9 n.6
Gosport, 54, 55*t*
Grantham and Stamford, 165–166 n.3, 178*t*
Gillingham and Rainham, 142
Gravesham, 120–121, 120*t*, 121*t*
Great Grimsby, 26–27, 52*t*, 71 n.4
Greenwich and Woolwich, 52*t*
Hackney, 55*t*, 142
Hackney South and Shoreditch, 52*t*
Haltemprice and Howden, 52*t*
Halton, 179*t*
Hampstead and Highgate, 55*t*
Hampstead and Kilburn, 55*t*
Harlow, 126–127
Harrow West, 55*t*
Hartlepool, 26–27, 142, 223
Harwich, 52*t*
Havant, 127–128
Hayes and Harlington, 55*t*
Hemsworth, 161–162
Hendon South, 55*t*
Hexham, 71–72 n.5
Hornsey and Wood Green, 50, 55*t*, 127–128
High Peak, 142
Holborn and St Pancras, 52*t*
Honiton, 52*t*
Hove, 52*t*, 112, 127–128, 176
Ilford South, 129–132, 134–135
Islington North, 52*t*
Islington South and Finsbury, 52*t*, 55*t*
Islwyn, 52*t*, 161–162
Kingston upon Hull East, 4*f*, 52*t*
Jarrow, 179*t*
Kensington, 10, 54, 55*t*
Knowsley, 176, 178*t*, 179*t*, 194–195, 199
Knowsley North, 52*t*, 55*t*
Leeds Central, 55*t*, 155*t*, 156*t*
Leeds East, 155*t*, 156*t*
Leeds North East, 70 n.3, 155*t*, 156*t*
Leeds North West, 5*f*, 14–15, 26–27, 70 n.3,
     126–127, 155*t*, 156*t*
Leeds West, 155*t*, 156*t*
Leicester East, 3, 51–54, 52*t*, 55*t*
Leicester North West, 4*f*
Leicester West, 3, 4*f*
Leigh, 71 n.4
Lewisham Deptford, 55*t*
Lincoln, 165–166 n.3, 166–167, 178–179
Liverpool Broadgreen, 70 n.3
Liverpool Riverside, 52*t*, 55*t*, 136, 178*t*, 179*t*
Liverpool Walton, 2–3, 3*f*, 69, 176, 178*t*,
     179*t*, 195–197, 199
Liverpool Wavertree, 70 n.3, 178*t*, 179*t*

Liverpool West Derby, 178*t*, 179*t*, 195–197
Louth and Horncastle, 165–166 n.3,
     166–167, 178*t*
Ludlow, 71–72 n.5
Makerfield, 179*t*
Manchester Blackley, 70 n.3
Manchester Central, 52*t*, 55*t*, 69, 136,
     139–140
Manchester Gorton, 131–132
Manchester North East, 16–17
Manchester Withington, 5–6, 5*f*, 70 n.3, 125,
     129–131, 136
Manchester Wythenshawe, 52*t*
Mansfield, 10, 26–27, 71 n.4, 125, 133
Merioneth, 71–72 n.6
Meirionnydd Nant Conwy, 71–72 n.6
Merthyr Tydfil and Rhymney, 142
Mid Derbyshire, 52*t*
Milton Keynes South, 139–140
Montgomery, 71–72 n.6
Montgomeryshire, 71–72 n.6
Morley and Leeds South, 155*t*
Morley and Outwood, 127–128
Newcastle-upon-Tyne, 16–17
Newcastle-upon-Tyne Central, 70 n.3, 179*t*
Newcastle-upon-Tyne East, 55*t*
Newcastle-upon-Tyne North, 70 n.3
Newham North East, 55*t*
Newham North West, 55*t*
New Forest East, 126–127
New Forest West, 52*t*
Normanton, Pontefract and Castleford, 52*t*
North Cornwall, 71–72 n.5
North Devon, 71–72 n.5
North Durham, 161–162
North Norfolk, 46, 52*t*
North Shropshire, 71–72 n.5
North Swindon, 127–128
North Thanet, 52*t*, 162
North West Durham, 161–162
Nottingham North, 52*t*
Nottingham South, 55*t*
Old Bexley and Sidcup, 52*t*
Oxford East, 55*t*, 126–127
Oxford West and Abingdon, 55*t*
Peckham, 52*t*
Pembroke, 71–72 n.5
Pendle, 52*t*
Penistone and Stocksbridge, 156*t*
Penrith and The Border, 71–72 n.5
Portsmouth North, 129–131
Preseli Pembrokeshire, 71–72 n.5
Preston, 52*t*, 136

constituencies (*Continued*)
Putney, 54, 55*t*
Rayleigh and Wickford, 52*t*
Ribble Valley, 52*t*, 179*t*
Richmond (Yorks), 71–72 n.5
Richmond Park, 54, 55*t*
Richmond upon Thames and Barnes, 55*t*
Rochford, 52*t*
Romford, 142
Rossendale and Darwen, 69
Rother Valley, 10, 10–11 n.8, 161–162, 223–224
Rotherham, 4*f*, 71 n.4
Ryedale, 71–72 n.5
Scunthorpe, 52*t*, 111–112, 184 n.1, 211
Sedgefield, 11, 134–135
Sefton Central, 52*t*, 152, 162–163, 178*t*, 179*t*, 186*t*, 188, 191
Sheffield Brightside, 52*t*
Sheffield Central, 52*t*
Sheffield Hallam, 5–6, 5*f*, 14–15, 26–27, 54, 55*t*, 70 n.3, 129–131
Shipley, 142
Sleaford and North Hykeham, 165–166 n.3, 178*t*
South Holland and the Deepings, 165–167, 165–166 n.3, 178*t*, 202, 208, 214
South West Norfolk, 71–72 n.5
Southport, 178*t*, 193–194, 199
Southwark and Bermondsey, 52*t*
Stalybridge and Hyde, 69
St Albans, 54, 55*t*
St Helens North, 178*t*, 179*t*
St Helens South and Whiston, 178*t*, 179*t*
Stockton North, 179*t*
Stoke-on-Trent Central, 10, 71 n.4, 128–129, 142
Stoke-on-Trent North, 51–54, 52*t*, 71 n.4, 89–90, 125, 142–143
Stoke-on-Trent South, 51–54, 52*t*, 71 n.4, 129–131, 142
Streatham, 55*t*
Tamworth, 126–127
Telford, 111–112, 129–131
Thirsk and Malton, 71–72 n.5
Tooting, 55*t*
Totnes, 52*t*
Twickenham, 54, 55*t*
Vale of Clwyd, 223–224
Vauxhall, 52*t*, 55*t*
Wakefield, 71 n.4
Wallasey, 178*t*

Walsall North, 51–54, 52*t*, 128–131, 142–143, 162
Walthamstow, 55*t*, 125, 129–131
Warley West, 51–54, 52*t*
Warwick and Leamington, 7*f*, 7–8
Washington and Sunderland West, 127–128
Weaver Vale, 199
Wentworth and Dearne, 155*t*, 156*t*
West Bromwich East, 128–129
West Bromwich West, 51–54, 52*t*, 128–129, 133, 142–143
West Dorset, 71–72 n.5
West Ham, 55*t*
Wigan, 179*t*
Wimbledon, 54, 55*t*
Windsor, 112
Windsor and Maidenhead, 52*t*
Wirral South, 162–163, 178*t*, 191
Wirral West, 178*t*, 188, 191, 199
Wokingham, 52*t*, 54, 55*t*, 112
Wolverhampton North East, 128–129, 142–143
Wolverhampton South East, 51–54, 52*t*, 128–129, 133
Woolwich, 16–17
Workington, 2*f*, 11, 11 n.9, 71 n.4, 223–224
Worthing, 51–54, 52*t*
Worthing West, 52*t*
Wrexham, 11, 52*t*, 71 n.4
Wyre, 52*t*
Wyre and Preston North, 52*t*
Wythenshawe and Sale East, 179*t*
York Outer, 52*t*
contextual effects, 18, 18–19 n.19, 37–38, 37–38 n.1, 60, 221
Corbyn, Jeremy, 10, 25–26, 31, 185, 187, 188, 195, 196*f*, 216
cosmopolitan
industries and jobs, 54, 55*t*, 86*t*, 100–101, 101*f*, 125, 148–149
measurement, 86, 86*t*, 114–115, 114*t*, 124*t*
places, 5–6, 5*f*, 101–102, 102*f*, 116*f*
versus left behind places, 49, 50*t*, 85–86, 85–86 n.2, 123, 224
counties
Cheshire, 193
County Durham, 216–217
Derbyshire, 162, 169–172, 176
Devon, 174–175
Essex, 142, 162, 167–168
Greater Manchester, 10–11 n.8, 63–64, 142, 169–173, 176
Hampshire, 169–172, 174–175

Kent, 142, 162, 169–172, 174–175
Lancashire, 10–11 n.8, 167–168, 174–175, 191–193, 198
Lincolnshire, *see* Lincolnshire
Merseyside, *see* Merseyside
North Yorkshire, 174–175
Northumberland, 1–2
Nottinghamshire, 152–155, 169–172
South Yorkshire, 157–159, 161–162, 167–168, 169–173, 176, 216–217, 220–221
West Yorkshire, 142, 157–159, 161–162, 169–172
cultural capital, 49–50

D
dealignment, 89–90
dealignment (class), 18–19, 25–26, 39–40, 94–95
deindustrialization, 32, 39–41, 40 n.3, 42–43, 47, 48–49, 54–57, 119, 134–135, 142, 148, 191
deprivation, 2–3
household deprivation, 50*t*, 87*t*, 107*t*, 123–124
left-behindedness, 4, 28–30, 48, 86
places, 30–31, 49
voting in general elections, 103–104, 104*f*, 147
disenfranchisement, 209–210, 214

E
ecological fallacy, 18, 228–229
economic growth, 30–31, 39, 148–149, 217
Eden, Anthony, 7–8
education and qualifications
expansion of higher education, 38–39, 41–42
places, 54, 55*t*
values, 38
voting in general elections, 24, 24*f*, 102–103, 103*f*, 109–110, 220–221
efficiency (of vote distribution, electoral), 18, 32, 61, 63, 63–64 n.1, 75–79, 78*t*, 80, 129–131, 218, 222–224
embourgeoisement, 142, 143*t*
employment and occupations
cosmopolitan, *see* cosmopolitan
low-paid, 39–40, 43, 48, 142, 217
low-skilled, 44–45, 119–120, 125, 142, 148, 221–222
managerial/professional, 54, 55*t*, 95*f*, 112, 138–139, 142–143, 219–220, *see also* social class

manufacturing, 38–40, 43, 48–49, 50*t*, 51–54, 52*t*, 62, 86*t*, 93–94, 96, 97*f*, 111, 142–143, 148, 219
precariousness, 3, 30, 43, 89–90, 105–106, 106*f*, 113, 115, 142, 211, 217, 225
public sector, 5–6, 40–41, 54, 176–177
routine/semi-routine, 40–41, 48–49, 50*t*, 51–54, 52*t*, 86*t*, 93–94, 93*f*, 95*f*, 124*t*, 126*f*, 147
semi-skilled/unskilled, 120, 121*t*, 125, 126*f*, 142
service sector, 3, 38–40, 43, 147
ethnic diversity, 38–39, 43–45, 86*t*, 98–100, 99*f*, 100*f*, 128–129, 129*f*, 144, 224–226
ethnic groups
Asian, 44
Caribbean, 44
Roma/Travellers/Gypsies, 208
white British, 45, 48–49, 163–164, 209–210
ethnic minorities, 25–26, 54, 55*t*, 58–60, 218–220, 226
ethnic segregation, 44–45
European parliament elections, 216, 224
European Union (EU), 8 n.4, 29, 206–207, 214
EU referendum, *see* referendum
extreme right, 220

F
financial crisis, 123, 223
first-past-the-post, 27

G
geographical mobility (out migration of younger people), 86*t*, 99*f*, 99–100
globalization, 40 n.3, 42–43
Green Party, 6, 14*f*, 222–223

H
health, 192
deprivation, 48, 50
healthcare, 39
poor health, 2–3, 133
left-behindedness, 87*t*
voting in general elections, 103–104, 104*f*, 108, 112, 134*f*
heartland(s), 2–3, 9–11, 14, 17, 26, 30, 75, 80, 89–90, 112, 120, 148, 151–181, 215–216, 217–218, 222–226
Herfindahl index, 26, 28–29, 86*t*, 124, 124 n.2, 128–129, 128–129 n.5
housing
affordability, 46, 123, 123 n.2, 124*t*, 136, 148–149, 220, 223

housing (*Continued*)
  price/income ratio, 51–54, 137
  prices, 123
  'Right to Buy', 134–135
housing tenure
  owners, 49–50, 50*t*, 51–54, 89–90, 94 n.5,
      112, 117*f*, 118*f*, 120, 120*t*, 121*t*, 123,
      124*t*, 134–135, 135*f*, 143–144, 144*f*,
      145–146, 148–150, 191, 219–220, 225
  private renters, 49–50, 50*t*, 112, 134–136,
      136*t*, 148–149, 220, 225
  social renters, 2–3, 49–54, 50*t*, 85–86, 87*t*,
      103–104, 104*f*, 107*t*, 108, 109*f*, 110*f*,
      120, 120*t*, 124*t*, 131–132, 132*f*,
      133–136, 146–147, 181*t*, 183*t*, 225

I

identity, 9, 16 n.34, 16, 18–19, 28, 37–38 n.1,
      37–38, 42, 43–44, 191–195, 197–201,
      207–208, 214, 221, 228, 229
immigration, 28, 43–45, 46–47, 49, 58–60, 200,
      202, 206–211, 214, 226
income/wealth/affluence, 5–6, 7–8, 26, 38, 43,
      46–47, 58–60, 62, 75, 89–90 n.4, 137,
      138*f*, 138–139, 148–149, 152, 188–191,
      192–193, 214
Independents, 212
Index of Multiple Deprivation (IMD), 2–3
Industrial Revolution, 16, 17 n.18, 35, 45
inequality, 40–41, 43, 47–48, 49–50, 192–193

J

Johnson, Boris, 185, 216

K

knowledge economy, 38–39, 44–45, 119, 125,
      217

L

Leave vote, 10–15, 12*f*, 13*f*, 29, 75, 207, 214,
      216
left behind
  conceptualisation, 30–31
  demographically left behind, 1–3, 2*f*, 10–12,
      48–50, 50*t*, 85–86, 86*t*, 93–94, 107*t*,
      111–112, 123–124, 124*t*, 125–131,
      147–148
  economically left behind, 1–3, 3*f*, 48, 50,
      50*t*, 85–86, 87*t*, 103–104, 107*t*,
      123–124, 124*t*, 131–134, 146–147
  precariously left behind, 1–3, 4*f*, 48–50, 50*t*,
      85–86, 88*t*, 104–106, 107*t*, 123–124,
      124*t*, 134–137, 148–149

'levelling up', 30, 47–48
liberalism (social liberalism), 57–60, 59*f*,
      222–224, 226
Liberal Party, 16–17, 62, 63–64, 192–193, 215
Liberal Democrats, 5–6, 14–15, 14*f*, 26–27, 62,
      71–72, 83*t*, 112, 192, 199–201, 222–224
Lincolnshire
  explanations of Conservative
      over-performance and Labour
      under-performance, 176–180, 201–214
  spatial analysis of Conservative
      over-performance and Labour
      under-performance, 161*f*, 162, 164*f*,
      165–167, 166*f*, 169–175, 173*f*, 175*f*
Liverpool Echo, The, 191, 196*f*, 208, 221

M

Major, John, 1–2, 41–42, 85
marginal constituencies, 75–79, 77*f*, 78*t*, 79*f*,
      212–213, 224–225
May, Theresa, 10, 185, 210, 216
Merseyside
  explanations of Labour over-performance
      and Conservative under-performance,
      176–180, 187–201
  spatial analysis of Labour over-performance
      and Conservative under-performance,
      161*f*, 162–165, 164*f*, 165*f*, 169–176,
      173*f*, 175*f*
methodology/methods
  areal interpolation, 90–92, 122, 227
  boundary changes, 69–70, 90–92, 122–123,
      138, 227
  harmonization, 51, 90, 106–108, 114*t*
  interviews, 34, 184–186, 186*t*
Local Indicators of Spatial Association (LISA),
      167
Miliband, Ed, 25–26, 187, 210

N

New Labour, 5–6, 71, 191–192, 216, 218
North-South divide, *see* cleavages

P

pavement politics, 192
places (types of)
  coalfield/coal-mining towns, 1–2, 10–11 n.8,
      11, 16 n.16, 76, 148, 151–156, 157–159,
      161–164, 167–173, 176, 180–181,
      216–217, 220–221
  coastal/seaside towns, 16 n.16, 17, 26, 30–31,
      40–43, 46, 51–54, 69, 75, 89–90
  commuter belt/towns, 42, 54, 224

core cities, 49–50, 69–70, 70 n.3, 70*f*, 218
cosmopolitan, *see* cosmopolitan
high-tech towns, 38–39, 42–43, 217
inner cities, 69, 72–73
left behind, *see* left behind
market towns, 26, 75, 126–127
Middle England, 222
mill towns, 10–11 n.8, 16
new towns, 17
periphery, 26, 37, 38–39, 40–43, 46–47, 50*t*,
        51–57, 58–60, 72–73, 75, 80, 217,
        225–226
ports, 16–17, 44–45
post-industrial cities, 33
post-industrial towns, 2–4, 26, 33, 58–60, 75,
        88, 89–90, 126–127, 155–156, 216–217
spa towns, 14–15
suburbs, 5–6, 5*f*, 7–8, 17–18, 26, 38, 42, 69,
        72–73, 75, 112, 121, 186*t*, 192–194,
        213, 218, 222–223, 224–225
university towns, 6–7, 7*f*, 8, 11, 17, 26,
        38–39, 41–42, 46–47, 54, 69, 75,
        216–218, 222
villages, 157–159
villages (coal-mining), 10–11 n.8, 26,
        152–156, 216–217
places (cities, towns, areas, local authorities)
        [not constituencies]
    Barnsley, 152–155, 155*t*, 156*t*, 157–159
    Birmingham, 33, 42–44, 51–54, 128–129,
        151–152, 155–156, 162, 172–173,
        174–175, 216–217
    Blackburn with Darwen, 44
    Blackpool, 40–41, 46–47
    Blyth, 1–2
    Boston (Lincolnshire), 44, 186*t*, 206–210,
        212, 214
    Bourne, 204*f*
    Bradford, 44, 176
    Brighton, 26–27, 140–141, 176
    Bristol, 6, 7–8, 26–27, 54, 140–141, 152, 222
    Cambridge, 42–43, 46, 49
    Cardiff, 54, 140–141
    Chester, 193
    Clyde, the, 9
    Crosby, 189*f*, 190*f*, 191–192, 193–194
    Deeping St James, 186*t*, 203*f*
    Ealing, 44
    Eastern Europe, 44, 206–207, 214, 221–222
    East Lindsey, 46, 186*t*
    Edinburgh, 72–73
    Fens, the, 205*f*
    Glasgow, 8–9

    Grimsby, 184 n.1, 211
    Hebden Bridge, 10–11 n.8
    Home Counties, the, 11, 222–223
    Harlow, 40
    Hatfield, 40
    Hillingdon, 44
    Hounslow, 44
    Hull, 152–155
    Kirkby, 201
    Knowsley, 194–195, 199
    Leeds, 26, 42–43, 54, 140–141, 152–159,
        155*t*, 156*t*, 176, 180–181, 197–198,
        216–217, 222
    Leicester, 3, 44
    Lincoln, 212–213
    Liverpool, 26, 45, 51–54, 69, 140–141,
        155–156, 162–164, 176–177, 186*t*,
        187–201, 213, 216–218, 221–222
    Luton, 40
    Maltby, 10–11 n.8
    Manchester, 6–8, 10–11 n.8, 26, 42–43, 46,
        49, 51–54, 63–64, 69, 128–129,
        140–142, 155–156, 169–173, 176,
        180–181, 197–198, 216–218, 222
    Marseille, 197–198
    Naples, 197–198
    Newcastle–upon–Tyne, 16–17, 54, 155–156,
        169–172
    Nottingham, 46, 54, 212
    Oxford, 46, 54
    Pennines, the, 155–156, 169–172
    Rother, 46
    Scunthorpe, 184 n.1, 211
    Sefton, 186*t*, 193–195
    Sheffield, 6, 7–8, 51–54, 155–156, 176,
        197–198, 216–217, 222
    Slough, 40, 44
    Southport, 193–194, 199
    South Hams, 46
    South Holland, 186*t*, 201–204, 207
    South Wales, 148, 152, 157–159, 161–162,
        167–173, 176
    Spalding, 186*t*, 205*f*
    Stevenage, 40
    Stoke-on-Trent, 142, 174–175
    Thames Estuary, the, 162
    Todmorden, 10–11 n.8
    Walsall, 174–175
    Walton, 199
    Welwyn, 40
    Wirral, the, 193–195, 199
    Wolverhampton, 174–175
Plaid Cymru, 71–72, 84*t*

polarization (geographic), 43, 69–75, 80,
    85–86, 222–223, 225–226
population density, 32, 50*t*, 63, 63–64 n.1,
    72–75, 74*f*, 80, 218, 225–226
populism, 229
poverty, 2–3, 30, 48
precariat, 43, 49–50, 50*t*, 88*t*, 89–90 n.4,
    104–105, 105*f*, 107*t*, 113, 115, 123,
    124*t*
precarity
    in employment, 43
    in housing, 119, 123
    and left behindedness, 85–86
    and voting, 105–106, 108–109

R
radical right, 37
realignment, 8–15, 8–9 n.5, 16–17, 25–26,
    28–29, 34–35, 39–40, 58–60, 79–80,
    216–219
great recession, the, 216
Red Wall, the, 4, 10–11, 10–11 n.8, 31, 88–90,
    112, 151–155, 151–152 n.1, 157–159,
    180–181, 216–217
Referendum Party, the, 26–27
Reform Act 1867, 215
Reform Act 1918, 16–17
regeneration, 142, 192–193, 221
regional patterns of voting, 63–68
religion
    Catholicism, 45, 176–181, 178*t*, 179*t*, 181*t*,
        183*t*, 190*f*, 198, 201, 221
    Christianity, 177–178
    Judaism, 45
    Protestantism, 187–188
referendum
    2016 EU referendum, 6–7, 8, 10, 75, 221–223
    2014 Scotland referendum, 8–9, 216
Remain vote, 6–7, 10–15, 222–223
resentment, 33, 119–120, 217–218, 220, 229

S
Scottish National Party (SNP), 8–10, 8–9 n.5,
    9*f*, 26–27, 65*f*, 80, 84*t*, 216, 218
Scottish independence referendum, *see*
    referendum
Self-selection, 28, 37–38, 37–38 n.1, 39, 49, 187,
    187 n.3

Social Democratic Party (SDP), 192
SDP-Liberal Alliance, 199–200
Socio-economic decline, 11, 30–31, 33, 120,
    138–139, 141*f*, 146–147, 191, 201–202
sorting (geographical), 28, 37–38, 37–38 n.1,
    39, 42–43, 49, 225–226
students, 6–8, 42, 46, 129–131
'studentification', 135–136
Sun, The, 194–197, 214, 221

T
Thatcher, Margaret, 1–2, 39–40, 58, 78–79, 85,
    112–113, 149, 187, 191, 194, 197, 201,
    214
towns, *see* places (types of)
trade unions, 1–2, 11, 148, 176–177, 179, 197,
    206, 211, 214, 220–221, 229
Truss, Liz, 216
turnout, 113

U
UK Independence Party (UKIP), 1–2 n.2, 15,
    15*f*, 26–27, 48–49, 199–201, 207–210,
    214, 216, 221–222, 228
unemployment, 2–3, 8–9, 40–41, 45, 48, 50*t*,
    85–86, 87*t*, 103–104, 104*f*, 107*t*, 109*f*,
    110*f*, 117*f*, 120, 121*t*, 124*t*, 132, 133*f*,
    133–134, 138–139, 144*f*, 145*f*, 146–147
university graduates, 5–8, 24, 24*f*, 25*f*, 25–26,
    38, 42, 54, 55*t*, 102, 112, 129–131, 130*f*,
    144–145, 217–218, 222–224
urban-ness, 86*t*, 98–99, 99*f*, 107*t*, 109*f*, 110*f*,
    123–124, 144*f*, 145*f*, 150*t*
urban-suburban/rural (divide), *see* cleavages

V
values
    left-right, 57–58, 59*f*
    liberal-authoritarian, 37, 57–60, 59*f*
    nationalist-cosmopolitan, 37
volatility, 18–19, 26–27, 35, 216–217, 229–230

X
xenophobia, 207–209

Y
young professionals, 5–6, 192–193